UNSPEAKABLE HISTORIES

FILM AND CULTURE

FILM AND CULTURE

A series of Columbia University Press

EDITED BY JOHN BELTON

For the list of titles in this series, see pages 253–57.

UNSPEAKABLE HISTORIES

Film and the Experience of Catastrophe

WILLIAM GUYNN

COLUMBIA UNIVERSITY PRESS
NEW YORK

Columbia University Press
Publishers Since 1893
New York   Chichester, West Sussex
cup.columbia.edu
Copyright © 2016 Columbia University Press
All rights reserved

Library of Congress Cataloging-in-Publication Data

Names: Guynn, William Howard, author.
Title: Unspeakable histories : film and the experience of catastrophe /
William Guynn.
Description: New York : Columbia University Press, 2016. | Series: Film
and culture | Includes bibliographical references and index.
Identifiers: LCCN 2016002532 | ISBN 9780231177962 (cloth : alk. paper) |
ISBN 9780231177979 (pbk. : alk. paper) | ISBN 9780231541961 (e-book)
Subjects: LCSH: Historical films—History and criticism. | Psychic trauma
in motion pictures. | Catastrophical, The, in motion pictures.
Classification: LCC PN1995.9.H5 G85 2016 | DDC 791.43/658—dc23
LC record available at https://lccn.loc.gov/2016002532

Columbia University Press books are printed on permanent
and durable acid-free paper.
Printed in the United States of America

c 10 9 8 7 6 5 4 3 2 1
p 10 9 8 7 6 5 4 3 2 1

Cover design: Jordan Wannemacher
Cover image: © Photofest

For Stefanie

CONTENTS

UNSPEAKABLE HISTORIES

INTRODUCTION

Making Experience Speak

"**FILM AND** the Experience of Catastrophe," the subtitle of this volume, refers first of all to the nature of the seven films I chose to study, all of which represent catastrophic events of the twentieth century—the Age of Extremes, as Eric Hobsbawn has named it—from the Holocaust to the Cambodian genocide. The subtitle also emphasizes the notion of historical experience that will be at the center of my inquiry. Indeed, I will posit a fundamental difference between historical *experience*—the inside of events, if you will—and their objective *representation*. If representations of the past are at heart discursive and intellectual, the experience of past events is phenomenological, anchored to immediate perception and the domains of mood and sensation. How can such internal experiences of the past, I then ask, be realized through film? My intention is to show that film is exceptionally capable of evoking the affective dimension of the past and equally adept at unearthing the atavistic emotions that belong to myth and ritual. In so doing, film may ease, at least fleetingly, the sense of loss we often feel at the utter pastness of the past. It is even capable, I will attempt to show, of triggering moments of heightened awareness in which the barrier between past and present falls and the reality of the past we thought was lost is momentarily rediscovered in its material being.

Philosophers of history have categorically denied that one can have any sort of direct experience of the past "for the simple reason that the past no longer exists," as Dutch philosopher Frank Ankersmit points out.[1] Nor has the recovery of past experience ever been the ambition of historians. Quite the contrary, historiography explicitly dissociates itself from experience, which occupies a disquieting zone of intractable impressions and emotions, alien to historical analysis as classically understood. The presumed task of historians is to isolate historical facts from raw experience—sift through the evidence—and then align the significant facts, brushed clean of extraneous material, in a meaningful (that is, causal) sequence. Thus historiography is seen as providing an *explanation* of the evolution of significant events. As French historian Henri-Irénée Marrou put it, "History becomes intelligible only in so far as it shows it is capable of establishing, of detecting the relationships that link each stage of human development to its antecedents and its consequences."[2] History as a narrative form is, then, supremely cognitive: it makes the past intelligible, shapes it, and discerns the relationships that structure its evolution. Indeed, as Ankersmit observes, historical writing is judged by the extent to which one historian's representation is more successful than another's according to the most recent state of the evidence: "That is to say, we can compare representations only to each other and never to the past itself."[3]

Such an intellectual endeavor is alien to the rediscovery of experience, which demands not analytic detachment but an intuitive and engaged sensibility. In the following discussions, I prefer to use the term "evoke" rather than "represent" when speaking of experience. As Ankersmit observes, representation has "all the support (and the deadweight) of a representational tradition behind it," whereas experience must rely on the "privilege of authenticity"[4] and the receptive intelligence of the researcher. Experience must do without readymade cognitive structures. Speaking of Johan Huizinga, the only historian to propose a theory of historical *sensation*, Ankermit describes Huizinga's notion of contact with historical realities, which is always triggered by material objects. It is "one of the many variants of ekstasis," an uncanny experience of *truth* that takes you unawares and thrusts you into a sphere where the usual protocols do not apply: "This contact with the past that cannot be reduced to anything outside itself is the entrance into a world of its own."[5]

The task of evoking historical experience devolves, then, to the more "eccentric" historians, who are less wedded to the analytic method, and to artists—literary, theatrical, visual, and in our case cinematic—who are less bound than historians by epistemological constraints and more open to noumenal (internal) realities. The look cast by such artists and historians is directed as much inward as outward. They are particularly sensitive to the evocative power of still visible traces of the past—a letter, a photograph, a ghetto street, a landscape, a prison cell, a killing ground, to cite examples from the seven films I study here. The experience of the past such objects may provoke is the contrary of an apperception. It involves an irrational encounter between the historian or artist in a state of alertness and a fragment of past experience that quickens under his or her gaze. As we will see, such fusional moments also occur to the subjects of memory—those who bear witness to the past in the documentary films in this study and in whom a present memory and a past reality suddenly coalesce. We observe this fusion expressed in the reflexive movements of the body, the nuances of facial expression, and the timbre of the human voice.

As I hope to show, the recovery of historical experience requires us to abandon certain defenses. We give up the cognitive distance of historical analysis that allows us to interpret the past rather than experience it; such analysis creates a historical context that overrides any direct contact with the past. We also forgo, at moments of particular intensity, the reassuring mastery of narrative that reduces the undifferentiated flow of life to the discrete and meaningful units of the story the historian (or the memoirist) is "reconstructing." Disarmed of these defenses, the researcher, the artist, the filmmaker, the reader/viewer, or the witness may come face to face with the past. It is not because, as Ankersmit puts it, "the past and present have now come infinitesimally close to each other but because we have momentarily returned to that primeval phase in which present and past were not yet separated."[6] The discursive strategies of interpretation, contextualization, and narration are, from the point of view of such experiences, instruments of avoidance. This is particularly true with regard to unsettling historical moments that continue to smolder in individual and collective consciousness. Indeed, the past is not necessarily over and done with. It is quite capable of reigniting and breaking through into the present.

THE GROANINGS OF A CIVILIZATION

Recovery of experience can be harrowing and is particularly so in films that speak about traumatic events in the catastrophic twentieth century. All the films evoke unresolved historical situations— unresolved for the communities that experienced them and for the historians who attempt to understand them—situations that continue to inflict individual and collective pain. Historiography, with its economic, social, or political instruments of analysis, is not intended to speak to such distress. The function of art, on the other hand, is precisely to speak about experience, including historical experience. It is not bound to construct a model—an imitation of past events; it does not adhere to the idea that it is only through such a construction that, as literary theorist Jean-Marie Schaeffer puts it, "we discover the properties of the object that constrain it."[7] Art has other, less intellectual modes that probe the body of history and are capable of hitting a nerve. Intuitive yet unsparing, art can stage the return of the historical past.

Experience is, then, by definition subjective—whether the experiencing subject is individual or collective. Experience refers to something the subject has directly observed and lived through. It is not abstract like the rational reconstruction of the past from the heights of historical consciousness. Historical experiences submit to the course of time, are embedded in concrete places and social milieus, and lodged in the private and collective consciousness that can bring them to light. Experience is, in sum, anchored in the materiality of the past. Historical discourse, on the other hand, speaks about experience as if it were irremediably separate, alienated from us by the very fact that it constitutes an object of study. Getting too close to the object of study is dangerous: empathy is the enemy of historical method. Scientific history is not suited to describing subjective experience because its concepts and its language position it at a remove from the world of concrete memory and the sensations and emotions that form the specific content of experience.

To narrate the past, which is what historians do, is to shift from being in the world to giving an account of the world, to shift from a position inside physical/mental life to a position outside and above it. Experience cannot be reached through the application of a conceptual apparatus, like historical materialism, for example, which assigns elements of experience ("facts") to the a priori categories of an analytic grid the historian establishes in advance. To put it plainly, the social sciences—economics, sociology, or politics—in their search for meaning of one sort or another inevitably *denature* experience (I use the word in its literal not pejorative sense). Although without a historical understanding of the past historical experience might well be inaccessible, experience cannot be explicated into existence. Indeed, explanation and experience are intractable adversaries; the one necessarily wins out over the other.

These theoretical propositions may sound abstract, and I would like to pause here to clarify what I mean by historical experience by citing an example from a work by essayist and memoirist Daniel Mendelsohn: *The Lost: A Search for Six of Six Million* (2006). *The Lost* is a remarkable piece of research into the fate of six members of Mendelsohn's Jewish family who lived and died in Ukraine under Nazi occupation. Mendelsohn thinks he knows what he is looking for: traces of the fate of his maternal grandfather's eldest brother, Schmiel Jäger, and Schmiel's wife and four daughters, whose photographs have the lure of the "unknown and unknowable." He wants to find out *what* happened, to be able to piece together a *story* that will give substance to that still skeletal branch of his family tree. In the last pages of the book, Mendelsohn's search leads him to the back garden of a house in Bolechow, the town where Schmiel's family lived and which on a previous visit he had scoured for memories. By miraculous happenstance. Mendelsohn, on the point of leaving the town in total frustration, is introduced to an old woman who was witness to the fate of Schmiel and his daughter Frydka. She takes him into a neighboring garden and points to the place near an ancient apple tree where Nazis summarily executed the father and daughter. Mendelsohn's experience is not what he had expected. He finds himself in the *place itself*, exposed to the sudden recovery of a moment in time he thought had been lost:

> It is one thing to stand before a spot you have long thought about, a building or shrine or monument that you've seen in paintings or books or magazines, a place where, you think, you are expected to have certain kinds of feelings. . . . It is another thing to be standing in a place that for a long time you thought was hypothetical, a place of which you might say *the place where it happened* and think, it was in a field, it was in a house, it was in a gas chamber, against a wall or on the street, but when you said those words to yourself it was not so much the *place* that seemed to matter as the *it*, the terrible thing that had been done, because you weren't really thinking of the place as anything but a kind of envelope, disposable, unimportant. Now I was standing in the place itself, and I had had no time to prepare. I confronted the place itself, the thing and not the idea of it.[8]

As this passage reveals, historical experience refers to the inchoate sphere of human realities and interactions that come before language consigns them to a structured domain of interpretation, whether narrative, conceptual, or figurative; without *what comes before*, these instruments of discourse would have nothing to organize. Historical experience—and the intuitive understanding we have of it—is preverbal and pre-logical. When we confront a past reality, we are *unprepared* as Mendelsohn puts it. Experience never assumes the status of an example or a historical fact; it does not enclose itself in a context; nor does it pose as one term of a transparent metaphor. Experience does not stand in for anything else; it cannot be subsumed without ceasing to be itself. It is what it is.

Pragmatist philosopher Richard Shusterman distinguishes experience from discourse in the following terms:

> We can understand something without thinking about it at all; but to interpret something we need to think about it. This distinction may recall a conclusion from Wittgenstein's famous discussion of seeing-as: "To interpret is to think, to do something; seeing is a state."[9]

An experience of the historical past occurs, then, when the context the historian constructs or the narrative structure of memory loosens its hold. In a sudden and fleeting apprehension, the human subject grasps, in the literal sense of the word, a concrete fragment of past existence. Experience cannot be defined; it can only be pointed at. As I can point to the gesture of a Jewish survivor (in Hersonski's *A Film Unfinished*) seated in a screening room, who covers her face with her hand when the footage of the Warsaw Ghetto where she lived as a child is not only intolerably brutal but entirely too *close*. Or to cite a recent example, in a television interview with CNN's Anderson Cooper, a woman who fled from North Korea ten years ago is absorbed in watching footage of mass demonstrations and suddenly finds herself pulled back into that world. To her horror, she identifies with the inculcated adoration of the despotic rulers from whom she had chosen to escape. In all such cases, the distance between present and past is suspended in a flash of renewed experience.

With gesture, as with inarticulate sound, we are in the realm of preverbal speech—the kind of unvoiced reaction that characterizes many of our relationships with the world, with others, with ourselves. Much of what is deepest and most intense in our experience has little to do with language as such. Experience manifests itself, rather, in the manner of what Wittgenstein calls the *groan*, an inarticulate sound that escapes from us as if the pain of experience were speaking on its own.[10] By metaphoric extension, we can say that entire communities express themselves in modes that rely, at least in part, on instinct and intuition. Following Wittgenstein, Ankersmit forcibly argues that civilizations also groan and that we find such "inarticulate" expression in the work of "enthusiastic" artists, be they poets, painters, novelists, or filmmakers, or even historians who deviate from the classical tenets of the discipline.

> These groanings may overwhelm us with an unequaled force and intensity, and they may be perceived in the *basso continuo* accompanying all that a civilization thinks and does. It means, rather, that we should not interpret them *as being about something else* in the way that the true statement is about some state of affairs in the world. We should take

them for what they *are*, that is, as the groanings of a civilization, as the texts in which the pains, the moods, and feelings of a civilization articulate themselves. *In this way these groanings are essentially poetic: just like a poem they do not aim at truth but at making experience speak. And this is how we should read them.*[11]

MYTH AS A MODE OF UNDERSTANDING

Wittgenstein is concerned with the *articulation* of historical experience that comes about through the rituals of art. Here, to articulate is to understand, not intellectually but affectively, the meaning of events. In contrast to the unpredictable ways in which memories of experience often surge into consciousness, ritual is a way of organizing—of imposing structure on—the inchoate and random world of past and present experience, particularly at the moments of upheaval and distress that are our concern in this study. It goes without saying that ritual and historical structures have little in common. As Israeli historian Joseph Mali argues, myth, the source of all ritual, offers "the primal 'order' in human life and history,"[12] which is quite the opposite of the discursive order that history imposes. T. S. Eliot describes thus the function of myth in the work of James Joyce: "It is simply a way of controlling, of ordering, of giving a shape and significance to the immense panorama of futility and anarchy which is contemporary history."[13] Eliot, writing in 1923, is talking about the survival—and the necessity—of myth in the modern era that has already seen the devastating cultural dislocation occasioned by the First World War.

From the anthropologist's perspective, Clifford Geertz argues for the universal relevance of myth not only for "pre-scientific" civilizations but for the modern and contemporary worlds. We need, he contends, "mythic models of emotion" that can enclose experience in structures that are both familiar and ineffable: "In order to make up our minds we must know how we feel about things; and to know how we feel about things we need the public images of sentiment that only ritual, myth, and art can provide."[14]

From the point of view of historical theory, Ankersmit describes history and myth as quite distinct modes of representation. History achieves its mastery over the past through association. It configures events in a causal/chronological series; it domesticates experience through narrative. Myths, on the other hand, are obdurate blocks of narration about a civilization's past that are impervious to historical method; they can be cited or retold in new guises, but they resist absolutely being integrated into any historical account of a community's past. "These mythological pasts," Ankersmit argues, "cannot be historicized since they are *dissociated* pasts, and, as such, beyond the reach of even the most sustained and desperate attempt at historicization. They must be situated in a domain that is outside civilization's historical time." What they provide is a legacy of immutable emotions and ritual structures capable of sustaining a community in the direst straights. "They possess," Ankersmit tells us, "the highest dignity: They are civilization's historical sublime."[15]

Indeed, myths, as Mali argues, are living social forces that a community in danger may call upon. They "become significant precisely in moments when common traditional meanings of life and history have become indeterminate, as in wars or revolutions, and their social utility is to sustain the structural tradition of society by some dramatic reactivation of its original motivations."[16] They also become significant in times of "memory crisis," which cultural theorist Richard Terdiman defines as "a sense that [the people's] past had somehow evaded memory, that recollection had ceased to integrate with consciousness."[17] As we will see, all the films in this study are pervaded by crises of memory: they struggle against historical neglect and political prohibition, they object to the artificial and self-serving mythologies of power, they expose the mendacity and distortions of sanctioned narratives, and they strive to rescue historical testimony from the brink of oblivion.

Above all, mythic narratives reach into the wells of collective memory whose images the individual subject has no immediate recollection of but which can be brought to the surface under the force of circumstances. The obverse of historical memories, they require no authentication. They are closer to the "primitive" structures of the unconscious. Their goal is to reenact some "forgotten" experience using the instruments of imagination and fabulation. Wittgenstein asserts that the human being is a "ceremonious animal" and that mythic ritual produces a "deep and sinister" effect on the inner self.[18] These organized sequences of images and actions are not biographical details the subject remembers. As T. S. Eliot suggests, they come from elsewhere: "Such memories may have symbolic value, but of what we cannot tell, for they come to represent the depths of feeling into which we cannot peer."[19]

For scientific historiography, myth as a mode of understanding past realities is irrelevant: it is a relic of pre-scientific thought. The historian is considered to be engaged in constructing a credible and rational account of events based on facts alone; he or she orders sequences of events according to plausible causes and effects. Myth, on the other hand, evokes the past as a storied world inhabited by fabulous characters who take legendary actions. Myth is atavistic. It "reverts" to the ancient and the ancestral, those suspect domains inaccessible to historical analysis, and to a state of the world in which the cosmic link between the human and the natural has not been severed. Indeed, historians have taken myth as the antipode of history. As an "explanation" of events, it replaces objective observation with primal emotions and collective fantasies. In Marxist thought, for example, myth is motivated by retrograde ideologies and needs to be eradicated to clear the way for a scientific understanding of history.

In general, for the historical discipline, mythological thought is pre-logical and pre-modern, that is, thoroughly retrograde. It harkens back to the dark times when human societies sought refuge from realities that overwhelmed comprehension. Before the scientific revolution divorced the subject who investigates from the object of investigation, mythical thinking kept historical communities in thrall to primitive stories that embodied a system of beliefs close to the sacred.

Mali, however, argues that historiography's rejection of myth is at best misguided. First, it eliminates from its purview authentic representations of the experience of past societies: "who they thought they were, where they came from, and where they went."[20] Second, it denies the fact that mythology is not just a relic of the past but an essential (if often unacknowledged) aspect of contemporary life. In the work of German philosopher Walter Benjamin, Mali tells us, myth is "a category of absolute conceptual and historical primacy, the key to all further inquiries into human affairs."[21] For Benjamin, myth exists in latent form in the most rational of modern societies. It is an irrepressible compulsion, a desire to return to "archaic" states of being and experiences that are thought to be lost to modern societies.

Let me suggest the implications of this analysis for the chapters to follow. This study is about two ways that historical film may turn away from the methodical realism of classic historiography and draw on sources one can only characterize as psychic. Both approaches respond to deep-seated compulsions. In the first, the subject of memory abandons all defenses in order to bring back to the surface of consciousness long suppressed experiences and relive them at his or her peril. In the second, the subject as a member of a collectivity recalls, in the literal sense of the word, mythic structures that organize the chaotic and often intolerable experience of the group.

SEVEN FILMS ABOUT CONVULSIVE HISTORY

In choosing films for this study, I was mindful of Mali's exhortation that a modern historiography should be judged on what it succeeds in saying about the cataclysmic events of the last century. This was the turbulent age that historian Eric Hobsbawn calls the "short" twentieth century: the cycle of violence that began in 1914 with the First World War and concluded with the final collapse of Soviet Communism in about 1990. I was particularly interested in films that approached their subjects from the point of view of the late twentieth and early twenty-first centuries. They were to be films that stood at a remove from the events they relate—some more distantly than others. They were, at the same time, to be films whose ambition was not simply to narrate events but to *recover*, often in flashes of insight, how these events were experienced by the people who lived through them.

Before going further, I should identify the films under study, each of which occupies a full chapter in this book.

Yaël Hersonski's *A Film Unfinished* (2010)
Andrzej Wajda's *Katyn* (2007)
Andrei Konchalovsky's *Siberiade* (1979)
Larisa Shepitko's *The Ascent* (1977)
Patricio Guzman's *Nostalgia for the Light* (2010)

Rithy Panh's *S-21: The Khmer Rouge Killing Machine* (2003)
Joshua Oppenheimer's *The Act of Killing* (2012)

Hersonski's *A Film Unfinished* appears among the recent flood of films about the Holocaust, be they documentaries or fictions, some more or less serious, others more or less trivial. The phenomenon has occasioned a great deal of debate about *traumatic realism* (to borrow the title of Michael Rothberg's excellent study) and how it is possible to represent what passes historical understanding. What is particularly compelling about Hersonski's film is that it reawakens the living experience of the residents of the Warsaw Ghetto through the last of its survivors, using a complex, intertextual approach.

The next three films deal with aspects of the history of Stalinism, still an under-researched area fraught with its own history of suppression and taboos. This willful neglect is all the more startling in that the Soviet revolution and its aftermath extend the whole length of the "short" twentieth century, the ignoble demise of the Soviet regime marking the century's point of closure. The Stalinist era is also underrepresented in filmographies of Soviet historical films that are not deformed by the deadening aesthetics of socialist realism and the work of party censors.

Siberiade and *The Ascent* were both completed in late 1970s, toward the end of the Brezhnev era. Shortly after the coup against Khrushchev, Brezhnev had begun to reverse the Khrushchev "thaw" and suppress intellectual and artistic freedom. As historian Tony Judt puts it, "By any standard save those of its own history, the regime was immovable, repressive and inflexible," and presaged a period of "indefinite twilight of economic stagnation and moral decay."[22] *Siberiade* and *The Ascent* are both critical of Stalinist mythology (Shepitko's film was denied export to the West until 2005), yet, for obvious reasons, transgression in both films moves below the surface of narratives that seem to conform to officially sanctioned Soviet subjects. They are, however, transgressive in quite different manners. *Siberiade* is epic in scale, an attempt to represent the whole of the Soviet experience from 1914 to the 1960s. *The Ascent*, on the other hand, is something of a chamber drama in which a small set of characters plays out the destiny of partisans captured by

Nazi invaders. From the perspective of the twenty-first century, Wajda's *Katyn*, in contrast, is a frontal attack against one episode of Stalinist atrocities: the Soviet dictator's murder during the Second World War of nearly the entire Polish officer corps. Made possible precisely by the fall of the Soviet empire, *Katyn* is haunted by Wajda's personal memories of hopelessly waiting for the return of his own father from a Soviet POW camp.

Patricio Guzmán's *Nostalgia for the Light* is about landscape and memory (to borrow another book title, this one by Simon Schama) in one of the most desolate places on the planet, the Atacama Desert. There, several histories converge: the history of pre-Columbian people, the history of the exploitation of native miners in the nineteenth century, the history of Pinochet's crimes, and the history of the cosmos. The convergence of these pasts, translated into luminous images, is held together by Guzman's personal voice and his poetic strategies.

The approach to the representation of genocide that Rithy Panh adopts in *S-21: The Khmer Rouge Killing Machine* is quite unprecedented. He reunites the few remaining victims and their more numerous perpetrators in the empty buildings of Pol Pot's infamous prison of the film's title where the former suffered and the latter inflicted pain. A master of documentary mise-en-scène, Panh stages encounters between the past —lying fallow in written, verbal, and photographic evidence, and in the psyches of mass murderers—and the present, seemingly mired in the depths of denial.

In *The Act of Killing* Joshua Oppenheimer has created an innovative approach to the study of mass murder, in this case the Indonesian genocide of 1965–1966. Like Panh, he calls on the torturers and executioners to bear witness to their crimes. However, instead of directly confronting the assassins, he asks them to reenact cinematically their history of violence in whatever manner they see fit. Enamored of the Hollywood film, the cinematic modes of representation they choose indulge fantasies we may find deeply disturbing. Nonetheless, they lead to revelations about this bloody history and its political consequences while exposing the psychological mechanisms that allow murderers to murder en masse.

STUCK IN THE THROAT OF HISTORY

Under what conditions is it possible to *forget* the kinds of traumatic events that haunt the seven films in this study? There are, Frank Ankersmit argues, four types of forgetting: (1) forgetting what is irrelevant to our current or past identity; (2) forgetting aspects of events whose relevance we have not understood (as in the neglect of economic factors in pre-Marxist historiography); (3) forgetting what is too painful to be admitted to consciousness; and (4) forgetting—shedding—an old identity in order to assume a new identity in a world that has been utterly transformed.[23]

Ankersmit designates the third and fourth types of forgetting as trauma1 and trauma2. He describes trauma1 in psychodynamic terms: the traumatic experience has been relegated to the unconscious where it survives as unacknowledged memory and continues to afflict the subject's existence. This is the paradox of an experience that is at once forgotten and remembered. Ankersmit extends the status of traumatized subject to the collective actors of history. In history, trauma is a shared experience, and, as the seven films I study demonstrate, the individual who bears witness to his or her suffering gives voice to the suffering of whole classes of victims. In trauma1, closure is possible (if often not realized) because the traumatic experience may be successfully absorbed into the life story of an individual.

Such a reconciliation can be conceived in collective terms only by analogy. As Paul Ricoeur so perceptively put it, we can think of a social group as a quasi-person by *oblique reference* to the individuals that make it up: "It is because each society is made up of individuals that it behaves like one great individual on the stage of history and that historians can attribute to these singular entities the initiative for certain courses of action,"[24] or, I would add, their subjection to the actions of others. Once transmuted by the binding power of narrative—once one's story has been told—traumatic experience "will lose its threatening and specifically traumatic character." What has been achieved, as Ankersmit puts it, is a *"reconciliation* of experience and identity . . . guaranteeing the continued existence of both." But there is, he insists, a terrible cost to pay: the subject, whether individual or collective, must contend with fearful demons and make a "most painful descent into the past."[25] In the case of collectivities, this descent into the past necessarily takes place in the public sphere where testimony—like the kind we find in the seven films studied here—exposes the pain of traumatic events.

Trauma2 is of a quite different order because the unconscious—personal or collective—is not at all in play. The subject of history consciously *abandons* a former identity anchored in a world of traditions and modes of thought that have ceased to exist. Ankersmit gives us examples of these transformational moments: Europe after the French Revolution, the radical social and economic consequences of the Industrial Revolution, or the impact of the Death of God on "our *outillage mental*." We enter these brave new worlds on condition that we shed our anachronisms—that is, everything that is obsolete and antediluvian about our prior existence. The loss of identity is profound; it provokes an irreparable sense of loss, but here no reconciliation is possible: "This, then, is the kind of trauma that we will carry with us after History has forced us to confront it; it is a trauma for which no cure is to be found."[26] Civilizations, he argues, do not die natural deaths: "moving to a new and different world really *is* and also *requires* an act of violence, in fact nothing less than an act of suicide."[27]

In the seven films under study, we are certainly dealing with the overturning of worlds, not by acts of suicide but by violent acts of murder: the Nazis' decimation of European Jewry (*A Film Unfinished*); the Soviets' brutal repression of Polish nationalism (*Katyn*); their suppression of the mythological foundation of traditional cultures in the name of the proletarian revolution (*Siberiade* and *The Ascent*); Pinochet's assassination of leftist Chileans in the name of "democracy" and liberal capitalism (*Nostalgia for the Light*); the systematic torture and murder of perceived class enemies, driven by a perverse and barbaric "left" (*S-21: The Khmer Rouge Killing Machine*) or by the anti-Communist right and its gangland agents in Indonesia (*The Act of Killing*). What "wholly new worlds" do these savage events of the twentieth century propose? How is it possible to forget such traumas? How do we live with "all the scars on our collective soul" that continue to give us pain? How do we become reconciled to the unacceptable?

Recovering historical experience, as I will describe it in the following chapters, has nothing to do with reconciliation or with the recognition and acceptance of events that have radically changed the shape of the world. Reconciliation, recognition, and acceptance are achieved through narratives, personal or collective, that lead us, however painfully, to an ending from which we are permitted no meaningful retreat. This is the heart of the historiographic project: to substitute a reconstruction, a synoptic model, for the reality of past experience. We may relapse into bouts of melancholia or nostalgic fantasy—palliatives that are sometimes necessary in the process of forgetting—but we ultimately acknowledge historical finality.

Each film in this study centers on a traumatic moment. Each of these moments is a manifestation of arrested development in which the subject can look neither backward nor forward. He or she is stuck in the reality of living time, unable to "process" the overwhelming character of events and the excruciation they cause. Indeed, all seven films seem incapable of dénouement: the knot cannot be unknotted nor can it be simply cut. None of the films is a "cure" for a historical malady. Rather, they all plunge us into the immediacy of a reality that sticks in the throat of history.

DYNAMIC AESTHETIC EXPERIENCE

It is quite apparent to any viewer that these films are not typical commodities in the marketplace of mass culture. They are, rather, exceptional films made by exceptional filmmakers—exceptional in the kinds of experience the filmmakers bear witness to and in the kinds of response the films evoke in the spectator. I do not mean to suggest that such films are rare, but they do rely on a particular kind of dynamic that binds the artist and the spectator in an "experiential activity through which [works of art] are created and perceived."[28]

This notion of dynamic social exchange motivates the approaches I take to the films—approaches that are only now beginning to emerge in the study of nonfiction films. First, I emphasize the *person* of the filmmaker, the subjectivity with which he or she approaches the material to be included in the film. Far from being a product of the text (as the poststructuralists would have it), the filmmaker is directly invested in the experiences the film evokes, and frequently that investment is autobiographical: it is the search for an experience of the past in which he or she is directly implicated. Although this emphasis on the filmmaker might seem like a variation on auteurism, notions like formal achievement, style as personal expression, or the filmmaker's oeuvre are beside the point. "Art," in the modernist sense, is not what these filmmakers are looking for (even if the films do provide rich aesthetic experiences).

Second, I found it important to pay close attention to the way the films work, and therefore close textual analysis is an essential tool. My intent is not to study the films as closed textual systems but to identify how they provide public access (so to speak) to intimate lived experience. As I have argued, historical experience for the film's public does not emerge from a broad representation of events that gives the impression that we have grasped their meaning. Rather, experience emerges as moments of insight, fragmentary illuminations, in which we feel the past is present to us. This way of looking requires a different model of the experience of art, one provided, I believe, by American pragmatist philosopher Thomas Dewey and his successors.

Thomas Dewey protested most cogently against the aestheticism that isolates art in a realm of its own, divorced from "every other form of human effort, undergoing, and achievement,"[29] Indeed it is the pragmatist model elaborated in his *Art as Experience* (1934), with its insistence on the sociohistorical dimensions of art, which provides a model of aesthetics relevant to the nature of the films we are considering. For Dewey, experience in the world is primary; it comes before any external human agency begins to frame it. It privileges, as Richard Shusterman argues, the "dynamic aesthetic experience over the fixed material object which our conventional thinking identifies—and then commodifies and fetishizes—as the work of art."[30] Art, history, and culture are part of daily life and its traditions before they become objects of cognition for historians, art historians, or anthropologists. They belong to common experience: "Indeed, such heightened experiences are frequently remembered not only *as* shared but *because* they are shared."[31]

Against classic historiography, Dewey contends that experience does not become meaningful only when it is transmuted into language (it is *understood* before it is *interpreted*); indeed, language may serve to devalue it. He argues for an aesthetic theory that reconnects the intense experience of art—with its formal structures, its sensory materials, and its sense of closure—with all human activity, the actions of daily life that human actors perform or are subject to. Art provides *an* experience, as Dewey puts it, distinct from the flow of experience that characterizes human life. Life is nonetheless the source, and to understand art, one must first turn away from it—back to the social world from which it emerges.

Art, then, is the *expression* of experience, which is the continuous interaction between human beings and their environment. It is distinct from the *description* of the world that is the objective of the social sciences. Unlike the scientific statement that relies on language, meaning in the arts is inherent in the object the artist produces. Art is concrete and "local." It combines the sensuous materials of art and the materials of experience, in "a fusion so complete as to incorporate both members in a single whole."[32]

The pragmatist model establishes a deep correspondence among the act of expression, the expressive object, and the public that "beholds" the object. The producer and his or her product are, as Dewey would say, "organically connected," and, for their part, the members of the public who receive the product do not passively undergo the experience of art. In response to the appeal of the object, they envision an experience analogous to the artist's: "For to perceive, the beholder must *create* his own experience. And his creation must include relations comparable to those which the original producer underwent."[33] In other words, the process of reception is deeply interactive. Shusterman describes in the following terms how works of art are understood by the public:

> As Wittgenstein labored to teach us, meaning is not a separate object or content, but merely the correlate of understanding. And understanding something is not the mirror-like capturing or replication of some fixed and determinate intentional object or semantic content. It is fundamentally an ability to handle or respond to that thing in certain accepted ways which are consensually shared, sanctioned, and inculcated by the community but which are nonetheless flexible and open to (divergent) interpretation and emendation.[34]

The pragmatist model of art Shusterman describes has, I believe, important implications for the analysis of historical films this study proposes. An interactive approach, which credits the spectator with such an active role in the production of meaning, argues against the pre-digestion of historical materials through discursive techniques, notably through the overriding *voiceover of history* (listen to the voice-track of 90 percent of historical documentaries featured on public television or the History Channel), or through the rhetorical play with which the filmmaker fabricates *equivalents* for the historian's representational language. Consider the mechanism of the synecdoche as it appears in Ester Shub's *Fall of the Romanov Dynasty* (1927), a film that virtually invents the rhetoric of the compilation documentary. In one of Shub's dialectical montages, for example, several shots of peasants at work in the fields stand for the whole laboring class in the countryside. These motifs are juxtaposed against shots of the landlords' excessive riches and their life of leisure. Through this rhetorical gesture, class warfare is materialized in the figure—the antithesis—made possible by parallel editing. The concrete realities the camera documents are thus appropriated by a structure of meaning determined in advance.[35]

Such discursive techniques are alien to the films in this study. Indeed, historical interpretation is not the objective of the filmmakers I have chosen to discuss. Consciously or not, they resist the work of interpretation because it is too detached for them, too removed from the experience that still hovers above the cataclysmic events their films are meant to evoke. They are after something I would call revival, if we can strip the word of all religious connotation. Through film, the past can still reemerge, not the diminished whole of it as it is grasped in the retrospective gaze of the historian, but in intense flashes of involuntary memory.

NEW HISTORY, NEW HISTORICAL FILMS

Frank Ankersmit has observed a recent cultural shift in historical study. He describes it as "a moving away from comprehensive systems of meaning to meaning as bound to specific situations and events."[36] In other words, it is not the discourse of history—the analytic construction of narratives based on facts—that preoccupies the researcher; it is rather the past itself and the ways in which "people in the past experienced their world" that are becoming a central focus of historical research. In Ankersmit's terms, the movement in the discipline is no longer "centrifugal"—outward toward the domain of cognition and language where historians alienate themselves from the material past. It is "centripetal" in the sense that research moves toward the center, which is the experience of the past itself.[37] It is a movement to break out of what Nietzsche called "the prisonhouse of language."

This shift in the practice of historiography that brings historians closer to their objects of study risks overturning historiography's classic position on subjectivity—namely, that the presence of the historian in his or her text is a *contamination* one regrets in the name of science and that one attempts to reduce to a strict minimum. In contrast, Ankersmit's theory of history focuses directly on the question of subjectivity, and his conception of it is iconoclastic. He postulates that the border between the subject (the historian) and the object (past events), which classic historiography and professional practice would guard inexorably, is porous by nature, "unstable and, in fact, impossible to define."[38] And it is not just the subject that intrudes on the object; the object also intrudes on the subject. The contamination of one by the other is inherent in any historical text, *as it is in life itself.* This second proposition cuts to the heart of Ankersmit's universalist notion of the presence of history in human culture. History, he argues, is part of us as we are part of history: its roots "reach into the deepest parts of our mind and are impossible to isolate completely from what and who we are ourselves."[39] To the extent that it is meaningful, the past is very much alive in us since we live through it, and Ankersmit insists on the intimacy of the relationship:

> The past—and I do really have in mind here a past stretching out to the very roots of our civilization—is as such not an entity that only historians come across in their academic researches but a companion permanently closer to us than even our parents, our wives and husbands, or our most intimate friends. It is our second self, and all of our life is a continuous fight with history.[40]

If the past is not the exclusive domain of specialists called historians whose regulated practice produces the only authentic historical representations—if history is, rather, a collective possession whose expression is the vital concern of living human communities—then we should be open to redefining what constitutes an appropriate object of historical representation and receptive to innovative strategies for evoking the past, including the cinematic.

In the succeeding chapters of this book I will attempt to describe seven such innovative approaches to the historical film. What unites the seven filmmakers is a common refusal, embodied in their texts, to give in to the idea that past experience can hope to survive only if it is reduced to language. They do not simply desire knowledge about the past; they desire to recover something of the past in its being. They search for "protuberances," as Ankersmit calls them, the lingering traces of historical life that are not yet caught in a system of signification. When the search is successful, images and sounds quicken, and speech and language become part of the human sensorium.

HISTORY AND THE ERRATIC IMAGE

This is the moment to speak about the specificity of the cinematic image that historians and social scientists, even the most enlightened, so often find disturbing. They are disconcerted by the "floating chain of signifiers" that semiologist Roland Barthes identified in the photographic image, which may evade meaning if it is not *anchored* by language—the verbal language imposed by the caption, the discursive language of causality, or the narrative language of before and after.

French historian Marc Ferro, much of whose work on film is collected in the volume *Cinema and History*, was perhaps the first to propose a serious methodology for approaching the historical study of film. He begins by deploring the bias of historians against visual media: "[Film] does not enter the historian's mental universe." "The language of film appears unintelligible," "like that of dream,"[41] and possesses none of the rigor of verbal language. But that, for Ferro, is both the point and his point of departure. In contradistinction to his more traditional colleagues, he argues that "there is material there [in films]—one which certainly does not claim to constitute a beautiful, harmonious, and rational ensemble as does History—which can help to refine or destroy History."[42] That material belongs to the "unexpected and involuntary," all that the visual field is susceptible of revealing about the reality the camera captures.

Ferro proposes what he calls the "counteranalysis of society"[43] through film, which he models on Freudian psychoanalysis, although his subject is not the individual patient but the more expansive field of unacknowledged historical intentions (history's patient, if you will). Ferro talks about *lapses* on the part of "a creator, an ideology, or a society" that frequently appear in films. Counteranalysis, he argues, consists in the historian's probe into the "unconscious" of the image: the latent messages a film contains either because, in one way or another, the filmmaker said more than he or she intended to say, or because the camera, that undiscriminating instrument, captured significant realities that were "irrelevant" to the discourse the filmmaker was constructing. Take for example Ferro's study of the ideological meaning of the four dissolves in the anti-Semitic melodrama *Jüd Suss* (1940) in which, he says, the filmmaker, Veit Harlan, "was betrayed by his art," or the "hidden" messages of documentary footage that Ferro analyzed in his television series, *Parallel Histories*. As we will see, these moments of "excess" provide a rich source of revelation in many of the films in this study.

I should point out, however, Ferro's deep distrust of film as a medium for representing the historical past: "It is easy to think that film is not suited to represent past reality and that at best its testimony is valuable only for the present; or that aside from documents and newsreels, the reality it offers is no more real than the novel's."[44] Filmmakers are not historians, he argues, because they are untrained in the discipline and lack critical objectivity. Moreover, all historical representation in film is by nature fictional because filmmakers are primarily concerned with aesthetics and drama: "History, as it was lived, or as it took place, does not obey the laws of melodrama or of tragedy."[45] Most damagingly, filmic representations of history are immutable (not open to correction and revision) and tend to fix (fictive) images of events in the mind of the public—images that historians must then struggle to dislodge.

Like Ferro, what I am interested in in this study is the *unbound* image, to use another Freudian term, or more precisely, the unbound audiovisual traces of the past that historical film may uncover and put back in play. As I hope I have made clear, my argument is not that the "irrational" traces of the past must be salvaged by the language of historians who interpret them according to their categories of analysis. On the contrary, I posit the inherent value of the vestiges of experience and of the mythic structures through which they are often expressed. I will be particularly attentive to the spillovers, the excesses, and the sense of the uncanny that the cinematic signifier often catalyzes and that may refer us to the sites of historical repression. I am looking for the moments when the *unexpected* and the *involuntary* surface and the desire to recover what has been lost overwhelms the need to understand.

ॐ

Before continuing, I would like to acknowledge the debt I owe to the innovative writers—historians, philosophers, and film scholars—whose work I think is relevant to expanding approaches to the study of the history film.

I have already cited Israeli historian Joseph Mali, whose *Mythistory: The Making of a Modern Historiography* champions myth—the archenemy of historiography since Thucydides—as the deepest expression of a people's aspiration and the motivation for all historical action. I have also revealed the great debt I owe to Dutch philosopher Frank Ankersmit, whose *Sublime Historical Experience*, among other works, demonstrates that the past, far from being irrevocably lost to us, may in fact be recovered and re-experienced in the present.

To cite other influences: British historian Simon Schama's *Landscape and Memory* shows that history can be recovered from landscape if the historian is not content with the superficial lay of the land but excavates deep into its many layers of meaning. Another is not a new historian but an "old" theorist, Walter Benjamin, whose notions of the illumination and the mimetic faculty suggest an intimate exchange between the subject of experience and his or her object, a closing of the distance that the science of history would impose between the observer and the observed. Finally, I would like to acknowledge the work of American historian Timothy Snyder, whose *Bloodlands: Europe Between Hitler and Stalin* opens our eyes to the two regimes' parallel ambitions and policies of mass murder and shows what is at stake in the representation of violent events.

Since the historical film calls on two separate disciplines, film scholars in the field have by necessity become to some extent historians, and historians have become film scholars. First among these hybrids is Robert Rosenstone, the self-described postmodern historian, who champions the (brave and scandalous) notion that there is more than one way of writing history and that audiovisual media are capable of telling us different but legitimate stories about the past, using their specific modes of communication so distinct from the written word. Moreover, Rosenstone has led the way in analyzing the modes of historical representation in film—the dramatic film, the documentary, the experimental film—and the various techniques of narration the historical film employs. Finally, Rosenstone raises, in his eloquent but radical manner, one of the issues that is at the heart of this study:

> For us [historians], the ideal "history" seems to be the history produced by scholars of the academy; one comprised of a soundless, colorless, motionless, and largely emotionless world of words on a page. One has to wonder: just whose history is this? Why do we so rigorously preclude all these affective elements that comprise our daily life?[46]

Historian Natalie Zemon Davis is a serious advocate for the cinematic expression of history. In her defense of the historical potential of the feature film, Davis examines the classic opposition between poetry and prose in which Thucydides embraces critical inquiry and documentation and Homer is given license to please his audience with fictive invention. This dichotomy, Davis asserts, is perpetuated in the commonsense opposition between documentary film (a pragmatic, truth-seeking discourse) and the feature film (imaginary narratives liberated from the constraints of the real and the true), and it is this polarity, she continues, that needs to be called into question. Davis argues that the film medium is particularly adept at "micro-history," or exploring a "telling example in depth." Indeed, its strength is that it can "show—or more correctly, *speculate* on—how the past was experienced and acted out, how large forces and major events were lived through locally and in detail."[47] Moreover, Davis is among the few historians who insist on the importance of the techniques a medium puts into play in its representation of the past.

There are of course the many film scholars who have slowly brought the historical film out from the shadows, defining a place for it as a genre, or a group of genres, and describing its modes of representation. I will mention the work of two scholars here because of their particular relevance to my study.

The first is Robert Burgoyne, who defends film's particular forms of "historical thinking": "the powerful sense that what is being rendered on-screen is not an imaginary world, but a once existing world that is being reinscribed in an original way."[48] Burgoyne's work on film as a way of reshaping national identity, although mainly focused on the American cinema, informs my analysis of the films in the following chapters. I also would cite his pioneering work on "generational memory," or "the discovery of new objects of memory by each generation."[49] Burgoyne's concept of "emotional archaeology" and "somatic empathy"— that the emotional "content" of history is an appropriate, even necessary part of filmic representations of the past—resonates with the work I present here.

The second scholar is Alison Landsberg, whose *Prosthetic Memory: The Transformation of American Remembrance in the Age of Mass Culture* is an important theoretical breakthrough that audaciously links words like "emotion," "sensation," and "sensuality" to the experience the spectator *should* derive from viewing a historical film: "In the process that I am describing, the person does not simply apprehend a historical narrative but takes on a more personal, deeply felt memory of the past event through which he or she did not live."[50] Moreover, Landsberg's notion of "transferential spaces," which invite people to enter into "experiential relationships to events,"[51] opens up areas of analysis of our transactional relationships with representations of the past. Landsberg is talking about American culture and the "commodified forms" through which "mass-mediated representations" become the potential "grounds on which social meanings are negotiated."[52]

What I am studying in *Unspeakable Histories* is less "rational" than the historical emotions Burgoyne and Landsberg seek to delineate. Burgoyne would rethink historical reenactment to include the emotional "content" of history. Landsberg's metaphor of the prosthesis—the historical film, the museum that is "worn on the body" and sutures the spectator into historical events—describes the spectator's position physically but also discursively inside of narrative. *Unspeakable Histories,* on the other hand, concerns those moments in the experimental films I have chosen when mediation loses its hold and the spectator comes face to face with the uncanny experience of recovering the past or recovering a long suppressed mythological emotion. The experience I describe is fusional: the historical (and commonsense) distinction between past and present breaks down as the subject suddenly realizes that he or she is implicated in an object from the past and the other way around. It is, to use Frank Ankersmit's comparison, like an ecstatic kiss. This is the (paradoxical) existential moment in which the subject becomes acutely aware of the past as *being,* a condition that is invisible to the analytic historian.

ON THE EXCEPTIONALITY OF THE SELECTED FILMS

It is not unreasonable to suggest that the phenomenon of historical experience, as I have described it, is rare in film and that I have chosen works that are to a large extent sui generis. Indeed, all the films I study could be characterized as experimental, idiosyncratic, and responsive to particular historical circumstances. In short, they are one-of-a-kind films, products of the unusual historical sensibilities of their directors, and they are unlikely to spawn imitations.

Admittedly, I have avoided discussing generic aspects of the films—which do indeed exist—and I have not attempted to discern parallels between the films, which might suggest that historical experience in film has its own special structures. What I wanted to do was uncover and describe what is powerful yet ineffable in these particular films—those *fleeting* moments of historical experience or the resurgence of mythical speech that do indeed arise in quite special circumstances.

I will now contend, however, that these exceptional films are more common than one might suppose.

There is, I would argue, a predilection in film for the representation of experience. Certain features of the cinematic signifier—its substance, its concrete depiction of space and time—"predispose" it to the representation of the tangible. Films become discursive, in the historiographic sense, only through the intrusive gestures of the filmmaker, and those (so visible) efforts, as Marc Ferro observes, are only partially successful in controlling meaning. For Ferro there is a kind of "pull" of cinematic material toward revelations about the past. When Ankersmit goes about describing historical experience—his own—he chooses to analyze his response to an unexceptional painting of Francesco Guardi and examples of rococo ornamentation! How much more likely it is that we will find multiple examples of historical experience in films, particularly those made by filmmakers possessing a fine sensibility toward historical events.

It is in some respects easier to demonstrate that many films have mythological content, whether latent or manifest. Myth is by definition a "social" phenomenon, part of the "collective unconscious." Myths are possessions of a community, however individual filmmakers make use of them. We can expect to find diverse examples of mythological representations in films in certain social contexts, particularly in response to repressive state authority, as I will demonstrate in chapters on *The Ascent* and *Siberiade*, or to crises of memory. Or myths may appear as rejoinders to a still palpable history of subjugation. Postcolonial cinema is replete with oppositional mythologies, for example in sub-Saharan films since Ousmane Sembene.

Finally, in any study that attempts to illustrate a new theoretical approach, one must make a selection of texts. Given the nature of the phenomena I set out to describe, it is understandable, indeed unavoidable, that I would choose films on a subjective basis. In moments of unusual intensity, each film produced in me the sensation of a direct contact with the past—what I describe as a *frisson*, in the full Baudelairian sense of the word. While my selection of films was personal, my intention was to analyze how these texts produced the effects I felt—effects I believe are shared by most viewers. Although I focus on seven specific films, there are many other films that produce what I call a historical sensation and that I could have chosen for the purposes of this study. Allow me to cite the following examples that come to mind.

A Film Unfinished is unusually complex and self-conscious in its approach to historical material, but there are many other testimony films I could have used. I remember vividly the frisson I felt at the end of Claude Lanzmann's *Sobibor* as the seemingly endless rolling titles specified the arrival time of each of the trains bringing victims to the death camp. Similarly, I could have chosen Marcel Ophuls's *Hotel Terminus* or numerous films from the Israeli cinema that are preoccupied with history and testimony.

Katyn is not an exceptional film in Andrzej Wajda's work. *Kanal* (1956) would have been an equally striking subject; so would another film from Eastern Europe—that region of frequently endangered nations so focused on their own histories. Miklos Jancsò's *The Roundup* (1965) or *The Red and the White* (1967) would be finc examples. Larissa Shepitko's *The Ascent* is remarkable for its intimist approach, a feature that brings to mind Yosef Cedar's *Beaufort* (2007). Elem Klimov's *Come and See* (1985) is in many ways quite experimental in its representation of the resistance and would lend itself to the kind of analysis I am proposing. Andrei Konchalovsky's *Siberiade* is certainly one of a kind, but the mythological impulse that drives the film also underlies works like Theo Angelopoulos's equally epic *The Traveling Players* (1974–75).

I would associate Patricio Guzmán's *Nostalgia for the Light* with other poetic films that dwell on the aura of historic places. Michael Haneke's *White Ribbon* (2009), for example, evokes the historical mood in Germany in the period immediately before the Great War. Rooted in a contemporary situation heavy with history, Abderrahmane Sissako's *Waiting for Happiness* (2002) describes Mauritania as the oneiric place of transit for immigrants desperately seeking passage to Europe.

Rithy Panh's *S-21* and Joshua Oppenheimer's *The Act of Killing* are startling examples of documentary mise-en-scène as a technique for recovering the past, but, as I point out, the tradition goes back at least to the films of Jean Rouch, such as *Chronique d'un été* (1960). These deeply ethnographic films demand lengthy preparation on the part of the filmmaker, and they provide irreplaceable testimony on contemporary culture. Panh's more recent *The Missing Picture* suggests that contact with the living past may take place even through the medium of stick figures, just as Art Spiegelman's *Maus* demonstrated the evocative power of the narrative cartoon.

Finally I would point out the importance of not isolating the phenomena I am describing from the larger cultural context. In the arts, literature, and not just in history, we are obsessed with authentic experience: Fernando Botero's *Abu Ghraib*, second-generation Holocaust narratives, poet Philip Schultz's *The Wherewithal*, museums of genocide or of the resistance where authentic traces are intended to transfigure us. . . . What we are seeking in works such as these is the rediscovery of the living past, however painful and disruptive it may be.

1

YAËL HERSONSKI'S
A FILM UNFINISHED

There are wounds with which we should never cease to suffer, and
sometimes, in the life of a civilization, illness is better than health.
—FRANK ANKERSMIT, "REMEMBERING THE HOLOCAUST"

N HER interview with Laliv Melamed, Yaël Hersonki identifies the
initiating event that would lead her toward *A Film Unfinished* (2010): the
sudden recovery of a family memory. In the 1960s her grandmother,
a Polish Jew, was interviewed by oral historian Ida Fink about her experiences in Poland during the Second World War. Hersonski knew that
Fink collected oral history for Yad Vashem, where her grandmother's
testimony might be found. It was, she says, "like a forgotten black box."
When she "rescued" the testimony from the archives, she tells us there
was a period in her grandmother's past about which she was unwilling
to speak. Hersonski cites the brief passage: "We escaped the Warsaw
Ghetto in 1943 to a little village near town. On my time in the ghetto I
don't want to talk." For Hersonski this reference to the Warsaw Ghetto
was totally unexpected: "The nationalized memory of the Holocaust always directs us toward Auschwitz. This is when I'm realizing that my
understanding is like a cracked peel and that the archive holds great
lacunae."[1]

Subsequently Hersonski stumbled on a Nazi documentary film
called *Das Ghetto*, whose ostensible intention was to produce a record
of Jewish life in Warsaw in the spring of 1942. It was obvious, however,
that the Germans had exploited the (quite literally) stunning footage of
misery and death for their nefarious purposes. *Das Ghetto*, which had

never reached the German public for which it was intended, would enable Hersonski, through careful analysis and the interrogation of documents and witnesses, to recover something of the experience of the ghetto about which her grandmother had kept silent. In the process she would expose how the Nazi propagandists had exploited the crafts of editing and staging to construct the film's anti-Semitic message.

THE DISCOVERY

The opening voiceover of *A Film Unfinished* describes the discovery of an underground archive of Nazi films:

> A full decade after the end of the war, East German archivists began for the first time to sort through what remained of Hitler's propaganda machine. Thousands of films discovered in the exact location where they had been stashed, a concrete vault hidden in a forest. It's also there that one lone copy of a film was found over one hour long, with no sound track, no opening or closing credits, only a brief title: "The Ghetto."

This is the film of Hersonski's title, which remains unfinished in two senses. First, *Das Ghetto* was never completed. It exists as a rough cut: it has no soundtrack (the text of which is lost or was never made) and therefore lacks the voiceover commentary that would certainly have firmly anchored the meanings of its brutal images in the Nazi narrative of the Jewish Problem. Second, the film is unfinished historically because its representations have not been subjected to historical analysis nor confronted by the victims of the history it presumably tells. As Hersonski's voiceover maintains, "From the frenzy of propaganda, the images alone remain, concealing many layers of reality." It is the mission of *A Film Unfinished* to dig down into these layers and force them to give up their substance. Under the pressure of testimony and the skill of the editors, the truths of these images are brought to the surface.

Das Ghetto was discovered, then, in underground archives in 1954. The voiceover in *A Film Unfinished* contends that the Nazi documentary was taken at face value for many years. Its pose as an authentic document of life in the Warsaw Ghetto in May 1942 remained unchallenged, despite the film's distortions and fabrications and the blatant anti-Semitism it exudes at nearly every moment. Yaël Hersonski set out in *A Film Unfinished* to counteract any naive reception of the Nazi film. Archives, as historian Jacques Le Goff has pointed out, are always *monuments*, funded by institutions dedicated to preserving a certain vision of history from the bias of power. When confronted with such monuments, the historian must always ask, For what purpose have these documents been assembled and whose interests do they serve? No "historical" archive was as perverse and mendacious as that produced by Nazi propagandists, and none calls more urgently to be deconstructed.

Das Ghetto, like all historical documentaries, reveals more than its filmmakers intended. Allow me to briefly recall what I have already discussed in the introduction about the approach to film analysis that historian Marc Ferro advocates. Ferro argues that the task of the historian involved in analyzing films is much like that of the psychoanalyst in relation to the individual patient: he or she strives to release the repressed content latent in filmic representations. The cinematic image is especially apt for such revelations because, Ferro points out, the author of images maintains only a partial control over the material he or she intends to use for specific purposes. The unanticipated, the involuntary, the excessive can surface under the pressure of historical analysis and lead to understandings of events the filmmaker never foresaw. Hersonski is such a historian, and she is keenly aware of the probative power the filmmaker can exert in the process of working on film documents. There is, she observes, "a certain duality that emanates from the doubleness of the gaze. On the one hand, every image is produced by the person who conceives it; and on the other hand you have the camera, the mechanism, which simply records." What it records are images that go far beyond the filmmaker's intentions, inadvertently revealing "layers of memory and cultural constructions." And this "split between the cameraman and what his camera recorded" exposes an "excess of intentionality, an authorless testimony" that the analyst may bring into play.[2]

The analyst's first task is therefore deconstructive. For Hersonski, a formidable editor, deconstruction of *Das Ghetto* develops through the complex intertextuality of her film. The text of the *Das Ghetto*, its image track, is juxtaposed to (is confronted by) sets of texts that come from different sources. Some are contemporary with the film production itself:

1. Adrian Wood, a researcher collaborating with Cooper Graham at the Library of Congress, who led an exhaustive search for existing filmed documents about the Nazi regime, unearthed previously unknown footage, including thirty minutes of outtakes from *Das Ghetto.*

2. Credible testimony on the events of May 1942 was recorded in a series of nine notebooks by the president of the Warsaw Ghetto's Judenrat (Jewish council), Adam Czerniakow, who kept a daily chronicle of his experiences with the German administration, including preparations for the filming of *Das Ghetto.*

3. Historian Emanuel Rinkelblum, a Polish Jew, recruited a host of residents of the ghetto to keep diaries of daily observations of events. He established a library of these journals that survived the war, known as the Oyneg Shabes Archive. They constitute one of the most important sources of information on techniques and effects of Nazi claustration.

4. One of the Nazi film crew was located after the end of the war, and his interrogation by a judge has been preserved in an archive in Ludwigsburg. As we will see, the fragmented "reconstruction" of this testimony appears at intervals in *A Film Unfinished.*

Another set of texts emerged from the production of *A Film Unfinished* itself:

1. In the process of preparing and shooting *A Film Unfinished*, the filmmakers were able to elicit testimony from several Jews who survived the Warsaw Ghetto and the Final Solution.

2. And, finally, there is the text of Hersonski's voiceover. Intermittent and discreet, it is not a master discourse in the tradition of classic documentary but one other element in the film's complex, intertextual play.

REPRESENT OR BETRAY THE HOLOCAUST?

Before discussing the textuality of *A Film Unfinished*, it is important, I believe, to raise the much debated issues involving the representation of the Holocaust. In his *Traumatic Realism: The Demands of Holocaust Representation*, Michael Rothberg contends that there are two major approaches to the study of genocide, which he identifies as *realist* and *antirealist*. The realist position involves both reference (the assembling of facts that document events from the past) and narrative (the organizing of events in their logical sequence). Narrativist history assumes that the events of genocide are knowable in the historical sense and that they can be organized into an unbroken narrative that establishes a chain of cause and effect. It follows that the Holocaust—or at least large episodes of the Holocaust—may be grasped in a *synoptic view* (to use historian Louis O. Mink's term): the historian—and the reader in his or her wake—brings "together in a single act . . . the complicated relationship of parts which can be experienced only *seriatim*."[3] These "stories of a particular kind"—the discourse of professional historians—are structured both chronologically and causally so that the *this-and-then-that* turns into the *that-because-of-this*. If the Holocaust can be compared to other historical events, then we should be able to reach an understanding of it by the objective causal argumentation that is at the core of the historical method. It is possible according to this positivist approach to encompass the Holocaust in the historian's enlightened gaze and thereby give it meaning.

The antinarrativist position rejects the possibility of understanding the Holocaust according to any existing historical method and its categories of analysis. Antinarrativists hold that the Holocaust is not knowable (at least in the terms proposed by the narrativists) or might be knowable "only under radically new regimes of knowledge."[4] Unknowable, in contrast to the knowability of ordinary events, it is also unrepresentable, at least within the limits of traditional narrative discourse. As Rothberg puts it, "This tendency removes the Holocaust from standard historical, cultural, or autobiographical narratives and situates it as a sublime, unapproachable object beyond discourse and knowledge."[5] The most radical exponent of this position in film is Claude Lanzmann, author of *Shoa* and other films on the Holocaust. Lanzmann argues that any attempt to represent and therefore to understand the Holocaust—including citing documentary images or other documents from the period—inescapably reproduces the logic of genocide and is therefore an obscenity.

The resistance to narrative is rooted in the fear that discursive explanations will domesticate the traumatic past, settling it, so to speak, into a conclusive pastness. The danger is all the more worrisome as the living generation of witnesses to the Holocaust disappear from the scene of history. Historian Saul Friedländer, in his classic essay *Reflections of Nazism: An Essay on Kitsch and Death*, argues that the Holocaust has been subject to two sorts of exorcism. The first is the work of revisionist historians who "traffic in facts" in order to suppress the "unbearable past" they seek to deny. The second is the historian's attempt to integrate the Shoah into the structures of explanation that hold for the "ordinary" events of history:

> To put the past back into bearable dimensions, superimpose it on the known and respected progress of human behavior, put it in the identifiable course of things, into the unmysterious march of ordinary history, into the reassuring world of the rules that are the basis of our society— in short, into conformism and conformity.[6]

Friedländer is disturbed by the neutralizing effect that language— even the best-intended—has on historical experience. "At the opposite extreme [of revisionism]," he argues, "systematic historical research, which uncovers the facts in their most precise and most meticulous interconnection, also protects us from the past, thanks to the inevitable paralysis of language."[7] The "bureaucratic" prose of historical analysis drains the catastrophic events of their historical reality. Language, Friedländer tells us, became flagrantly inadequate when historians sought to represent the events of the First World War, and language is utterly impotent when it seeks to represent Auschwitz. He is particularly skeptical of Marxist historians, who would like to explain the Holocaust according to the social and economic factors that are the basis of the materialist interpretation of history. As Friedländer puts it, it is possible to analyze the rise of the National Socialist movement, their accession to power, and Nazi politics in Marxist terms only up to 1936, after which the usual categories of analysis are overwhelmed by the deranged ambitions and perverse intentions of the Nazi program for conquest:

Afterwards nothing seems to respond anymore to this scheme of analysis, and if one wants to maintain it, it is necessary to eliminate the central role of Adolf Hitler; the foundations and stages of his racial policy; his war in the West, especially his declaration of war on the United States; and finally his policy of exterminating the Jews. In sum, what's left is a Nazism without Nazism.[8]

Moreover, the language of historical representation operates primarily on a grand scale. It creates group protagonists or identifies historical figures whose impact on events can be demonstrated through analysis. It recounts collective actions, motivated by momentous social, political, and economic forces, which take place in constructed space and conceptual (rather than chronometric) time. As for the human individuals caught up in events, historical analysis vacates the field of real experience that cannot be understood in abstract terms or contained within the structures of historical narrative. When historical writing takes its distance, what is left out of its field of vision? What becomes of the *substance* of history, of that material world resonating with subjectivity and emotion?

Frank Ankersmit argues that the Holocaust was the ultimate challenge to Hayden White's thesis that form—the form of story the historian chooses to *emplot* a set of historical events—determines meaning. The so-called linguistic turn in the discipline of history sought to subjugate the real past to plot forms and culminated in what Ankersmit sees as a disregard for the constraints on discourse imposed by the reality of the past. "No event in the whole of human history," he tells us, "tolerates less its obfuscation behind the veil of text and language less than the Holocaust."[9]

APOSTASY: CASTING OUT THE JEW

Recently, several historians have argued that the Holocaust must be understood in terms of cultural history. David Nirenberg's groundbreaking work, *Anti-Judaism*, asserts that much of Western culture emerges from a mythic opposition to the Jew, not the real Jew but the Jew as symbolic figure. Despite the diversity of the periods he studies—from antiquity to the modern era—he traces the continuity of the rhetorical opposition that pits the "spirituality" of Christianity against the "materialism" of Judaism. The Jew was consistently imagined as dominated by the body and thus corrupt, grasping, sexually aggressive, and incapable of moral judgment. The enduring caricature of the "Eternal Jew," whether in medieval sculpture, the anti-Semitic iconography of late nineteenth century France, or in Nazi propaganda films like *Jüd suss*, turns moral defects into physical deformities. Such anti-Semitic representations were not confined to the "darker" moments of history. Indeed, they were fully present in the brightness of Enlightenment thought, for which the Jew posed the central anthropological problem: Are Jews human or do they belong to a lower order? The figural Jew also "explained" the emergence of capitalism and all its disruptive effects, including humankind's enthrallment to the new god: money. The hapless Jew is not only responsible for modernism; he is also a historical anachronism that needs to be expunged. In his discussion of Hegel, Nirenberg remarks that "Judaism after Christ will always remain for him a type of necrophilia: a dead man walking, an indigestible remnant from the guts of history."[10] As Nirenberg makes clear, Karl Marx, in his (often avoided) essay "On the Jewish Question," blames the Jew for the emergence of ruthless capitalism: "What is the worldly cult of the Jew? *Haggling*. Which is his worldly God? *Money*."[11] Indeed, Marx propagated the confusion between the real and figural Jew. Worse, according to Nirenberg, "his conflation elevated the specific and particular 'Jewish Question' posed by Bruno Bauer, about the social emancipation of the Jews, to a universal and revolutionary question, with its solution (in Marx's emphatic words) 'the emancipation of society from Judaism.' "[12]

There is no question but that the Nazis adopted the essential tenets of anti-Judaism that Nirenberg describes: the debased figure of the Jew (whose bearded face betrays a cunning smile), his subhuman status, his instrumental role in the creation of the evils of modernism, and, paradoxically, his anachronism. It is quite possible to grasp the Nazi program for the emancipation of Germany from the Jews in these terms. Indeed, it is essential to see *Das Ghetto* as a document bearing witness to the evolution of Nazi thought at the exact moment when the party was implementing the strategies of the Final Solution.

Alon Confino, in his recent *A World Without Jews: The Nazi Imagination from Persecution to Genocide*, makes the case—and a convincing one—that one is better able make sense of the Nazi era if one approaches it as mythistory (although he does not use the term): "A history of the Holocaust must include the history of emotions and imagination of Germans during the Third Reich, for the fundamental reason that the persecution and extermination was built on fantasy."[13] The Jew was an imaginary, not a real enemy. The Nazis imagined their triumph over the past through transgressive acts against the Hebrew Bible and the People of the Book. For Confino, Kristallnacht (November 9, 1938)—the culmination of the popular anti-Semitic demonstrations that had increased in number and virulence since 1933—was an emblematic moment: Germans everywhere engaged in the apostatical gesture of defiling and burning Torah scrolls by the thousands. The Book had to be destroyed so that another Genesis could arise: a new narrative of creation that placed the Homo Germanicus at its center.

Confino argues that making a world without Jews was a Nazi goal from the beginning, indeed the essence of its program. Its strategies—encouraging emigration, creating a social space where Jewish presence was forbidden, stripping Jews of their livelihood and their place in German culture, deporting Jews toward the East—all sought to eradicate the presence of Jews, or at least to make them invisible. One solution in Poland, where there was a much more significant Jewish population, was to wall them in. There is, Confino argues, no rupture between the earlier Nazi policies and the implementation of the Final Solution between the fall of 1941 and the winter of 1942. There was simply the decision to proceed more rapidly to the massive eradication of the Jews. This is precisely the moment that *A Film Unfinished* and the object it deconstructs, the Nazi film *Das Ghetto*, evoke: the human consequences of the Nazi program to "slowly" murder Jews through starvation and, looming on the horizon, the menacing shadow of Treblinka and mass annihilation.

DISSENTING VOICES

The intertextual strategy that *A Film Unfinished* puts in place is self-evidently a form of discourse. However, it clearly sets aside the ambition of historiographic representations and the synoptic view by means of which history gives order and meaning to events. While the film includes a voiceover commentary, which does indeed at times provide a broader and longer perspective on events, it does not pretend to subsume the various experiences of the Holocaust in a master narrative.

Hersonski's film pays close attention to detail, to the particularity of testimony, returning discourse to the scale of human experience: "because in the details," she argues, "you can reach what is humane, and once you enter the humane, things become much more complex."[14] The texts spoken by witnesses retain their specificity: the events they evoke are inseparable from the particular moment in which they occurred, the particular space in which they took place, and the particular subjective point of view from which they were experienced. Hersonski, a remarkable editor, constructs a polyphony of individual voices, each of which maintains its integrity and its tangibility. It is in the relationship between these voices and the malignant representations of *Das Ghetto* that the discursive work of the film emerges.

A Film Unfinished is, in the first instance, a work of refutation that exposes the fabrications of Nazi propaganda in *Das Ghetto* by confronting them with testimony of different sorts. In this sense the film is analogous to a judicial procedure conducted by the filmmaker/narrator to expose the lies that the images seek to tell. *Das Ghetto* was shot silent and much of the work of refutation takes place as an adversarial relationship between voice and image. Even the diegetic sound that Hersonki adds is not intended to blend with the image but to break it open: "I wanted to produce an entire world of sound that is not woven into the images but hovers over them."[15] Thus Hersonski the editor makes a discourse out of what the images propose as self-evident truths: "The editing felt as a certain act of speech, speech that comes on top of the original footage's silence."[16]

The voice appears in several modes: the narrator's voiceover commentary, the vocal reenactments of documents (such as diary entries), and direct testimony by witnesses. The voiceover commentary is exegetic. It performs the function of historian—the "centripetal" historian of *Das Ghetto*'s production and the historical situation of the Jews who haunt the images we see. It intervenes to specify what testimony alone cannot. In the opening sequence, for example, the camera tracks down an

EXAMPLE 1.1
A STREET SCENE

VOICEOVER	IMAGE
1. [*No voice.*]	High angle of a crowded intersection at the ghetto gate; shots of a line of Polish rickshaws; a crowded street.
2. May 1942, the Warsaw Ghetto.	Medium shot of a two-seater rickshaw with a passenger and a "driver."
3. Two and half years have passed since the ghetto was established.	An old Jew passes the camera in medium close-up.
4. In three months those we see here will be sent to their death. Here are . . .	Medium close-up of a woman looking at the camera (slowed to a jerky frame by frame).
5. . . . images where these people are still fighting for their lives.	Ghetto residents advance toward the camera carrying their belongings.
6. What the film doesn't tell us is that nearly half a million were trapped here in a walled in area of less than . . .	Passersby advance toward the camera in medium shot.
7. . . . three square miles in conditions of unparalleled overcrowding and typhus.	A crowd entering a building.

underground corridor toward darkness and an illuminated "escape" sign: the film's investigative character and its goal are thus represented metaphorically. At the same time, the voiceover does the work of exposition: "This is the story of a film that was never completed. A film designed to serve as propaganda for the Third Reich, that empire infatuated with the camera that knew so well to document its own evil passionately, systematically, like no other nation before it." We soon learn that we are in the underground archive in a forest where the Nazis preserved reels of documentary footage and where the unfinished film on the Warsaw Ghetto was discovered.

At crucial moments in Hersonski's film, the narrator's voice establishes the historical context for testimony. It discusses the historical situation of the ghetto; identifies the roles played by particular actors, such as Adam Czerniakow or Heinz Auerswald, the SS Commissioner for the Jewish Residential District; speculates on the intentions of the German filmmakers and describes their methods; reveals the fictionality of material staged for the film by the German crew; discloses how the German courts after the war interrogated Willy Wist, the only member of the film crew whose name came to light; and describes the plight of ghetto residents in the first massive deportation to Treblinka two months after the shooting of the film.

The voiceover thus often plays in counterpoint to sequences of shots drawn from *Das Ghetto*. It contextualizes the present of the images. For instance, let's look at the first sequence that appears after the titles for *A Film Unfinished*, as represented in example 1.1. The voiceover speaks about what the images don't tell us or avoid telling us. Where they were taken, on what date, in what historical situation. Who these people are. What they have been subjected to. What destiny awaits them. The here-and-now of the image expands to embrace the ghetto's past, its scale and its aftermath.

DISRUPTING THE TRANSPARENT IMAGE

The Nazi filmmakers' intention in *Das Ghetto* was to produce what could be taken as a transparent document of daily life in the Warsaw Ghetto in 1942, at least for the anti-Semitic German audiences who were already inured to malignant representations of the Jew, indeed embraced such representations in the conduct of their daily lives. Hersonski's strategy is to break apart the film's transparency and bring to light undisclosed "layers of reality" by confronting the images of *Das Ghetto* with other documents that contradict their apparent meanings. *A Film Unfinished* makes extensive use of archives of testimony by contemporary witnesses who observed the filming of *Das Ghetto* in the disquieting moments preceding the first deportations to Treblinka. The first of these are the diaries of Adam Czernikov, president of the ghetto's Judenrat, the Jewish council set up by order of the Nazis to manage "what had become the holding pen [for Jews] before the Final Solution." As Hersonski's voiceover describes Czernikov's mission to document his daily life, the image emphasizes the documents' importance with a repeated gesture framed in close-up: a hand places the volumes of the diaries on a table, one after the other.

A second major set of documents was the project of historian and ghetto resident Emanuel Rinkleblum, who undertook to organize "a vast underground archive, documenting the annihilation of one of Europe's largest Jewish communities." Rinkleblum "understands" that scholarly writing will never be competent to communicate what happened, "it can never grasp or express the ghetto reality."[17] He called on all willing individuals to keep a personal journal, which he took charge of compiling: "Our guiding principle was that the work should be multifaceted. We aspired to present the whole truth, as bitter as it may be." The first quotation from an observer's diary speaks of the historical mission he assumes in documenting his experiences "until I am no longer physically and emotionally capable." The image that accompanies this witness's statements seems at first unrelated. In a street scene of no apparent significance that Hersonski has reduced to slow motion, a tall, relatively well-dressed man walks toward the camera. As he approaches, he stares into the lens. The look into the camera becomes increasingly emphatic as the shot advances frame by frame. If the images in *Das Ghetto* cannot be changed, they can be subjected to manipulation. They can be forced to produce unintended meanings. Thus, the look of this passerby, so fleeting in the original shot, becomes an assertion of presence, a look that contests the "transparent" gaze of the Nazi documentarists.

As I remarked earlier, the fact that the Nazi propagandists had not yet endowed *Das Ghetto* with a voiceover commentary (about whose virulence the images leave little doubt) opened the possibility of the sustained counterpoint *A Film Unfinished* develops. Let us look at an example. On the image track we find the juxtaposition of two sequences. The first takes place in the sumptuous bedroom of a vain Jewish woman preparing for an evening out (the Czernikovs' apartment was the featured location for shooting scenes involving the Jewish elite). Shot 1 shows the woman examining herself in the mirror of an armoire; in the background we see a tall double window flooded with light. The camera pans with her as she crosses to her dressing table. Shot 2 is a medium close-up of the woman in a satin negligee seated in front of the mirror arranging her hair. She smiles with self-satisfaction and picks up a hand mirror to examine the back of her head. She primps and applies lipstick. Shot 3 shows the woman, again in medium close-up, smoking and gazing at her image.

The second sequence, which follows immediately on the first, takes place in the utter misery of a ghetto bedroom where we see two emaciated couples. Shot 1 shows a wasted young woman who gets out of bed. Shot 2 shows a second bedroom with two beds. In the first a woman sits knitting while her husband sleeps wrapped in filthy blankets. The camera pans toward the second bed where an emaciated couple lies in the immobilized state of the starving. Shot 3 re-presents the second couple in a close shot. A man—we assume a member of the film crew—enters the frame from the position of the camera and gives a crust of bread to the man on the bed, who manages a slight smile.

It is obvious—at least to spectators who have not been conditioned by the forms of Nazi propaganda—that the first sequence has all the elements of staged fiction. The mise-en-scène is replete with redundant signifiers of superior social class. The actress's gestures are fluid and polished, and her movements across the space of the bedroom and before the mirror are analytically edited. The three-point lighting further underscores the theme of luxury. And so forth. The second sequence belongs to documentary. There are some obvious elements of mise-en-scène—the crew has asked the young woman to rise from the bed—but there is no doubting the physical and emotional state of the starving figures nor the authenticity of the setting. The scene is illuminated from the front in harsh light that lays bare a repugnant reality of degenerate, socially promiscuous, polluted humanity. Most repugnant of all, for us, the cruel gesture of offering a crust of bread to the starving.

Such stark oppositions, frequent in the film, are part and parcel of the Nazi propagandists' crude rhetoric of causality. The Rich Jew's narcissism is responsible for the Poor Jew's degradation, and such representations were intended to be credible, at least to an audience of anti-Semites. As if the blatant contrast between the two sequences were not enough to unmask the filmmakers' intentions for modern audiences, the soundtrack provides an even stronger disavowal. The voiceover reads an entry from Czernikov's diary. In parallel with the first sequence of images, we hear: "May 5, 1942. In the afternoon, the filmmakers were busy. They brought in a woman who had to put on lipstick in front of a mirror." Against the second sequence of images, we hear the continuation of the same diary entry: "In addition to all this, there are persistent rumors about deportations, which appear not to be unfounded. Kommissar Auerswald ordered us to provide a contingent of nine hundred people."

The discovery of outtakes from *Das Ghetto*, "frames from the raw footage left on the cutting room floor," provided the material for another intertextual strategy. These "images that were never meant to be seen revealed repeated attempts to stage events over and over again until the takes seem credible enough," the voiceover informs us. The multiple takes "documenting" the "same" event obviously belie their authenticity: the juxtaposition between the shots included in the film and those that were excluded exposes the artifice of a fictional mise-en-scène. Consider, for example, this sequence from *A Film Unfinished* made up of outtakes showing two ragged boys in front of a butcher shop window. Take 1: the camera pans down to discover the two hungry children looking in the window. Take 2: the camera pans up as a woman enters the shop and the boys approach the window. Take 3: a closer view in which the camera pans up to show the boys at the window. Take 4: the camera pans up as in take 3 but from a different angle. The children—doubtless victims of the Nazi plan to starve ghetto residents—are exploited as actors. Their actions are staged and re-staged from different angles. The motifs of the outtakes create far from subtle melodramatic contrasts—the ragged children, the enticing yet attainable riches in the butcher's window, the wealthy customer who breezes into the shop—which recall scenes from D. W. Griffith's Biograph period.

"HERR WIST, LET ME REFRESH YOUR MEMORY"

In one quite complex case, *A Film Unfinished* makes use of "fictional" reconstruction. In nine sequences that punctuate the film, it restages the interrogation of *Das Ghetto* cameraman Willy Wist by a German magistrate years after the war, "when the German courts began to prosecute local war criminals," as the voiceover tells us. Two actors read passages from the four transcripts of the hearing that have been preserved. In the institutional setting of the courthouse corridor and the interrogation room, the camera maintains its detachment from the characters either through distant long shots or obfuscating close-ups. We are not intended to identify with the characters, whose bodies are fictional, and Hersonski resists creating any impression of full presence. The place and the actors are represented as fragments of the scene—extreme close-ups of components of the tape recorder or of pieces of the actors' anatomy. For example in reconstruction 1, we see a fragment of the tape recorder and the microphone, then the camera pans right to show us a hand and part of an arm belonging, we suppose, to the witness being deposed, Willy Wist. Strangely, although everything is about what Wist is saying, we never see his mouth. Even when "Wist's" face is visible, we see only part of it, which is decentered, that is, cut off at the edge of the frame. Moreover, as if visibility were prohibited, the face is either out of focus or obscured in shadow. The image seems as evasive as the witness.

We can interpret Hersonski's motivation in the following terms. First, she purposively avoids the excesses of docudrama, which foregrounds full diegetic effects—the "presence" of the past in the mode of fiction—to the detriment of the documented reality, in this case the text of Wist's interrogation. It is a strategy of discretion that does not refuse to reconstruct places, actors, and action but radically reduces their real effect. A minimum of fiction. No whole bodies, and particularly, no faces to identify with. There are, of course, the actors' voices that reproduce the words spoken by the historical Wist and his interrogator. But since the voices are only minimally anchored in the scarcely seen figures on the image track, the audience focuses its attention on the spoken testimony.

As the judge draws out the witness—"Allow me to refresh your memory"—another set of images emerges against the voiceover: the Warsaw Ghetto. Wist is saying, "It is probably true that I was in Warsaw in May 1942," and, in response to this admission, the image track gives us a Nazi guard examining the papers of a group of Jews, a close-up of a *Passierschein* in the guard's hand, then a longer shot of the Jews entering the Ghetto. Wist is obtuse ("we cameramen had no idea what awaited us there"), obedient ("we were simply told curtly that we should film there"), and (disingenuously) unable to put two and two together ("I never knew what the purpose of the films we shot was") (from reconstruction 2). Yet each time Wist says, "I remember . . . ," the image gives us concrete representations that confirm, belie, or extend his (often hazy) recollections, as shown in examples 1.2 and 1.3.

EXAMPLE 1.2
A RECOLLECTION CONFIRMED

VOICE	IMAGE
1. In this context, I remember being told to film a large pile of feces in the courtyard of one of the buildings.	Very long shot of the courtyard of an apartment building in the middle of which appears a large mass.
2. I remember thinking to myself that either because of the winter or because of the overcrowding, the sanitary installations had stopped working.	The camera pans down from a balcony toward the courtyard showing washing hanging and open windows. A second pan of the same scene in a longer shot.

EXAMPLE 1.3
THE IMAGE BELIES

VOICE	IMAGE
1. Goldpheasant (the nickname the crew gave to the official who gave them their assignments) sent us to various scenes or groups of people.	A crowded street; passersby. Then the camera reveals, through a doorway, a woman seated on the floor doing her washing in a basin.
2. He never gave us any explanation concerning the meaning of our filming. He simply said that he wanted us to film this or that.	Long shot of a family in a squalid interior sitting on a filthy palette that serves as a bed. The camera pans right to reveal another palette and two more children. The pan continues toward yet another palette where we see, in medium close-up, an emaciated mother and child.

In sequences like these we often see the reversal of the relationship between image and sound found elsewhere in the film. It is Wist's testimony that lies and evades and it is the visual documents that contradict.

TRANSCENDING THE SADISTIC GAZE

This is perhaps the moment to recall what has become an obvious historical truth: that malignant discourses like *Das Ghetto* were part of the ambitious project that Minister of Propaganda Goebbels developed to justify the Nazi program to create a world without Jews. As Nirenberg compellingly demonstrates, the "Jew" was not an ethnic reality but an abstract figure against which positive advances in the West, whether Christian or humanist, were to be measured. Indeed, the "Jew" remained a constant reference even in cultures where real Jews had long been driven out. In Goebbels's narrative, the Weimar state had been infected by "rampant Jewish intellectualism," and "Goebbels expected his audience to understand what this 'Jewish intellectualism' was, and to perceive how it menaced them as individuals, as classes (students, workers, burghers, soldiers), and as a German nation. He also expected them to be moved by this understanding to political action."[18] Moreover, the Jew was the embodiment of the moral degradation brought into being by the new exchange economy at the root of Germany's social and economic ills.

This allegorical Jew—whose flesh can still be mortified—arose as the arch-antagonist in a perverse social narrative. Confino summarizes the tenets of European anti-Semitism in the following terms: the Jews are "racially inferior, religiously deviant, physically deformed, sexually polluting, psychologically treacherous, makers of bolshevism and liberalism."[19] Indeed, what we see in *Das Ghetto* is a rehash of such well-worn figures of anti-Semitism, a malicious social typology that gives cover to the film's sadistic representations. The avaricious, grasping, heartless Jews (portrayed by actors, brought in for the purpose) eat well, indulge in frivolous amusement, and ignore the human misery that surrounds them. Indeed, they are responsible (the film's contrastive montage suggests) for the ills of ghetto life: the mass starvation and death that the film chillingly documents. Poor Jews are the very figure of misfortune: hapless, utterly unredeemable, the degenerate victims of their genetic destiny. They constitute, from the perspective of the Nazis' racial scientism, a defective mental and social type.

Contemporary audiences of *Das Ghetto* are horrified by the images of the collection of the Jewish dead deposited on ghetto sidewalks, the stocking of their corpses in sheds, their transportation on handcarts to the cemetery where a slide dumps them into mass graves. As a gauge of German indifference to suffering, however, Timothy Snyder reminds us that this gruesome process was a major attraction for certain German tourists visiting Warsaw.[20] The German public, which had demonstrated its violent anti-Semitism in street demonstrations, was by and large complicit in demanding the Jews' containment and isolation, whatever the consequences might be. The ghetto and the yellow star were necessary measures against the specter of racial contamination.

We should also not forget, as Nirenberg points out, that such voyeurism was not new but rooted in the ethnic tourism already practiced in the Enlightenment. The "enlightened" tourist would visit scattered enclaves of Jews in France, Italy, or the Ottoman Empire in order to observe the Jew's contemptible "difference." Nirenberg cites, for example, the commentary of a seventeenth-century visitor to the Avignon ghetto: "The Jewish quarter is a place filled with infection which I would gladly have left behind had it not been for the fact that curiosity drove me to see it. . . . It is not possible to see anything as disgusting as this whole place, as repulsive as their apartments, nothing as wretched and as stupid as the people: all these afflictions have justly befallen them for their crimes."[21] It is such representations that *Das Ghetto* strives to replicate.

SEEING WITH YOUR OWN EYES

In the intertextual confrontations *A Film Unfinished* organizes, it is often a text from the past that is pitted against another text from the past. These ironic juxtapositions reveal the hand of the editor, who takes charge of extracting new meanings from old texts. Or it is the hindsight of the voiceover that comments on images from the past in documentary's impersonal mode—impersonal in the sense that the voice is not embodied in a person who recounts from his or her subjective point of view but from a position that transcends the direct experience of history. This is the phenomenon of documentary's voice without a body that I have discussed elsewhere.[22]

Testimony of eyewitnesses is of a wholly different order from historical representation. Shoshana Felman and Dori Laub, in their *Testimony: Crises of Witnessing in Literature, Psychoanalysis and History*, emphasize the special character of the recollections of eyewitness participants: "Why is it that the witnesses' speech is so uniquely, literally irreplaceable? 'If someone else could have written my stories, I would not have written them.' "[23] Testimony is the direct expression of personal experience that cannot be borne by a third party; no hearsay, as relayed or summarized in a voiceover commentary, for example, has the same evidential standing. Seeing with one's own eyes represents for Felman and Laub a specific "topographical *position* with respect to an occurrence."[24] Historically, testimony has had a privileged standing in the Western tradition of the laws of evidence because it places the witness at the scene of an action under scrutiny. Even at great distances in time, as in the case of the survivors' testimony in *A Film Unfinished*, memory retains enormous credibility. The honest witness speaks with an authenticity that cannot be matched by "experts" who were not present at the event and can only attempt to reconstruct it, always partially, through deduction. What the witness lacks in global vision, he or she more than makes up for by the rich detail of experience.

If such has been the status of memory in Western judicial systems, quite the reverse obtains in the historical science. History, especially since Leopold von Ranke, has mistrusted memory as a source of testimony. In his influential introduction to *Places of Memory*, historian Pierre Nora contrasts the scalpel-sharp representations of history with the unreliable, misty representations of memory: "Memory, being a phenomenon of emotion and magic, accommodates only those facts that suit it. It thrives on vague, telescoping reminiscences, on hazy general impression or specific symbolic detail. It is vulnerable to transferences, screen memories, censoring, and projections of all kinds."[25] This characterization of memory does not, however, fit the present-day testimony we find in *A Film Unfinished*. Here, memory is not a nebulous narrative of events cobbled from reminiscences and warped by desire. We are in the presence of the *act* of memory. Confronted with the concrete documents that *Das Ghetto* provides, living witnesses recover a power of recall anchored in specific details—details that cause them significant pain. Reticence is no longer possible.

In *A Film Unfinished* there are two types of testimony. As I have shown, there is *past* testimony, such as the diaries kept by inhabitants of the ghetto, which the filmmaker uses to refute the mendacious representations of *Das Ghetto*. But there are also witnesses from the present—survivors of the Warsaw Ghetto who appear in a screening room to watch the images the Nazi documentary provides and give testimony on the past of an entirely different order. What is crucial in such testimony has nothing to do with editing or mise-en-scène. The filmmaker has set up the situation, chosen how to frame it and when to show which face of the encounter between witness and film, and selected what is to be included in or excluded from the final cut. What counts is the meeting between the present and the past and the potential fusion between the two. Indeed, Hersonski tells us, it was important not to call on the well-worn narratives of national or even personal memory, but to fix the witnesses' gaze on specifics, that is on their own experience:

> I noticed that when my questions dwelled on details and challenged what they remembered, for example: if this or that crew member wore a hat, in what angle they positioned the camera, all these specifics come together to an image that was scorched in their minds. The rest is a story they've been telling themselves as years pass by. Somewhere deep inside there was an image and I tried to reach that image.[26]

RESTORING EXPERIENCE

If *A Film Unfinished* is a work of refutation, perhaps more important, it is a work of restoration: the restoration of a certain experience of the past. The word "restore" cannot be taken in its usual sense because past experience cannot be restored as a building or work of art can be returned to its presumed original state. It can have no stable existence in the present. It is, rather, ephemeral, fleeting. Historical experience appears, unbidden, as a glimpse, a flash: the brief encounter between the past and the present. It is the recognition of something forgotten or repressed that was too painful to assimilate at its occurrence and comes to the surface of consciousness belatedly. The filmmaker may orchestrate these moments of recognition by bringing survivors into the screening room to see *Das Ghetto*, or she may manipulate its footage using techniques of slow motion or frame-by-frame advancement to amplify what might have passed unnoticed. However, if she is hoping to gain access to historical experience, she needs to refrain from contextualizing it. Which explains the discretion of the narrative voiceover in *A Film Unfinished*. "I'm trying not to lend the image a single meaning," Hersonski tells us, because by naming the image we lose our ability "to question things" and "to remain alert, morally alert."[27] We lose what the image preserves of the experience of the past.

What is immediately striking in the testimony of survivors is the apprehension they feel at re-experiencing what memory has repressed. In testimony 1 (of the thirteen sequences devoted to survivors bearing witness before the images of *Das Ghetto*), we see a series of close shots of an old woman seated in a screening room, the beam of the projector emanating from its source in the background. Alternating with the woman's looks off screen is a series of shots representing inhabited spaces (a crowded stairway, city streets with passersby, a tram, close-ups of individuals). A point-of-view series brings together the witness and the film in the familiar structure of seeing/seen. It also brings together the present and the past. The woman cries out, "Oh God! What if I see someone I know?" Then, chillingly: "I keep thinking that among all these people I might see my mother walking." We feel the fear of and the desire for recognition: that the distance between this woman's present and the past she has held in abeyance might suddenly dissolve. The past whose replication she is seeing has not been softened or semanticized by narrative or description. It is there in the hardness of the cinematography (the "camera" as Hersonski puts it) that resists the clumsy manipulation of the rhetoric of German propagandists. The image retains its openness and indeterminacy, in which the real of the past has more of a chance of surviving.

In Ankersmit's words, the past and the present come together. Their surfaces are each other's negatives, each bearing the imprint of the other. The difference is that the present is totally absorbed in the past and sees nothing else—the witness stares at the screen, registering the sensations he or she experiences—while the past remains impassive, unmoved by the encounter it forces on the present.

> Everything surrounding us in the present is pushed aside and the whole of the world is reduced to just ourselves in this specific memory—where the memory sees us, so to say, and we see only it. The past event in question can present itself with such an unusual intensity when it was in one way or another incompletely and not fully experienced when it actually took place: We finish, so to say, in the present a task that we had prematurely laid down in the past itself.[28]

Against the mesmerizing image, which may at any moment cross the threshold between the harrowing and the traumatic, the survivor has no defense.

Let's take one example of such a passage. A witness is seated in the screening room and watches the unfolding film, which functions as an unsparing mnemonic device. She endures the shots of corpses, dead from disease or starvation and dumped on the sidewalk and against buildings in the ghetto. The movements of well-dressed Jews striding by the corpses (and across the frame), apparently oblivious to what lies at their feet, were staged by the film crew, a crude and mendacious representation of Jewish iniquity. The witness responds by explaining that ghetto residents were indeed inured to suffering: "No one looked, it was impossible. We became indifferent to the suffering of others, because otherwise it was impossible to live."

The grim realism of the footage provokes the sudden rush of memory in a second witness, again an old woman, seated in the screening room. It is a short, urgent narrative—an atom of historical experience, as Ankersmit puts it (see example 1.4). The images of corpses have hit a nerve: the subject does not simply recount the past; she re-experiences it. The involuntary gestural language—she places a hand over one eye as if to shield herself from the image at the same time as she acknowledges it—exposes the intensity and pain caused by what she is seeing.

EXAMPLE 1.4
TRIPPING ON A CORPSE

VOICE	IMAGE
1. When it was already dark and I was walking . . .	Corpses lying on the pavement; passersby.
2. . . . down Karmelitzka Street, which was crowded with people, I tripped on something and lost my balance.	Close-up of the witness speaking.
3. When I opened my eyes, I saw I had fallen on a corpse.	Another corpse.
4. My face was nearly touching his, and I was shaking. It was as if all the corpses which I had previously avoided looking at were there in the face of this one man.	Return to a close-up of the witness, her hand over one eye. She massages her eye.
5. It was a human being!	A barely clad corpse, lying against a building.

With gesture, as with inarticulate sound, we are in the realm of pre-verbal speech—the unvoiced reaction to events—that characterizes many of our relationships with the world, with others, and with ourselves. Much of what is deepest and most intense in our experience has little to do with language as such. Experience does not involve itself in the cognitive processes that allow us to determine if statements are true or false. Nor is it, at least initially, bound by the language of narrative that places an experience in a chain of events. It resembles what Wittgenstein calls "a deep inarticulate sound in response to pain or fear." It is the "groan": the wordless utterance that expresses an immediate and uncontrolled response to a stimulus. Ankersmit's formulation, already cited in the introduction, is worth repeating here because it so precisely defines what texts like *A Film Unfinished* are about:

We should take them for what they are, that is, as the groanings of a civilization, as the texts in which the pains, the moods, and feelings of a civilization articulate themselves. *In this way these groanings are essen-*

tially poetic: just like a poem they do not aim at truth but at making experience speak. And this is how we should read them.[29]

A Film Unfinished does more than set matters right by explaining and exposing a piece of Nazi propaganda. It puts us in touch with the reality of the Warsaw Ghetto.

STARTLED BY PHANTOMS

I would like to conclude by describing a type of direct experience Hersonski's film provokes in the viewer without the intermediary of witnesses. The effect is achieved by the filmmaker's manipulation of the image. Hersonski wanted to change the way the spectator looks at the images: "I had a few techniques I used to alter or reorient the gaze, like slow motion, pause resize."[30] The process resembles certain rhetorical figures, like *emphasis* or *hyperbole*, both of which describe the willful exaggeration of expression. Such an exaggeration is achieved when the filmmaker uses slow motion or frame-by-frame advancement, as I described above, to arrest the images' fleeting character. The images the filmmaker chooses to *dilate* suddenly appear in relief. The gesture is imperative: take the time to look at this, and the audience is drawn, *nolens volens*, into an experience that is profoundly disturbing.

Let's look at an example. The third sequence reconstructing Willy Wist's interrogation begins with a tracking shot of the emaciated face of a Jew in a crowd. The German cameraman describes his distant relationship to the Jews he photographed: "On the one hand, I was unable to have much contact with the Jews because the SS immediately pushed them away." A woman in the image gives a direct prolonged look into the camera as Wist continues: "On the other hand, they brought us Jews they deemed appropriate for filming. . . . I want to point out that the Jews were frightened of the SS. There were no incidents during the shooting." Wist's self-defense stops, and there follows a sequence of five "portraits" of Jews, men and young boys, who are in an advanced stage of emaciation. They are framed in close-up against a neutral background. Each portrait has the quality of a mug shot, as the subject appears first in profile and then turns his head to face the camera or starts facing the camera and then turns aside. It is as if this sequence, like others in *Das Ghetto*, were attempting to establish a typology of male Jewishness, a kind of perverse phrenology, like that fostered by the Institute for Hereditary Biology and Racial Hygiene at the University of Frankfurt. Hersonski reduces the series to slow motion so that we have a long time to observe the faces and their unnatural movement. The subjects' look into the camera is wary, grim, and beyond anger. Fluttering eyelids react painfully to the light; the eyes seem deadened and at the same time penetrating. We read the tragic passivity, the pathos of the faces, as an accusation that shatters the ideological project of *Das Ghetto*.

Yet something more is happening: another experience of the past is taking place. The contact we feel with the subjects is intense. We are startled by these phantoms that are looking directly at us across the temporal void of seventy years. Their faces, which could not have suspected our presence, engage with us, and we are totally absorbed by the look that was not meant for us. We are suddenly directly implicated in the past: we look at them, they look at us. The present suddenly *recognizes* the past. These faces are no longer cynical representations in a Nazi film; we can no longer simply observe them. They are what they were: living beings, whose plight now strikes us to the depth of our souls. This exchange between past and present is perhaps illusory and fleeting but it comes to assuage our sense of loss and to set in motion a profound empathy.

Empathy, as Alison Landsberg so cogently observes, is a way of negotiating difference. These victims—these bodies so different from ours—are suddenly in our likeness. Intuitively we seize on their lived experience as if distance no longer separated us from them. This experience has nothing to do with reason and cognition; we are in the irrational domain of emotion and sensation. Moments like these, which abound in *A Film Unfinished*, stand outside the strategies of contextualization the film employs and offer an understanding of historical reality that historiography would deny. They break apart the chain of history to allow access to autonomous fragments of experience, exposed in their semantic nakedness.

2

ANDRZEJ WAJDA'S *KATYN*

For the important thing for the remembering author is not what he experienced, but the weaving of his memory, the Penelope work of recollection. Or should one call it, rather, a Penelope work of forgetting? Is not the involuntary recollection, Proust's mémoire involontaire, much closer to forgetting than what is usually called memory?
—WALTER BENJAMIN, "THE IMAGE OF PROUST"

THE SUBJECT of *Katyn* (2007) is the massacre of nearly the entirety of the elite Polish officer corps at the hands of the Soviet secret police (the NKVD) during the Second World War. As Andrzej Wajda acknowledged, the film project had haunted him for a long time. In 1940 his own father had been one of the twelve thousand officers massacred at Katyn, a spa in Soviet Russia converted into an execution ground for Polish POWs. He was thirteen years old at the time, and in the following years of the war and its aftermath, he had been the helpless witness to his mother's anguished waiting for the return of her husband and her eventual grief and early death. But Wajda could not have undertaken to make a film on such a taboo topic until the Polish People's Republic finally collapsed under the pressure of the democratic movement in 1989. As Piotr Witek affirms, "From the end of World War II until 1989, Polish cinema, like almost all fields of social life in Poland, was subject to overwhelming pressure and control from the communist state, which was watching over the purity of socialist orthodoxy in the work of scholars, writers, journalists, and filmmakers." The past was not open to interpretation: historical narratives followed the party line, and their mode of representation was an obligatory socialist realism. The fall of the People's Republic in 1989 brought about an ideological liberation: "History became both a subject of open argument and a free area of debate between different social actors: historians, journalists, artists, writers, filmmakers, and ordinary people."[1]

Katyn was, then, a deferred project. It came at the end of a career devoted to the representation of Polish history and the struggle for national independence, an artistic undertaking with few parallels in film history. Indeed, Wajda intended *Katyn* as the continuation and completion of his films about the Second World War, which had covered a broad range of topics: the German occupation and the stories of resistance; the persecution of Jews in ghettoes and concentration camps; acts of collaboration with the enemy, both German and Soviet. In his interview for Telewizja Polska, Wajda expressed hope that *Katyn* would constitute the last film of the Polish school, "a sort of farewell, the last movie of his type."[2]

HITLER AND STALIN IN POLAND

Germany began bombing attacks against Polish cities on September 1, 1939. This was the first attempt by a modern air force to terrorize a civilian population. Beginning on September 10, the German air force began the systematic bombing of Warsaw, the first time a major European city had been attacked in this fashion. On September 17, 1939, in coordination with the Third Reich, the Red Army, half a million strong, swept across Poland from the East toward their meeting with the Germans who were simultaneously invading Poland from the West. Their rendezvous points with German forces would establish the Molotov-Ribbentrop line, dividing Poland into two zones of occupation. In the treaty of September 28, 1939, Warsaw came under German control, and Lithuania was occupied by the Soviets. The Polish state, and with it the Polish nation, as such, ceased to exist.

Stalin spoke of his alliance with Germany as "cemented in blood." Indeed, sixty thousand Poles perished during the double invasion.[3] En route to their encounter with the German Wehrmacht, the Red Army met the Polish army fleeing the Wehrmacht and desperately looking for Soviet military support. Instead of assisting stateless Poland—the official pretense for invasion—the Red Army made the Polish forces prisoners of war. Although the ordinary soldiers were soon released, the officers remained in captivity. This was part of Stalin's strategy for crushing Polish resistance to the Soviet occupation: "decapitate" Poland[4] by eliminating its intelligentsia, a strategy the Germans also adopted. The Polish officer corps were made up not so much of military men as of highly educated intellectuals and professionals without whom the future of a free Poland was cast in doubt. The officers were taken by Soviet prison trains to locations in Ukraine (Starobilsk) and in Soviet Russia (Kozelsk and Ostashkov). From there, the NKVD, the Soviet secret police, transported the officers to isolated locations, where they massacred approximately twelve thousand of them. In the coming months the forces of the NKVD would arrest over 109,400 Polish citizens and send them to the Gulags.[5]

In what was formerly Western Poland, Germany ruled. Its goal was to rid Poland of the Poles, whether Christians or Jews, by deporting them to the East, and to annex the territory to its empire. The instrument of aggression against the Polish population was the Einsatzgruppe, whose mission was to pacify the country and eliminate the educated classes (the deportation of the entire professoriate of Krakow University is documented in *Katyn*). After annexing parts of Poland lying on the German border, the Germans left the rest of the zone as a "dumping ground for unwanted Poles and Jews."[6] In the East, the Soviets, whose motivations were strikingly similar, annexed "Western Belarus" and "Western Ukraine."

Despite significant differences, the ambitions and tactics adopted by Hitler and Stalin show strong parallels, as Timothy Snyder amply documents in his authoritative *Bloodlands*. As we will see, *Katyn* also raises the question of the comparability of the iniquities carried out by Stalinists and Nazis. As Snyder points out, it was Russian novelist Vasily Grossman who first had the courage, in *Life and Fate* (1959, published in the West in 1980) and *Everything Flows* (incomplete but published in the West in 1970), to represent points of comparison between the actions of the two regimes:

> He then broke the taboos of a century, placing the crimes of the Nazi and Soviet regimes on the same pages, in the same scenes, in two novels whose reputations only grow with time. Grossman meant not to unify the two systems analytically within a single sociological scheme (such as

Arendt's totalitarianism) but rather to relieve them of their own ideological accounts of themselves, and thereby lift the veil on their common inhumanity.[7]

Wajda also places Nazi and Soviet crimes "in the same scenes," so to
speak. On the one hand, he develops narrative parallels between the
German-occupied zones of Poland and the Soviet prisoner of war camp
at Kozelsk. In the film's second half, the Soviet occupation of Krakow
in the postwar period "mirrors" the German occupation of the city in
the first. Indeed, by means of this narrative rhetoric, one term of the
comparison contaminates the other: the Einsatzgruppe and the Gestapo,
whose iniquity had long been established by history, infects the Soviet
NKVD and the Polish secret police, instruments of oppression long ob-
fuscated by the Stalinist left's distorted history of socialism.

In his representation of the Soviet POW camp where the Polish officer corps is eliminated by a bullet in the nape of the neck, Wajda exposes what the Soviet Union and post-Soviet regimes had continued to
deny: that the Road to Socialism and its murderous trajectory had allowed Communism to "deprive groups of human beings of their right
to be regarded as human."[8] This essential narrative in twentieth-
century history—with its changing cast of perpetrators—will follow us
in a later chapter devoted to Rithy Panh's exposure of genocidal incarceration under the communist regime of the Khmer Rouge. I was not
unaware of the ironic parallel I was drawing by devoting the subsequent chapter to the "anticommunist" genocide perpetrated by the fascistic Suharto regime in Indonesia.

THE CRIME AND THE LIE

In his interview with Telewizja Polska entitled "Post-Mortem: A Conversation with Andrzej Wajda," the Polish filmmaker stated that *Katyn*
was "about two things: the crime and the lie." The crime to which Wajda
refers—the Soviet massacre of the Polish officers—is emblematized in
the Polish collective consciousness as Katyn, the forest spa near which
mass graves were discovered in April 1943. At the time of the massacres,
Katyn was in Soviet territory, which was subsequently captured and

occupied by the Germans. Minister of Propaganda Goebbels was de-lighted by the revelation of Soviet crimes and crowed: "Katyn is my victory."[9] The documentary footage of the exhumation would make glorious propaganda against the Soviets with whom Hitler was now at war.

The lie came later, in 1944. Soviet authorities, who had broken off relations with the Polish government in exile, attempted to shift blame for the massacre to the Nazis. As the Soviet Union was winning the war on the eastern front, the British and American Allies, who needed Stalin, colluded in the lie. Everything turned on the date. If the massacre occurred in April 1940, as the Germans rightly contended, it was the Soviets who controlled the territory where it took place and thus could be held responsible. If it occurred in 1941, according to the Soviet revision, guilt could be deflected onto the Germans, who were then the occupying force. Indeed, Wajda incorporates into *Katyn* projections of two propaganda films—one German, the other Soviet; each asserts the guilt of the other party, using excerpts of the same documentary footage of the grisly discovery of mass graves and of investigators performing necropsy on the bodies. *Katyn* is an accusation against the Soviet state that had never acknowledged responsibility for the massacre and against the Russian state that continued to avoid admitting its guilt after the fall of the Soviet Union.

At the time of *Katyn*'s release in 2007, the Russian authorities had not fully acknowledged the lie. Under democratic pressure, an inevitable shift occurred. On April 2, 2010, the film premiered on Russian television in preparation for the first joint Polish and Russian commemoration of the massacre. One week later, numerous Polish dignitaries, including Lech Kaczynski, perished in a plane crash as they neared Katyn en route for the ceremony.

If *Katyn* were to tell the story of the crime, the story of the fate of Wajda's father, it would take place in the East and recount events of which Wajda had no direct knowledge. If the film were to tell the story of the lie, it would take place principally in the West—German-occupied Poland—and would be the story of the women who waited for the return of the Polish officers, their husbands, brothers, and fathers. This is Wajda's mother's story. Wajda was thirteen at the time of the Katyn massacre and nineteen at the end of the war. He had direct experience of the events the film renders as a narrative of waiting and saw his mother "wither away after the end of the war when she knew [her husband] wouldn't come home." Wajda decided, however, that the subject of *Katyn* was both the crime and the lie and that the film must take place in the West *and* the East. Indeed, at the level of the scenario, the film constructs a pattern of alternation between the two sites of oppression: events occurring in German-occupied Poland and those occurring in the POW camp in Russia and eventually at the execution site known as Katyn.

TO REPRESENT, TO DESIRE

At the moment of preproduction, Wajda is preoccupied with the lapse of time: more than sixty years separate the historical events the film seeks to represent from the here and now of Poland in 2007. For Wajda, Katyn is still an indelible personal memory from his childhood and a national tragedy that the Communist regime long excluded from public commemoration. As we saw in *A Film Unfinished*, the moment presses: the older generation is fast disappearing, and with them the living traces of the events of the war and its aftermath. For the younger generation, Katyn the event has entered the sphere of the historical where living memory has given way to mediated representations that establish an unavoidable estrangement of the present from the past. Despite the Russian Federation's persistent "amnesia" about this shameful event, historians in the post-Soviet era had already assembled the documents, put events in their proper order and in their proper context, identified the victims and perpetrators, and, with their synoptic gaze, grasped the "truth" of Katyn. It is one of the ironies of historiography that the comprehension of historical events—because of the critical distance it imposes—operates to detach the reality of the past from the discourse that seeks to represent it. All the documented experience of the war and the postwar period, under Nazi and Soviet occupation—the aggregate of historical traces of all sorts—recede before the organizing power of historical language.

The event named Katyn, narrated and thus interpreted, reinforces the perception that the human experience the name should evoke is retreating, that it has been "broken off" from the present. For Wajda, this loss of *being* is intolerable. As Robert Burgoyne maintains, what is lacking in "objective" history and what needs to be recovered from past events like Katyn is the "pathos of identification," the "somatic empathy" that would give the new generation access to the emotional experience of the past.[10] This involves, he argues, a reenactment of history, a "rethinking" that takes "the detour by way of the historical imagination."

What do we mean by the historical imagination? Among philosophers who have reflected on the subject, R. G. Collingwood has perhaps had the most influence on twentieth-century historiography. Knowledge of the past comes, he argues in *The Idea of History* (1946), from an ever-deepening identification with what once was. We do not identify with the outside of events—"everything belonging to [the past] which can be described in terms of bodies and their movement."[11] We identify with the *inside* of events, the *mind* of the past, as Collingwoood puts it, that encompasses not only thought and intention but, I would add, the emotional content of actions.

This is how Collingwood describes his methodical approach to historical representation, an approach that combines the rigor of analysis and the studied application of intuition: "The historian's picture of his subject, whether that subject be a sequence of events or a past state of things, thus appears as a web of imaginative construction stretched between certain fixed points provided by the statements of his authorities."[12] According to Collingwood, historians are not the free agents of imaginative fiction. They may not speak of what they cannot know, and, as he maintains, they are not at liberty to embellish historical facts with unsubstantiated details. They are duty-bound to respect the relationship—the vis-à-vis—between the historical text and the reality to which it refers. As literary theorist Jean-Marie Schaeffer puts it, there is an "isomorphic relation to the reality to be known, therefore by virtue of a resemblance (direct or indirect) between the two."[13]

Collingwood's theory of historical imagination is enormously ambitious. He talks of "revivification," accessing the "inside of events," and he means nothing less than bringing the past alive in the historian's mind. This is not, for him, exclusively a cognitive process; it necessarily involves the acuity of the historian's insight, since internal life cannot be observed directly. On the one hand, historians must "read" the actions and behaviors that have left traces in the historical record and they must take account of the social and economic contexts that frame these actions. But they must also, he argues, account for the intentions and emotional states of historical actors and their relation to the physical world they inhabit. The historical imagination is not, however, free-flowing; it obeys historic necessity, which the historian establishes through reflection and analysis. "We cannot but imagine what cannot but be there," according to Collingwood's formulation.[14] In this, the analysis of internal states is as necessary to the imaginative construction of the past as the directly observable face of events.

Collingwood's theory of history is, then, a theory of *presence*: that the historian becomes so immersed in the past he is studying that the thoughts that underlie the development of events and situations in the past become revivified in his own mind. We need to be cautious here because Collingwood's idea of historical representation approaches dangerous territory in the eyes of deconstructive theories of the late twentieth century. What becomes of historical time—the essential idea of the pastness of the past—if we are able to replicate in our minds the historical experience of characters and events in both their material and psychological dimensions? There is a sense, Collingwood asserts, "and one very important to the historian, in which they [the historian's apprehensions of historical events] are not in time at all."[15]

However, historical analysis—even with Collingwood's emendations—does not have the power to take us out of time. Living history exists paradoxically only in the past as experience. The patient exercise of the historical imagination cannot account for—cannot erase—the utter strangeness we experience when an object extruded from the past imposes itself on our consciousness, like the "mug shots" of starving Jews I cite toward the end of the chapter on *A Film Unfinished*. Such persons do not live in the mind of the historian; they live in the past. It is the indisputable realism of these shots that prepares the way for another sort of apprehension. Our relationship with the images is both direct and complex. We as spectators are not there with those phantoms, in their world, so to speak; we are exchanging looks with them across a breach in time. The look we cast is indeed *fusional*, as our emotional response makes clear. This does not mean, however, that we are, for that moment, unconscious of time; rather, we are, suddenly, utterly fixated on the temporal reality that separates us from them. We do not *understand* difference, we *live* it. This kind of close encounter with the pastness of the past is, as I have insisted, fleeting. No film can sustain for long this level of contact with historical experience.

In describing the historical imagination, we need to be mindful of what Arthur Danto called "the problem of *Other Periods.*" How do we determine "the degree to which we might succeed in achieving an *internal* understanding of what it would have been like to live in periods other than our own"?[16] Here Danto is referring to *sympathetic*, not cognitive, understanding (the notion of *Verstehen*). Internal knowledge of others, he argues, comes through empathy. We can understand the past only insofar as we identify parallels between our own internal lives and those of persons who have lived in the past, and "where similarity breaks down, external understanding alone remains possible."[17] Empathy can of course be developed, as the historian who studies a particular period achieves, by dint of research and acute sensibility, an unusual understanding of another world. That is, of course, the sign of a good historian. The same is obviously true of those who occupy the space on the edge of historical events with which they conserve a biographical connection. This was the case of the survivors in *A Film Unfinished*, as it is the case with Wajda or Rithy Punh, and indeed all the filmmakers I include in this study. For them, the past has not been resolved. It pulls them back into what is for them a still living reality.

But even here there appears to be an obstacle to recapturing the experience of others, or even one's own experience in retrospect. As Danto points out, historians and memoirists are not in a "state of innocence" about what the future had in store (I am setting aside for now the case of true repressed memory). In hindsight, they know events in a different way from those who experienced them, or in the case of memoirists, different from the persons they were when they experienced them. They cannot deny their position of narration—their retrospective gaze, as Louis O. Mink would put it—by attempting to hold this knowledge of events and their outcomes in abeyance: "*Not knowing how it is all going to end,*" as Danto tells us, "is the mark of living through events."[18] In history, narrators—like the filmmakers in this study—do know how things turned out, as do the majority of their audiences, and this knowledge colors the events they narrate. These are stories imbued with nostalgia, grief, or anger—the emotions generated by the filmmaker's backward glance. But there are also moments in all these films when we "forget" that we are positioned above the fray. Ecstatic moments when we react as if we do not know "how it is all going to end" and follow events in their unfolding, too close to see beyond them. It is possible in such moments to re-experience some of the terror of the unforeseen.

As he suggests in his interview with Telewizja Polska, Wajda understands that Poland is facing a *memory crisis* in which the recollection of the event he calls Katyn, with its far-reaching consequences, is no longer an active part of national consciousness. The modes of representation he adopts are not therefore intended to simply narrate historical events. It is not sufficient, for his purpose, to construct a rational model in which a causal sequence of events represented audiovisually stands for the real events known as "Katyn." For Wajda, *standing for* is not a discursive substitution. He is less interested in representing the outside of events, their historiographic contours observed from above; rather, he would turn inward and expose the inner life of events, their physical, mental, and emotional content. How was Katyn experienced by the people who lived through it? In what concrete places and in what ways did the Poles suffer occupation and resist oppression and censorship? How did the massacres damage the mythological integrity of the Polish nation?

As Frank Ankersmit observes, the symbolic language of history "presents us with an image of the world, but as such it can offer only the shadow of the terrors inhabiting the world itself and of the fears it may provoke."[19] To evoke the terrors of Poland in thrall to two occupying powers, historical traces must be reinvested with some of the attributes of real being. Wajda wants to *touch* the world he is representing, and he wants his public to understand that world *affectively*.

The material past—fugitive but real—is then Wajda's object of desire: the desire to put his audience in touch with experiences from a painful period that remains unresolved for him, and for Poland, both historically and psychologically. The Soviet murder of the Polish officer corps was the act that dismantled Poland's future; it was an event that eventually culminated in the Soviet domination of Polish society for forty-five years following the end of World War II. This crushing historical situation should not be forgotten, Wajda's film argues; it should be hypostatized and emblazoned in public memory. That is, after all, the primary task of historical film: to salvage the past even if it must be relived in the mode of infinite regret. *Katyn* is the *dramatic reactivation* of a historical moment. Wajda creates a compelling diegetic world in which the characters are at once collective and individual protagonists who act or are acted upon in extreme historical circumstances. They live in a world of intense emotion where the pathetic fallacy prevails: the characters, settings, and objects coalesce and are alive with meaning.

Wajda is, then, a complex human agency. He is at once a historian (by his rigor and his attention to the factual record), a living repository of historical experience, and the autobiographical subject that constructs his narrative. "I wanted to tell my story," he said in the interview he gave to Telewizja Polska, and it is doubtless for this reason that one feels a special intensity in the film. To tell his story is to undertake the (impossible) return to childhood. Wajda's impulse is nostalgic: to re-inhabit the space-time of loss and re-experience the pain of frustrated desire.

NOSTOS "RETURN HOME" + *ALGOS* "PAIN"

Although he avoids replicating his personal situation—Wajda does not directly represent himself—*Katyn* is infused with what I will term *autobiographical affect*: an emotional charge that spreads across the entire perceptual field of the film. This most intimate kind of subjectivity shapes all the film's strategies of representation; its presence is not localizable but is palpable everywhere in the text. The same can be said of the subjective character of nearly all the films in this study, but autobiographical affect is most explicit in *Katyn*, *Nostalgia for the Light*, and *S-21*. Wajda, Guzmán, and Panh invest themselves in their films. Victims of history, they are motivated by a devastating loss and seek reparation not only for themselves but for the "intersubjective communities" whose memories they take upon themselves. Whatever distance they may adopt as narrators of the stories they tell, like the dreamer in the dream, they permeate the worlds they stage.

Wajda's vision of the past has all the earmarks of nostalgia, and *Katyn* is a nostalgic film in the strongest sense of the term. It embodies what cultural historian Svetlana Boym describes as the central paradox of nostalgia: it would "repeat the unrepeatable and materialize the immaterial."[20] Nostalgic representations are irrational in that they superimpose, as Boym observes, images of the present over images of the past—a temporary suspension of irreconcilable elements.

Nostalgia is rarely, however, just a personal state of yearning. It is a collective phenomenon involving others—the family, the ethnic group, the nation—that constitute the social context of memory. Collective memory, on which all nostalgia is based, involves the notion of the "affective community," a group with which we are closely identified and whose solidarity allows individual memory to "take possession of itself." This is the notion that Paul Ricoeur eloquently formulated in *Time and Narrative* as "participatory belonging." Collective memory is a bond between generations: children's experience with their parents and grandparents, for example, gives access to the ethos of another time. Moreover, as Maurice Halbwachs puts it, the individual may elicit from memory perceptions of the past that belong to contemporary history:

> The world of my childhood, as I recover it from memory, fits so naturally into the framework of recent history reconstituted by formal study because it already bears the stamp of that history. What I discover is that by attentive effort I can recover, in my remembrances of my little world, a semblance of the surrounding milieu.[21]

As Boym observes, nostalgia is "a symptom of our age, a historical emotion." It centers on "the relationship between individual biography and the biography of groups or nations, between personal and collective memory." Moreover, nostalgia allows for open forms of figuration: "It charts space on time and time on space and hinders the distinction between subject and object."[22] In other words, such figurations upset some of the basic logical categories of conscious thought. Replacing ourselves in a time that has been lost to us is a poetic operation.

Nostalgic representations, then, can be only partially explained in rational terms. They are reconstructions of events—stories—drawn from the reservoir of personal memory, from the community of witnesses, and from the testimony of historical sources, as is the case with *Katyn*. As such they belong to what Freud called secondary process, in this case the discursive shaping of memory through the techniques of narration. Nostalgic representations are, however, also subject to the body—the body's physical being and response to events—and to deepseated emotions and reactions we cannot account for in rational terms. The "intentions" of the body and of emotional compulsion belong to what Freud called primary process and reveal the workings of the unconscious. Affective communities, as we have seen, may also be subjects of memory, and memory for the historian, as Pierre Nora asserts, has nothing to do with the objective gaze the historian adopts as a methodological principle. On the contrary, memory is emotional and instinctual; it "wells up from groups it welds together." Moreover, memory is "rooted in the concrete," as opposed to the rational units of historical narration. It dwells on "space, gesture, image, and object."[23] Memory does not discourse; it materializes.

Many contemporary historians resist the dichotomy between history and memory that Nora espouses. The skepticism he expresses for the intuitive faculties—those allies of a-historical emotionalism—would deprive historians of what should be, many contend, one of their fundamental aims: the recovery of the sensorial and psychological realities of the past. Ironically, it is the work of an "old" historian that points the way toward such innovation in historical writing: Johan Huizinga. The Dutch historian's *The Waning of the Middle Ages* is still as provocative as it was when it first appeared in 1919, and his emphasis on historical sensation remains strikingly modern. As French historian Jacques Le Goff puts it in the 2015 French re-edition of Huizinga's masterpiece (nearly one hundred years after the original), "Let's reread Huizinga. He is still an opener of doors that lead to what needs to be done in history."[24]

The magnificent opening passages of *The Waning of the Middle Ages* make it clear that Huizinga intends to evoke a whole range of sensations in his historical representation of fifteenth-century Europe. Moreover, Huizinga's depiction of the material realities of life brings to mind the psychological and moral structures—the mentalities—that organized perception in the medieval period. Consider a few examples.

In modern life, Huizinga observes, we no longer know the absolute contrasts between light and darkness or between noise and silence that were familiar realities in the medieval period. The opposition between wealth and misery or the disparity between sickness and health were more achingly felt then than now, as was the cold and darkness of winter against which "a fur-lined robe of office, a bright fire in the oven, drink and jest, and a soft bed" still offered a sense of the fullness of life. Indeed, Huizinga sees in these polarities the emotional resonance characteristic of the period: "Daily life received the kind of impulses and passionate suggestions that is revealed in the vacillating moods of unrefined exuberance, sudden cruelty, and tender emotions between which the life of the medieval city was suspended."[25]

Huizinga asks us, then, to imagine sensorial realities that belong to fifteenth-century experience. Image, sound, smell, taste, and touch emanating from the past, if unavailable to direct experience, can be reactivated in the mind. Consider, for example, Huizinga's description of the soundscapes of medieval cities and villages. "But one sound," he tells us, "always rose above the clamor of busy life . . . and, for a moment, lifted everything into an ordered sphere: that of the bells."[26] For the alert observer, signs of past experience can appear in unanticipated ways. In the chapter he devotes to "Art and Life," Huizinga describes the affective intimacy of Jan Van Eyck's painting of Arnolfini, represented in his bedchamber with his wife—a rare survival from the period of a painting evoking domestic intimacy. Great lord and ducal counselor he undoubtedly was, but Arnolfini and his wife were friends of Van Eyck, as the inscription he places above the mirror bears witness, a touching manner to sign his work: " 'Johannes de Eyck fuit hic, 1434.' Jan Van Eyck was here. Just a short time ago. The deep silence of the chamber still reverberates with the sound of his voice."[27]

What Huizinga wants to evoke is the *life* of the past, especially the life of the body, as Jacques Le Goff points out in the recent French re-edition of *L'Automne du Moyen Âge*. In his attachment to the image and the *imaginary* of a period, Huizinga brings history closer to ethnology, whose mission it is to discover the symbolic thought and the representations that are deeply inscribed in the cultural foundation of archaic societies.[28]

It is precisely this kind of historical imagination Wajda espouses. He believes it is possible to hear voices emerging from the past that carry with them the sensorial, emotive, and symbolic qualities of an era. The poetic imagery Wajda produces emerges from experience, not from logic or transparent rhetoric, and therefore remains open to intuitive associations. In relationship to the past, as Huizinga puts it, "We want half dreamt, unclearly delineated images, leaving free play to our imagination and this need is better satisfied by a visual than by an intellectual apperception of the past."[29]

Before proceeding to an analysis of the text of *Katyn*, I would like to return for a moment to Walter Benjamin and specifically to his short essay "The Mimetic Faculty" (in *Illuminations*). It is Benjamin's intuition that mimesis—the "gift for seeing similarities"—retains, even in the modern period, some of the power it had in prescientific cultures. As Michael Taussig suggests in *Mimesis and Alterity*, this is one of Benjamin's enduring themes: "the surfacing of the 'primitive' within modernity as a direct result of modernity."[30] Essential to Benjamin's concept, Taussig points out, is the double nature of mimetic activity: "To get hold of something by means of its likeness. Here is what is crucial in the resurgence of the mimetic faculty, namely the two-layered notion of mimesis that is involved—a copying or imitation, and a palpable, sensuous, connection between the very body of the perceiver and the perceived."[31] When one intellectualizes the process of mimesis, describing it in terms of representation and identification, one denies the importance of *contact*—the role of the body and its senses in the activity of imitation. Such has been the impact, Benjamin would argue, of the dominance of language and "rationality," inherited from the Enlightenment, which would detach the bodily subject from the experience of representation. We have become crippled by language, "the most complete archive of nonsensuous similarity."[32] Indeed, what is important in the notion of the mimetic faculty is the *exchange* that takes place in this double-layered activity in which the copy retains some of the power of the original.

Retaining some of the power of the original—that is the ambition of Wajda's film, indeed, the ambition of all the films in this study. Image-based communication, by dint of its mode of signification, is more sensuous (more sense-dependent) than language-dominated discourses and is therefore open to the more poetic strategies that characterize Wajda's filmmaking. The indexical quality of the cinematographic image—its existential relationship to the phenomena it photographs—is one embodiment of the mimetic faculty that binds perception and representation. The mimetic ideal is to strip away distance, even if always incompletely. Adorno tells us that in Benjamin's writing "thought presses close to its object as if through touching, smelling, tasting, it wanted to transform itself."[33] Wajda also presses close to his object in his desire for authenticity, as will become clear in the following section.

SEARCHING FOR AUTHENTIC OBJECTS

One should not confuse the search for authentic objects with the fantasy of the literal representation of history in film. As Robert Rosenstone observes, film "can never provide a literal rendition of events that took place in the past. Can never be an exact replica of what happened."[34] From the historical perspective, there is no "automatic privileging of the 'realistic' or naturalistic mode for representing the past," as Natalie Zemon Davis tells us.[35] Indeed, the relationship between a filmic representation and a historical event depends, I have argued, on acts of figuration that belong to the poetic realms of the metaphoric and the symbolic.[36] It does not follow, however, that concrete historical traces showing that "a man, an animal passed by here," as Paul Ricoeur puts it, are only meaningful once they are positioned as signifying elements in historical narrative. Traces are not empty signifiers. When they emerge from the experience of the past in an act of representation, they bring with them material fragments of vanished life. In "Uber Walter Benjamin," T. W. Adorno describes Benjamin's fixation on objects, in which he seeks to discover hidden signs of life just as he contemplates life around him for signs of its links to the primal: "He is driven not merely to awaken congealed life in petrified objects—as in allegory—but also to scrutinize living things so that they present themselves as ancient 'Ur-historical' and abruptly release their significance."[37]

We know that, in preparing the production of *Katyn*, Wajda was obsessed with authenticity. As in all his historical films, he was intent on reconstructing the everyday existence of a specific period: locations, objects, dress, and behavior observed in the finest detail. He instigated an uncompromising search for authentic historical materials—*indices* of the past, or to use Ankersmit's notion of historical artifacts, "protuberances" that have survived into the present. Their function is not to create a convincing veneer of an era; Wajda wanted no truck with historical spectacle. In his hands, objects are pregnant with latent meanings and susceptible of giving off the *aura* of a specific period. If we are sensitive to them, these indexical signs—material traces left by historical actors and their actions—can produce an experience in which we apprehend at once the present object and the past that adheres to it.

Wajda charged his costumers and set decorators with gathering every available vestige of life of 1940s Krakow, where much of the action is set. Indeed, they were so successful, his team contends, that no subsequent filmmaker could make a historical film using authentic artifacts from that place and time. Wajda's concern for authenticity applied equally to the actors he chose to impersonate his historical protagonists. In his previous films about the Second World War, actors had direct experience of the war, bringing to their interpretations the authenticity of their personal insights. To Wajda's regret, they had become too old to play characters from his mother's generation, and he had to rely on young actors who were not vestigial remnants of the past and who, he feared, might not be able to understand the historical circumstances of the period or the characters' predicaments. He was reassured, however, by the actors' power of empathy: the ability to share the emotions of others, in this case the characters he constructed, and thereby negotiate difference across the historical divide.

Among the traces, the most important are perhaps not objects but texts: the memoirs, journals, and letters that survived both the war and the postwar Stalinist regime that sought to suppress all evidence that might challenge its lie—that the massacres known as "Katyn" were the work of the Germans and not the Soviets. These texts are of course already narrative accounts whose voices speak to us across time. They furnish much of the narrative and emotional material that Wajda weaves into his film. If the texts are transposed, attributed to "fictional" characters, and framed by dramatic structures, they remain rooted in the urgent concerns of their autobiographical testimony. They bring with them the material experience of the past.

Wajda begins, then, with concrete experience, his own and that of other individuals, and with the material "protuberances" of the past that jut into the contemporary moment. He is much less concerned with the "gasier" constructs of historical representation: those abstract social actors playing on the grand stage of history. He embraces, rather, the ("archaic") Romantic attitude toward the representation of the past, in which past and present are involved in an exchange that has as much to do with emotion as with knowledge. The Romantic historian intervenes in the world of the past; this historian is, to cite Jules Michelet, in love with his or her subject ("the heart is moved"), and love is the force that draws the historian toward an intimate knowledge of it: he or she "sees a thousand things that are invisible to the indifferent public."[38] History makes the historian as much as the historian makes history. As Ankersmit puts it, "How we *feel* about the past is no less important than what we *know* about it—and probably even more so. '*Sentir, c'est penser*' [to feel is to think], as Rousseau liked to say, and this is where I fully agree with him."[39]

FACE TO FACE WITH MEMORY

If Wajda's *Katyn* constructs a remembrance of the past, we need to be careful in defining what kinds of memory-work are involved. It is useful to recall the distinction between voluntary and involuntary memory that Walter Benjamin draws from the work of Marcel Proust. These are, he argues, radically different modes of recollection that place the "memoirist" in quite different positions vis-à-vis the past. In the mode of voluntary memory, the remembering subject constructs a narrative chain of occurrences in which each remembered detail achieves meaning through its (subservient) role in the montage of events. This is memory as a constructed discourse. For Benjamin, the mechanism of voluntary memory is repressive in that it inhibits the immediacy of the remembered experience. A frequent instrument of defense against the shock of past realities, narrative memory functions to screen out what seems to endanger the organism; "assigning to an incident a precise place in time in consciousness at the cost of the integrity of its contents," turns "the incident into a moment that has been lived (Erlebnis)."[40] What has been lived and told (what has been "processed," in the language of popular psychology) is relegated to the safety zone created by narration.

In the mode of involuntary memory, the remembering subject is not willful; indeed, he or she is overtaken by sensations—images, sounds, tastes, touch—that arise unbidden. In Proust's *In Search of Lost Time,* involuntary memories spring up when the unsuspecting narrator tastes a madeleine or trips on a paving stone, objects that transport him into the experiential past. This is the memory of sensations as yet unorganized by the logic of the mind, unsubdued, as Benjamin makes clear.

> It is its characteristic that the information it gives about the past retains no trace of it. "It is the same with our own past. In vain we try to conjure it up again; the efforts of our intellect are futile." Therefore Proust, summing up, says that the past is "somewhere beyond the reach of the intellect and unmistakably present in some material object (or in the sensation which such an object arouses in us) though we have no idea which one it is."[41]

In *Katyn* characters are indeed overtaken by sensations provoked by instigating objects, particularly those that produce in the anxious families the sudden recognition of the experience of their murdered loved ones: the discovery of a wedding ring concealed in the lining of a coat, the borrowed sweater that at first conceals then reveals the reality of a murder, the diary entries that initiate the film's visualization of the Polish officers' final moments. Beyond these "narrativized" objects, there is, as we have seen, Wajda's confidence in the power of authentic objects to evoke a lost world.

TO NARRATE, TO SYMBOLIZE, TO EXPERIENCE

The more general question remains: In what specific ways and to what degrees does *Katyn* reactivate memory? I will argue that the action of *Katyn* is invested with both voluntary and involuntary memory, as Benjamin conceives them, and that Wajda employs three modes of representation to evoke the past.

The first I will call *representational* because it functions according to the principle of *standing for*. The film's actors stand for historical actors, whom they endow with a visible body and the readable signs of intention and emotion. The actions they perform for the camera stand for real actions in the past, as the settings stand for real historical spaces. We are intended to understand them as substitutes for (but not copies of) realities that are no longer accessible to consciousness.

I will call the second mode *symbolic* because it no longer functions as a description of past reality. Rather it rises above denotation—in particular the chronological chain of events the historian creates—to bring into play associations that are part of the shared culture of the community the film addresses, for example the Catholic iconography that infuses the sequences I will analyze shortly. Because these associations are largely understood spontaneously and, at least partially, unconsciously, they are read intuitively and are often charged with emotion.

The third mode, which I will call *experiential*, has nothing to do with historical narration or with symbolic figures. It provokes unmediated experience—a resurgence of historical memory that results in the recovery of a moment of the living past. The most striking examples in *Katyn*, as we will see, are the sequences of mass murder that conclude the film.

Representation takes a certain distance from its object in order to see it more clearly. The symbolic floats above the discursive, so to speak, because it calls into play transhistorical figures of meaning. The experiential is a moment of fusion—fusion of the past with the present, the subject with his or her object—and precludes narrative and symbolic structures. If the representational and the symbolic, as we shall see, frequently intertwine, the experiential stands apart: it is only what it is.

To produce narrative or symbolic meaning, one must blot out experience. As Ankersmit observes, "Where we have narrative, experience is impossible; and experience excludes narrative." Historical experience, as conceived by Huizinga,[42] involves the historian in an *ecstatic* movement out of the self (from the Greek *ekstasis*, "standing outside oneself"). No longer centered in the here and now, the historian stretches toward a "contact with the past." This movement toward the past may culminate in "a moment of rapture," in which representation gives way to the power of direct experience. Everything that separates past and present momentarily disappears.

> All spatial and temporal demarcations have been lifted; it is as if the temporal trajectory between past and present, instead of separating the two, has become the locus of their encounter. Historical experience pulls the faces of past and present together in a short but ecstatic kiss.[43]

A final note. We know that film has its own modes of representation and that it is not capable of rendering the past without recourse to them. All films—fiction or documentary—rely on narrative and rhetorical structures, on mise-en-scène, on the expressive use of the scale of shots and camera movement, and on the textual articulations produced by the work of editing. Otherwise films would be unintelligible. Such techniques and procedures help construct the plot—the *telling* that renders events comprehensible—and contribute to *binding* the images and sounds into a discourse. As we will see, Wajda is a master of these discursive strategies.

FUSING THE NARRATIVE AND THE SYMBOLIC

Let's first look at the film's opening sequence, which is preoccupied with exposition. Wajda chooses a chaotic moment: the invasion of Poland by the Soviets on September 17, 1939. The exposition is particularly dense because it needs to accomplish several tasks: lay out the historical situation; introduce several major characters; set up the narrative "problem"; and establish the film's major themes. From the opening images, the symbolic begins to play its key role. The clouds behind the titles slowly dissipate revealing a crowd of people immobilized on a bridge (long shot in deep focus). This is the first of the many metaphors the film deploys: memory emerges from oblivion, representation reclaims what has been lost. This group on the bridge (a) is looking, and in the reverse angle response we see another group of people (b) running toward them across the bridge. In the succession of shots that follow we hear a man from group (a) shout: "Where to folks? There are Germans behind us." Someone from group (b) responds: "Where are you going? Turn back!" and another: "The Soviets have entered!" Wajda represents the bridge as occupying one point on the Molotov-Ribbentrop line, the border established according to the Hitler/Stalin nonaggression pact signed in Moscow on August 23, 1939, which demarcated the Polish territories to be occupied by the Germans from those to be occupied by the Soviets.

The figurative meaning of the beginning of this sequence is clear, communicated through the opposition established by the reverse-angles. The literal representation of "these people, trapped between two unacceptable alternatives, hav[ing] nowhere to go," extends, by synecdoche, to the more abstract notion of the Polish predicament in 1939: the nation subjugated by two occupying powers. This space and these actions represented by means of narrative and cinematic structures stand for a broader historical reality. We should remember that any such symbolic exchange in which something material—this bridge and the chaotic encounter of the crowds—represents something immaterial—the historical predicament of the Molotov-Ribbentrop agreement—opens up all the associative power of poetic language.

As the crowd pushes forward toward the Russian side, this larger movement is broken into a multitude of details: bicycle handlebars, baggage, a close-up of a young woman followed by a close-up of a young girl, then other close shots of the evacuees, and so forth. We are turning from a relatively large-scale historical representation to a smaller scale where the mechanisms of individuation and identification take over. Here the subjective experience of events begins to assert itself. The close-ups of mother and child are at first anonymous "faces in the crowd" at the same level as other details, but, as they are repeated, mother and daughter become focalized as protagonists: the young mother (Anna) is in search of her husband (Andrzej), a Polish officer held captive by the Soviets; her daughter (Nika) attempts to save an abandoned dog tied to the side of the bridge. A third character appears—a woman in a car who stops to inform the young mother of the Soviet invasion and urges her to abandon the search for her husband. Hers is another "face in the crowd" we will subsequently recognize as the Polish general's wife, who will wait in vain for her husband's return. Not only are these individual characters pushed to the foreground of events; they are also endowed with an optical point of view. They perceive things through the mechanism of the point of view series, and we of course see these things through their eyes. This alternation of scales and of positions of narration is a classic structure of the historical film in which individuated action invests the historical situation with intensified feeling.

Later in the sequence the mother and child approach the field hospital in a churchyard, and here metaphor adheres to narrative. Anna sees a cross on which only one forearm of Christ remains hanging (sacrilege). The child recognizes her father's coat draped over what appears to be a body. The mother lifts the coat and sees the head of the statue of Christ with a crown of thorns. The poetic strategy is complex but quite intelligible. The (atheistic) Soviets are committing ravages against the holy body of Poland: Christ's body takes the place of the Polish officer feared dead, a substitution that extends to the Pole the aura of Christian sanctity. This kind of figurative substitution will recur frequently in the film. Moreover, not only does the body mistaken prefigure Andrzej's martyrdom but it also sets up one of the film's major narrative devices: the mis-recognition followed by recognition—so essential to Greek tragedy—that establishes a pattern of alternation between hope and despair. The most obvious example of delayed recognition plays out over large segments of the film. In the prison camp where Polish officers are held by the Soviets, Jerzy gives his sweater to his friend Andrzej, who is suffering from the cold. When Andrzej's body is found in the mass graves at Katyn, he is misidentified as Jerzy, whose name is embroidered in the sweater and who is declared dead. Anna therefore continues to believe that her husband is alive and is only disabused when Jerzy returns to Krakow to see his friend's widow, bringing her a gift of canned meat.

The question long debated is whether the kind of focalization I just described, which presents events from the narrative and even optical point of view of characters who are not "historically real," is a fictional device and therefore a betrayal of historiography. As in fiction, Wajda's characters, played by actors, appear and reappear in the course of the narrative: they carry the action and undergo emotions that cinematic structures like framing and editing make clear. That is, they are endowed with individual subjectivity. Since we can see inside them and see others "through their eyes," we no longer simply observe them from the outside. It is relevant to recall that Käte Hamburger defines the novel, and by extension novelistic film, as the only genre in which we are privy to the inner lives of characters—their thoughts, intentions, emotions—presented in the third person. In Hamburger's analysis, all proceeds from the position of the author: if the author directly represents events that have an existential relationship to the present in which he or she is writing, then we are dealing with a factual narrative; if such a relationship does not exist, we are dealing with fiction. Factual and fictional narratives are, accordingly, separate domains. As Gérard Genette puts it, "To enter fiction is to leave the ordinary field of the exercise of language, marked by the concerns of truth or persuasion that command the rule of communication and the deontology of discourse."[44]

What is disconcerting is that *Katyn* seems to partake of both. On the one hand, as I have described, the film employs many of the techniques we associate with the fiction film, in particular strategies of focalization and point of view. And all of these techniques sin against historical representation as the historical discipline conceives it. On the other hand, who could reproach Wajda, who is and has been both historian of the Polish nation and an activist fighting for the liberation of his country (precisely through the "fiction film"), of failing to represent the past from the position of the present or of failing in his obligations to history? Who could doubt the historical intentionality *Katyn* embodies?

In their introduction to *A Companion to the Historical Film*, Constantin Parvulescu and Robert Rosenstone raise this problematic in terms of institutions. Historiography as practiced by professionals in the discipline is a hegemonic institution; representations of the past are constructed according to established historical methods and are vetted by the body of university-trained historians. Filmmakers, they argue, do not operate under such institutional constraints; rather, they occupy a "secondary position" as challengers to the historians' representations of the past. According to Parvulescu and Rosenstone's analysis, film has a "hybrid social function" because films are at once "education and entertainment, document and fiction, an address of reason and emotion, scholarship and art, a public and a commercial enterprise." Their hybridity—so often the target of historians' critiques—disqualifies them as "serious" representations of the past. They occupy, rather, a "counter-hegemonic" position that allows, indeed fosters, discursive openness.[45]

This discursive openness appears in *Katyn*. In Wajda's historical films there is an underlying tension between the abstract and the concrete. As everywhere in cinema, the visual material produces convincing representations of the phenomenological world—moving photographic images cut out of space and time. A title may, for example, identify "a public square in Krakow," but the succession of shots of the square gives it the sense of real being. Indeed, this is one of the concrete historical spaces within which the actions the films represent took place. Moreover, in cinematic representation, the human characters are always particularized: this specific body and this distinctive physiognomy engaged in carrying out these discrete actions. Such figures seem to lack the defining feature that distinguishes historical narrative from fictional narrative: anonymity. Historical characters are not individual protagonists; they are members of social groups whose actions take place on another plane of narration. They are, to use Paul Ricoeur's formula, *entities of participatory belonging*.[46] The work of historical narration in film begins with this problem: How is it possible to show that recognizable human individuals, acting in specific settings, belong to a class of historical characters whose essential traits speak about the collective identity of the group faced with a particular historical situation?

Katyn is, on the one hand, historical *fiction* because its narrative combines real and imagined events; these events take place in a reconstructed space and center on fictional, not anonymous, characters, who are, moreover, played by actors. On the other hand, *Katyn* is undeniably linked to the present of its author, who, as we have seen, is determined to recount the historical events that marked his childhood. Even if Wajda acknowledges his responsibility for the "truth" of his representations, he does not shy away from the representation of inner states: the psychological experience of the past, *Katyn* suggests, is just as cogent, indeed as necessary, an element of historical representation as the observation of action and behavior. Instead of attenuating the subjective aspects of characters—as in the distancing effects Rossellini achieves, for example, in his historical films—Wajda accentuates his characters' emotions. It is as if these intense inner experiences were meant to radiate out to embrace the collectivity and thus historicize feelings that film cannot represent directly as belonging to a social group. This is, once again, a poetic device. The rhetorical exchange between the individual and the collective relies on a metonymic figure that expresses the relationship between two aspects of a field: the emotions of the focalized characters infuse the group of their peers, while the group lends the individuals its collective identity. In historical representation the group never functions passively as the simple background to individuated characters. Rather, it is the very definition of their social being.

Consider the following example of this figurative strategy. In the scene of a public square in Krakow, a crowd listens to loudspeakers disseminating the names of those discovered in mass graves at Katyn. I would add that the event represented in this sequence is meant to be taken as frequentative: we understand that these people, and others like them, have come repeatedly to this square to endure the agony of the wait. This representation thus stands for all similar events that are not represented, in the manner of the synecdoche in which a part stands for the whole.

The first three shots represent the crowd of anonymous listeners, a collective figure that is individuated briefly in shot 2 in the close-up of the reader's hands and, as the camera pans, the face looking over his shoulder. Only in shot 4 does the first focalized character (the university rector) appear, and a point-of-view series links her to the reading of the list of the dead (in this case, a student): the rector gazing off-screen/close-up of loudspeakers/return to rector's gaze. The second focalized character, the general's widow, emerges in shot 7. In shot 8 Anna appears, scans the list of the dead in the newspaper, and smiles. Shot 9

EXAMPLE 2.1
EMOTION IS CONTAGIOUS

IMAGE	SOUND
1. A long shot of cobbled pavement; the camera cranes up to a high angle of a crowd; we see the title: "Krakow, April 13, 1943." The camera moves higher to a close-up of loudspeakers.	"Zygmeut Szymkiewicz, major doctor, a letter from the Health Department." "Roman Zajaczkowski, land engineer. His service papers were found." Ambient noise.
2. A close-up of a newspaper held in the reader's hands. The camera pans across the figure to a close-up of a man looking over the reader's shoulder.	"Anton Darda, military rank unknown." Ambient noise.
3. Another long view of the square. Nazi flags fly in the background, and we see others in the crowd.	The reading of the list of the dead continues in this and all following shots, as does the ambient noise.
4. The woman we will later recognize as the university rector and Agnieska's sister climbs down from a carriage and turns to look in the direction of the loudspeakers.	The list continues. Ambient noise.
5. Close-up of loudspeakers from the rector's point of view.	The list continues. Ambient noise.
6. Return to the rector in close-up, in sharp focus among other less-defined figures. The camera tracks her as she moves forward.	"Ferdynand Marecki, his student card and a telegram attached."
7. A medium shot of the general's widow. The camera tracks her as she moves; she stops to listen.	The list continues. Ambient noise.
8. Anna runs to the kiosk. The camera pans with her.	Anna: "Goniec Karkowski, please." Vendor: "I got the latest." Ambient noise.
9. Anna opens the paper and reads. The camera pans with her as she walks. She stands in medium shot facing the camera, raises her head and smiles. She turns her head twice to look back, smiling, and disappears in an archway.	The list continues. Ambient noise.
10. The general's widow in medium long shot. She turns and moves away from the camera.	The list continues. Ambient noise.

reinforces Anna's emotion as she hesitates to leave the square and casts backward glances. The general's widow reappears in shot 10 as she turns her back to the camera and moves away. By metonymic transmission, the three women and the emotions they express stand for the experience of all the others. Moreover, the fluid camera movements—a linking strategy that appears elsewhere in the film—and the characters' movements within the frame—tie the three women and the crowd into the shared experience of anxious waiting. On the soundtrack there is only a brief snatch of dialogue (usually a prime tool of individuation). Instead we hear ambient noise and the loudspeakers disseminating without interruption the list of the dead disinterred at Katyn, the accumulation of names suggesting the generalization of experience.

I would call this strategy *collective figuration* in which the individual character and individual actions are to be taken as the narrative expression of larger-scale entities and actions. The episodic structure the film adopts is the clear sign of this figuration: we move between relatively autonomous groups of characters who represent different poles of the developing historical action: the domestic space of the wives and mothers, the collective space of the Polish prisoners, the university under Nazi threat, and so forth. The protagonists who inhabit these spaces are to some degree idiosyncratic but they are at the same moment representative—that is, they are *members of* their class—and as such, they express more general political and existential attitudes. In short, characters take on symbolic functions, as they do in many historical films: this is the rhetorical means of describing social entities and actions that are not easily represented in cinematic terms.

This is particularly apparent in the representation of life in Soviet-dominated Poland after the end of the war. Characters choose to belong to one side or the other of a great political divide. In one camp we have those who "want to live" and choose the present over the past, which means an accommodation with the People's Republic and, in particular, their complicity in the lie about the Katyn massacres. In the other camp are those who refuse to forget, who will tell the truth about Katyn, even if their resistance ends in death.

Take the example of two sisters, whose actions and attitudes make them polar opposites: Agnieska and the (unnamed) rector of the university (Wajda chose to name only a few of his characters to prevent the hunt for their "real" models). Agnieska thinks of nothing but telling truth to power, and she insists on inscribing the correct date of her brother Piotr's death at Katyn (1940, before the German occupation) on the tombstone she plans to have made for him, as Wajda did for his own father. To pay for the monument, she sells her long blond hair to an actress, who has recently returned from a concentration camp where her head was shaved. The actress has been cast as Antigone, the character of Greek tragedy who performs a forbidden ritual burial for her brother killed on the field of battle and, refusing to decant, is punished by being entombed alive. It is, however, Agnieska who assumes the role of the mythological heroine. She places the tombstone in the cemetery; she is arrested by the Polish police and is subjected to a Stalinist interrogation, which she contemptuously resists; she is then taken down a dark corridor and descends the stairs that lead into the underground.

Agnieska's sister, the rector, stands on the side of accommodation. Anna's nephew Tadzio appears in her office with a curriculum vitae that supports his application to study at the university's art school. Tadzio's CV includes the information that his father was murdered by the Soviets at Katyn. The rector attempts to persuade him to revise his application, asking him to choose life. He refuses. She admits him nonetheless, asking a professor to make him see reason, and reveals her fundamental pessimism: "There will never be a free Poland." In the next sequence, Tadzio rips down a Soviet poster, is pursued by the police, and eventually is killed in the street.

Another figure of resistance is the general's widow. She attempts to stop an open-air showing of a Soviet documentary that pins the massacre at Katyn on the Germans. Jerzy, one of the few survivors of the killings, takes her away, telling her he has chosen to live with the lie and pursue his life in the Polish army. Seated together on a bench in a park, engulfed in fog, they engage in a battle of conscience. The general's widow tells Jerzy, "The Soviets must lie to cover up the crime, but you don't have to." Jerzy responds, "I could just as well shoot myself in the head. We have to survive, forgive." After army officers pass by and Jerzy rises to salute them, she says, "You're the same as they are," and walks away into the mist. In the next sequence, Jerzy is drinking heavily in a bar and talking recklessly about Katyn. To silence him, a friend pushes him out into the dark where the tormented Jerzy does indeed shoot himself in the head.

Most sequences in *Katyn* are sustained by narrative and figurative structures like those I have just described. Codes of action align events in their sequential order and assure the text's readability; rhetorical structures specify the relationship between the individual and the collectivity or relate the details of a scene to a mythic symbology. But, as I have attempted to suggest, Wajda's discourse on history is far from transparent. Indeed, there are pauses in *Katyn* that interrupt the flow of action and create a state of reflection in which every detail of the scene, every action or gesture, every movement of the camera becomes part of a grand metaphor, the distillation of a historical moment. *Katyn* also confronts us with moments of historical experience that refuse to be contained within any narrative logic or any model of symbolic substitution. They do not refer us to codes; they return us to life. I would like to illustrate these quite different aspects of Wajda's text through the analysis of three sequences: the first depicts the celebration of Christmas in the prison where the Polish officers are detained. The second and third represent their massacre at Katyn.

THE SACRED BODY, THE BODY MASSACRED

Three sequences take place in Kozelsk, site of the Optyn Hermitage that the Soviets converted to a POW camp in 1939 and 1940. Irony of history: it was in this monastery that Dostoevsky in *The Brothers Karamazov* set the dialogue between an old monk and a young aristocrat who discuss whether morality can exist if God is dead.[47] We are clearly in the sphere of the mythological. The most significant of these sequences takes place on Christmas Eve, 1939. It begins with a long shot of the domed structure of the monastery church under snowfall as a Polish soldier looks at the sky above it where a star is shining. Wajda plays on the irony of the setting: the sacrilege (etymologically "the stealer of sacred things") of the deconsecrated church that, paradoxically, retains its identity as a sacred vessel. It holds within it the elite Polish officers—intellectuals and professionals, not military men—who constitute the hope for the future of Poland.

In the first interior shot we see the back of the soldier who moves toward the door of a room where the general is seated at a table, seen in deep focus. The general/priest is in his "sacristy," and the soldier announces: "General, I report that the first star has been sighted." The camera tracks back as the general moves into the church to begin his Christmas Eve speech. It is a symmetrical, enclosed space—the church's vaulting rises above the multiple tiers of bunks—that the composition of the following shots shows as centered and harmonious. Majestic crane shots take us above the heads of the soldiers emphasizing again the symmetry of space with the general at the center encircled by his men. He is the subject of several interpolated close-ups. His speech concerns the future: "You must endure, because there won't be a free Poland without you." The camera re-descends as the general begins singing: "God is born on earth / Powers tremble . . ." and his men join in, and then the camera regains its height. An exterior shot shows Soviet soldiers in a watchtower. Then we return to a long shot of the church.

The subject of the sequence is a ritual, which, like all authentic rituals, reaches into the depths of collective memory. (As we will also see in *The Ascent* and *Siberiade*, sacred myth, whether Christian or animist, is the vehicle of transgression against soulless Soviet materialism.) The rite's ceremonious character is reinforced by the repetition of motifs and the expressive use of the moving camera. The sequence is symmetrically framed and circular in movement: a long shot of the church inaugurates the sequence and rhymes with the last shot, which brings the rite to closure. The rising crane shot is repeated by the descending crane shot that follows. These parallel movements enclose the figure of the general, who conducts the service and delivers his sermon on the theme of the necessity of survival. Strikingly, the focus on the individual characters disappears: the men are at one with each other and with the space of the church. The sequence constitutes a "mythic model of emotion": it organizes and subdues the chaotic and traumatic experience of the group and suggests the possibility of transcendence. Thus the POWs become a sanctified body both in their religious faith and in their national solidarity. The sequence has extraordinary poetic resonance—a summation of everything that Poland is about to lose. It is against these representations of the sacred body that the massacre at Katyn forest takes on its savage character.

The massacre is prepared for by Anna's receipt of her husband's diary, somehow salvaged from the Katyn death trenches and delivered to her years later. Beginning with the film's second sequence, we know that Andrzej will bear witness to the events of the Polish officers' captivity. He moves among the multitude of soldiers. He is one of them but he also stands for them; he is their self-appointed witness. In a voiceover Andrzej says, "Surrounded by Soviet tanks, we surrendered weapons. They take us for POWs though there was no war with them." "I'll try to write from time to time to let you know what happened to me, if I died and didn't return." Later in the sequence, Andrzej tells his friend Jerzy: "I've decided to describe everything I've seen here day by day."

Andrzej's journal entries promise to repair the rift between past and present. They cover, beginning on April 7, 1940, the Polish officers' deportation by transport train, their arrival at Gniezdovo, their transfer to Black Marias, and their journey to the Katyn spa, during which we see a bulldozer digging trenches. Andrzej's narrative voiceover accompanies the images, which take on a subjective character expressive of his situation. In the sequence in the transport train, a tracking camera moves across the figures of the prisoners caught in a close and fragmented space. The sense of dread is reinforced by low-key lighting in which the dark interior of the prison carriage contrasts with small areas of the frame brightly lit by the windows. The penumbral effects are striking, as for example in a deep focus shot in which the darkened carriage and the figures of the prisoners are set off against the distant doorway, infused with murky light, where we see the figure of a guard. Andrzej's commentary ends uneasily: "They brought us to a forest, a kind of spa. A thorough search. They didn't find my wedding ring. . . . What will happen to us?" and we see Andrzej putting his diary back in his coat. After a brief sequence representing the arrival of three Black Marias at the spa, a single protracted shot shows us that succeeding pages of the bloodstained diary are blank as they rustle in the wind.

Despite the quasi-religious meanings the sequence at Kozelsk produced, Wajda affirms in an interview that he was not interested in "Polish martyrology." Like other films of the Polish School, *Katyn* was meant to be an accusation, and it was certainly Wajda's intention to strike the spectator with the visceral horror of the Katyn massacres and deny any sense of the victims' transcendence. Indeed, the two sequences that represent the massacres show a major shift in narrative point of view. The first occurs before the end of Andrzej's account of the events of the deportation, but, exceptionally, he is not a witness: the general and several officers are executed by the Soviet secret police. The second represents the shootings over the death trenches at Katyn, in which Andrzej perishes along with many others. In most of the film's other sequences the representation of the subjectivity of characters, particularly the anxiety of wives, mothers, daughters, or sisters awaiting the hoped-for return of their loved ones, is strongly represented by narrative and visual point of view—these are emotions that we share with them. By contrast, point of view disappears as the massacres take place: victims cannot be witnesses, and the perpetrators are pure instruments of brutality. In this sense the massacre is an unmediated experience.

The executions are unsparing experiences for the spectator. There is first the brutality of the images, cut together in what the French call a *montage sec*. The executions are carried out with mechanical efficiency. The repetitions of the same or similar gestures are caught in dehumanizing close shots: the binding of wrists, the moment of panic, the shot to the head, the hand that removes the gun from the executioner's hand and replaces it with another, the body pushed up a chute, the boot that steps in blood, and the bucket of water that washes the blood from the floor before the next victim is brought in. It is the brutality of the executioners' detachment from the enormity of their tasks that stuns us.

The second aspect of these brutal representations comes from our own detachment from the experience of the characters, our starkly unfiltered point of view. And our detachment from "Wajda," the instrument of historical memory that has organized, up to this point, our experience of the events known as "Katyn." Although we recognize Andrzej and Agnieska's brother Piotr among the anonymous victims of the second sequence, we no longer consider their subjective beings. They are living bodies, among so many others positioned above the trenches, soon to pass ignobly into death. We do not suffer through the victims—the sequences suppress pathos—but are restrained in our uncomfortable position of observers, all too close to the action. Our aloofness seems to put us in immediate contact with the event. Ankersmit describes the nature of historical experience in the following terms:

> The event is no longer a symbol that can be read or be given meaning in terms of something else (that is, its context)—it is just what it is, and nothing else, and therefore only and exclusively a *potential object of experience*. What withdraws itself from context, from all (narrative and contextualist) meaning, from all signification, *what is just there in its semantic nakedness*, can be only an object of experience to us.[48]

Who is the subject of experience in the final moments of Katyn? The question is complex. It is certainly we as spectators who are faced with this austere representation of a historical event. But it is also Wajda, the subject/historian, who withdraws all the narrative and figurative apparatuses that have served as context in the rest of the film. He is the traumatized subject who exposes himself to this horrific representation: the murder of the Polish nation and the murder of the father. The images he edits together deny all meaning. They demolish, without the slightest afterthought, the sacred edifice that Wajda constructed in the sequence that takes place in the monastery church at Kozelsk. He thus deprives himself of the mainstays of personal and historical understanding. As Ankersmit puts it:

> An experience in which the history of the experiencing subject (and the memory thereof) has no role to play—it is an experience without a subject. The subject has to divest itself from its *own* history which ordinarily contextualizes and historicizes his or her experience.[49]

Sometimes the real itself breaks through representation in a way that confounds us and takes us out of time as we experience it in the present. We are there, joined to a terrifying reality of the past. We are not asked to understand it. The distance imposed by narrative or the retrospective gaze of the historian has been wiped away. So have the rhetorical and symbolic figures that are strategies for producing historical meaning. All those screens have been overturned. We simply take in the reality of the massacres in its "semantic nakedness." It matters little that the sequences of massacre are not edited from documentary footage, which of course never existed. They are representations that do not simply compensate for the absence of the past, like all historical representations; they abolish all distance. Without indulging in undue speculation, it seems clear that Wajda needed to reconstruct this experience for deeply psychological reasons. It was not enough to understand the loss of his father in historical terms, with all the alienation that such understanding involves. Nor could he understand it personally through the memory of his own suffering or his mother's. He needed to place the murder of his father before his own consciousness in the most direct and brutal manner possible.

3

ANDREI KONCHALOVSKY'S
SIBERIADE

And here stands man, stripped of myth, eternally starving, surrounded by every past there has ever been, digging and scrambling for roots, even if he must dig for them in the most remote antiquities. The tremendous historical need of our unsatisfied modern culture, the accumulation of countless cultures, the consuming desire for knowledge—what does all this point to, if not to the loss of myth, the loss of the mythical home, the mythical maternal womb?

—FRIEDRICH NIETZSCHE, *THE BIRTH OF TRAGEDY*

N THE two films I will be discussing in this chapter and the next, Andrei Konchalovsky's *Siberiade* (1979) and Larissa Shepitko's *The Ascent* (1977), the reactivation of myth—the rediscovery of "primordial longings"—is absolutely central to their meanings. We are dealing here with a reaction not only against the limits of scientific understanding but against the reductive and inhuman form it takes in the Stalinist view of history, a view reaffirmed and perpetuated during the Brezhnev era from which these films date. Konchalovsky's and Shepitko's films stage a "reenchantment of the world" (in Walter Benjamin's formulation). In *The Ascent*, as we shall see, this takes place as a mystic *revelation* in which the world recovers a sense of wonder and human behavior achieves a transcendent heroism. In *Siberiade* reenchantment takes the form of a *haunting* in which primordial forces resist the progress of history and the "rational" human exploitation of the earth. Both films are about heroism in Soviet history: *Siberiade* represents the revolutionary spirit in epic terms, while *The Ascent* is an intimate psychological study of the heroic figure.

Konchalosky's *Siberiade* is an ambitious retelling of Soviet history from the prerevolutionary situation in Russia before 1917 to the massive reworking of the Soviet landscape in the hydroelectric projects and oil exploration of the 1960s. The film's running time is more than four hours. Its narrative point of view is unusual: with notable exceptions the story takes place in the isolated Siberian village of Elan—"the end of the world," as one character puts it—a place surrounded by endless primeval forests, the otherworldly habitat of irrational forces and shamanism. Elan is reachable only by boat along the immense expanse of its waterway. The noisy events of wars and revolution, of industrialization and collectivization, reach the village in the form of the tales told by revolutionaries, soldiers, and bureaucrats returning to revolutionize their compatriots—to enlighten the benighted and win them over to the "scientific" historical project of Stalinism.

As we will see, *Siberiade* evokes in Elan an animistic world alive with the forces of nature. Simon Schama tells us that all landscapes are shaped by our shared traditions, "built from a rich deposit of myths, memories, and obsessions."[1] The project of the socialist garden, on the other hand, which is designed to settle the conflict of Man against Nature, would overturn retrograde traditions and establish a program of rational exploitation of the natural world. Such "rationality," as Konchalovsky's film suggests, is calamitous, because it would subjugate nature, placing it in the dubious service of progress and industrial development. Can the historical *elsewhere* that is Elan become a landscape of resistance, a place where the laws of socialist history and economic exploitation are stymied by the living spirit of the natural world? Speaking of German art historian Aby Warburg, Schama emphasizes the mythic currents that can resurface in the most carefully planned landscape:

> Beneath its pretensions to have built a culture grounded in reason, he believed, lay a powerful residue of mythic unreason. Just as Clio, the Muse of history, owed her beginnings to her mother Mnemosyne [the Greek goddess of memory], a more instinctual and primal persona, so the reasoned culture of the West, with its graceful designs of nature, was somehow vulnerable to the dark demiurges of irrational myths of death, sacrifice, and fertility.[2]

A GENERATIONAL EPIC: SYNOPSIS

The long and complex narrative of *Siberiade* is structured around the conflict between two families: the rich Solomins, whose class advantage (as Kulaks) is expressed in the dumplings and meat they have hanging in an outbuilding; and the Ustyuzhanins, oppressed peasants who rebel against their condition and who, all males, are erotically attractive to young Solimin women. The story spans three generations of Ustyuzhanin fathers and sons and the beginning of a fourth, and the film's diegesis is divided into three parts representing five epochs, marked by intertitles. The film is narratively and historically very complex. The following is a synopsis of the plot.

The opening images are enigmatic: an immense derrick gushing oil is engulfed in flames and a man perishes in the conflagration; an old man looks at family photos on the wall of a room as the building shakes.

FIRST PART: KOLYA AND THE ROAD TO REVOLUTION

1. The prerevolutionary period centers on Afanasy, the crazed but potent Ustyuzhanin father who is obsessed with felling trees to build a road through the forest "up to a star." The road also leads toward the Devil's Mane, a haunted marshland feared by the villagers. The figure of the Eternal Old Man appears at this point to warn Afanasy of the danger of his project. His young son Nikolai, most often called by his nickname Kolya, encounters an escaped revolutionary bomb-maker, Rodion, who models himself on Tommaso Campanella, the defender of Galileo. As Rodion is carried away by the police, he inspires in Kolya the desire to "die for the truth."

2. The 1920s see Kolya as a young revolutionary. Class warfare rages, and Anastasia Solomin's brother, Spirodon, returns to Elan wounded by the "marauding poor." Kolya is involved in an erotically charged yet frictional courtship with Anastasia, who is after all the class enemy. Lovers' spite intensifies as Anastasia declares she can marry her cousin, Philip Solomin. The two young rivals then woo the flirtatious Anastasia. The angry Solomin males beat the upstart Kolya and cast him adrift on the river where Anastasia, defying her kin, swims to join him.

SECOND PART: THE 1930S AND 1940S

1. In the 1930s, Kolya returns to Elan with his young son Alexei. Kolya's mission is to involve the village in Stalin's plan for energy self-sufficiency in the Soviet Union. He informs Spiridon, Anastasia's brother, that she gave her life to the revolution. Kolya and Alexei go prospecting for oil in the Devil's Mane, where they become lost among flammable vapors and retreating ghosts. Some time later, the aggrieved Spiridon emerges from a building carrying a hatchet dripping with blood: he has murdered Kolya. Alexei, searching for his father, meets the bloody Spiridon, who attempts to embrace him. He spurns his uncle and casts himself adrift in the river, the banks echoing with his call, "Pa! Pa!"

2. The 1940s are divided into two sections. The first is named for the Solomin daughter Taya, who, while swimming with swans in a pool in the forest, discovers a young man on the bank, apparently dead or dying. It turns out to be Alexei, who has come back to avenge his father's murder. Thwarted in his revenge because Spiridon is in prison, Alexei visits his father's gravesite and plays a tango on the phonograph he has brought from the outside world. Taya pursues Alexei but their courtship is interrupted by a military officer who announces that the Soviet Union has been attacked by Nazi Germany. The underage Alexei volunteers for the front, leaving Taya disconsolate. The second section takes place on a battlefield somewhere in the Soviet Union. In a watery landscape of derelict machines of war, floating barrels, cadavers, and bombed bunkers, Alexei discovers a badly wounded captain (Philip Solomin), whom he drags to safety.

THIRD PART: ALEXEI, THE 1960S

Alexei, Nikolai's son, is the focus of this part of the film. Like his father before him, Alexei returns to Elan as a Stalinist zealot. He tells his father's murderer, Spirodon, that he will find oil, demolish Elan, and build collective housing. He encounters Taya and their flirtation begins again and is consummated in the woods. The head of the drilling project, Tofic, informs Alexei that they will not drill in the Devil's Mane but in the village cemetery. Alexei is angered by the sacrilege. He madly drives a tractor down his grandfather's road and into the Devil's Mane. He discovers the abandoned drillers' shack inundated by swampwater; once inside he has visions of his dead father.

In one of the few locations outside the village of Elan and its surroundings, we see Philip Solomin arriving at a monumental complex, an example of Soviet "grandeur." We recognize him as the captain that Alexei saved on the battlefield. Now a high-ranking bureaucrat, Philip attends a meeting of Gosplan, the U.S.S.R. State Construction Committee, where he attempts to salvage the oil drilling project and thwart the plan to build a dam and inundate the region around Elan, creating the world's largest hydroelectric plant. We return to the village where rivalry arises between Tofic and Alexei over Taya. The impetuous Alexei is responsible for a work accident that delays drilling.

FOURTH PART: PHILIP, THE 1960S

Philip returns to Elan and announces to his uncle Spiridon that "the whole place will be flooded." He encounters the Eternal Old Man to whom he expresses the shame he feels for his responsibility in ruining the land. Philip encounters Alexei and recognizes him as Nikolai's son and the soldier who saved him during the war. Philip returns to party headquarters to make the case for continued drilling. At the drilling site, Alexei notifies Tofic that he is resigning. Alexei asks Taya to leave with him. She says she cannot because she is pregnant. As Alexei makes his way to the dock to leave, we see the derrick gushing with oil. The derrick bursts into flame (reprising the film's opening images and anchoring them within the plot). We now know it is Alexei who dies in the flames.

At the headquarters of Gosplan, where discussions of the hydroelectric project are taking place, Philip receives the telegram announcing the gusher and the death of Alexei. In Elan, Taya announces to Spiridon that Alexei's family is not without issue since she is bearing Alexei's child. Philip arrives in the village as the cemetery is engulfed in flames. In a vision, Philip is inundated with images from the past: he is embraced by an uncle, young children, his cousin Anastasia, and finally Kolya.

THE "LONG JOURNEY" NARRATIVE

By 1979, when *Siberiade* appeared, the Soviet regime was bathed in an "indefinite twilight of economic stagnation and moral decay," as Tony Judt puts it. Shortly after the coup against Khrushchev in 1964, Brezhnev, who nurtured his own "cult of personality," began to eradicate the vestiges of the Khrushchev "thaw." He came down hard on the more relaxed intellectual and artistic atmosphere Khrushchev had sanctioned. "By any standard," Judt argues, "save those of its own history, the regime was immovable, repressive and inflexible."[3] Indeed, Konchalovsky's second film, *Asya's Happiness* (1966), was severely criticized because of its realistic (rather than socialist realist) depiction of a Soviet collective farm; it was banned and shelved until 1987. Goskino, the Moscow film studio, resurrected in 1963, became by 1972 and the administration of Filipp Yermash, a mighty conglomerate overseeing film export, co-productions, film festivals, journals, the VGIK (the Moscow film school), and Gosfilmofond, the state film archive. The 1972 resolution of the Central Committee on Cinematography issued a call—after the deconstuctivist tendencies of 1960s Soviet cinema—for a return to classical Stalinist values:

> There are too many grey, formless works in which contemporary and historical themes are worked in a superficial manner. . . . Persistent thematic planning will make possible the creation of films which will center on the positive hero of our time—man, for whom the struggle for the embodiment of the Communist idea becomes the personal aim of his existence.[4]

Brezhnev's was a shabby dictatorship, devoted to preserving the status quo in social life, sustaining the bankrupt Stalinist vision of history, and defending proletarian art from attacks by bourgeois deviants. It is in the context of political decadence and invasive censorship that Konchalovsky launched his ambitious project of *Siberiade*, which was both historically and aesthetically daring.

Konchalovsky's strategy, I will argue, is predicated on a feigned observance of the Stalinist norms of historical narratives. On the surface *Siberiade* appears to adhere to the narrative plot lines of Soviet socialist realism. Literary scholar Katerina Clark contends that the Soviet novel marks a return to the age of parable. The Soviet parable is, above all, a structure, crudely modeled on medieval hagiography, which describes the "positive hero's" movement from the realm of darkness into the realm of light. The "vertical axis" that imposes a ritual meaning on this narrative progression is no longer biblical scripture but Leninist/ Stalinist orthodoxy. "The Soviet socialist realist novel was, de facto, expected to provide a parable showing how the forces of 'spontaneity' and 'consciousness' work themselves out in history."[5] The hero whose trajectory we follow is typically a rebel against bourgeois privilege, untutored yet eager for revolutionary struggle. He is, however, in need of the enlightenment that comes from political awareness, embodied in the seasoned members of the vanguard.

Thus *Siberiade* incorporates what Russian historian Yuri Slezkine refers to as the "Long Journey" narrative. The standard version from the 1930s—the narrative persists in variations into the 1980s—begins when the Russians, armed with the words of Lenin, reach the native encampment where ignorance reigns. They throw the light of dialectical history on the inequality and abuse they find. In *Siberiade*, abuse takes the form of the class oppression that the Solomin family imposes on the Ustyuzhanins. As Slezkine characterizes the ideological transformation, "The long polar night and the darkness of ignorance retreated before the sound of Lenin's name and the voices of his emissaries."[6] In the struggle for hearts and minds, the eyes of the disenfranchised are easily opened, while the kulaks and shamans, who cannot be reformed, are cast out into the dark world of forest and tundra. The enlightened people "march on toward cultural and economic development."[7] Thus are the natives Russified. And under party guidance, the Russified native can make himself into a Communist revolutionary: either the boisterous, instinctual proletarian who pushes the masses toward progress; or the well-educated, reserved yet sensitive bureaucrat who is committed to rational persuasion. In *Siberiade,* Nikolai and Alexei represent the first type, Philip Solomin the second.

The stories and characters of the "Long Journey" narrative have their origin in the fabricated mythology of the Stalinist era. The propaganda agencies of the state labored to produce a cult of personality, Stalin's *charismatic authority*, to use Max Weber's well-known notion of the superhuman power attributed to a sanctified individual. The success of this effort was, at least in part, predicated on its parasitic link to an older mythification: the embodiment of all power, terrestrial and spiritual, in the figure of the tsar. As novelist Vasily Grossman puts it, the power of the tsarist state "was able in its great might, to control both the vastness of space and the secret depth of the hearts of enchanted human beings who willingly offered up to it the gift of their freedom, even of their wish for freedom."[8]

The Stalinist rendition proposes the myth of the Great Family, in which the all-powerful father figure (Stalin), imbued with pure revolutionary spirit, raises the political consciousness of the spontaneous figure of the son, harnessing his energy for the fight against the class enemy. Stalin had, of course, his surrogates—party stalwarts—who took charge of the political education of its multitudinous sons. In this highly coded mythical system, characters are reduced to their political and moral identity and thus represent, not psychological individuals, but reductive social categories. One-dimensional characters could offer only slight variations on the master plot of revolutionary transformation.

As my synopsis of the film indicates, *Siberiade*'s narrative is constructed around a series of father-son relationships. Nikolai's biological father, the presumably mad Afanasy, is replaced by the revolutionary Rodion, who, as he is being carted away by the police, gives the rash young Kolya the symbolic chain he wears around his neck and enjoins him to be ready to die for the truth of the revolution. Alluding to the work of the "heretical" Tommaso Campanella, who, like Rodion, spent four years chained to a wall, Rodion assures Kolya that Cities of Sun will replace the sinister swamplands of Siberia. As a young man, Kolya is beaten and set adrift on the river, which sweeps him toward the city and eventual enlightenment. The second generation repeats, with variations, the story of the first. Nikolai, now a seasoned cadre, retains nonetheless much of his impulsiveness (the son is perpetually childlike). He returns to Elan with his own son, Alexei, singing revolutionary songs as they approach the village by river. After his father's murder, Alexei flees, again by river. He too will come back to the village and continue his father's work, and will experience the obligatory setback as preparation for the climactic completion of the revolutionary task.

Like his father, Alexei retains the selfless impetuosity that will lead him to the final self-sacrifice.

As Svetlana Boym points out, the scene of the proletarian hero's death in the socialist realist novel became an essential feature of postwar iconography: it was "not just death as such, but a heroic feat, an ultimate victory."[9] Alexei's death by fire and Philip's homage to him at the Gosplan convention in the great hall serve to consecrate his place within "history." Thus we appear to arrive at socialist realism's apotheosis. As Katerina Clark puts it:

> The positive hero, or son figure, is the most burdened character of a Stalinist novel. In the account of his life, past, present, and future must be illumined, the forward movement of history proclaimed, and the legitimacy of the status quo endorsed.[10]

The revolutionary conflagration necessarily destroys the past. But it also brings the film's most nostalgic moment. In the burning cemetery, the triumphant Philip, who is proud to have saved his region, is overcome with visions, at once melancholic and joyful, of what has been lost. Do Stalinist history and the socialist realist aesthetic admit the possibility of such emotions?

It is immediately clear to any viewer that Konchalovsky's *Siberiade* is much more complex than prototypical Stalinist fiction, whose aesthetics were defined by notions "such as 'ideological commitment' (*ideinost*), Party-mindedness (*partiinost*), 'national/popular spirit' (*narodnost*), and so on."[11] Indeed, the film does not conform to the "simplicity and clarity of form" that imposes, as literary scholar Leonid Heller confirms, a "drastic reduction of components, that is, its willingness to make do with a limited number of concepts."[12] The ideal of classic socialist realist storytelling involved a transparent, unproblematic vehicle of communication—"a language as pure as water, through which the content of life is visible."[13]

Just as the sinister demiurges of myth rise to undermine the rationality of planned landscapes, the sensuality and indeterminacy of the cinematic image and Konchalovsky's poetic style trouble the "language as pure as water": what is visible of life is clouded by what one feels is stirring beneath it.

MYTH AS A SUBVERSIVE ACTIVITY

Siberiade is a transgressive film that sets up a clash between two mythological systems. The first is the product of political invention: it justifies the suppression of traditional cultures in the interest of constructing the enlightened proletarian hero, imbued with revolutionary fervor and committed to the victory of "scientific" socialism. The second mythology would sink its roots into an obscure, immemorial past where one intuits the presence of unknowable forces. If the first mythology, Stalinist, flattens and deforms experience in favor of the binary language of class struggle, the second exults in the phenomenal richness of the world that overpowers the rational and embraces libidinal forces, including the impetuosity of the revolutionary hero and his unbound energy. Stalinist myth proposes the inevitable forward march of history that knocks obsolescence off the road of progress. Archaic cultures and reactionary human impulses are overwhelmed by the seemingly unstoppable forces of historic causality.

In contrast to the aggressive activism of the Stalinist myth, primordial myth is often dormant—or "latent" to use the term common to psychology and biology. The recessive power of myth can, however, be reactivated and return the human animal to its place within nature. The world can be "reenchanted," to use Benjamin's metaphor, as it is in Konchalovsky's film. The myth of origins in *Siberiade* takes root in the taiga—that isolated domain of Siberian shamanism where life is ruled by cosmic (not historical) forces. Outside the village and outside time, the taiga is a deeply animistic world in which "the sisters weeping" can be heard after each tree is felled. "We live off living things," the mystical Afanasy explains, as he stands next to the living mountain lion he has suspended from a pole.

Siberiade's figure of the Eternal Old Man is the incarnation of natural forces. He lives outside society and is often seen in the company of deer and bears. His forest hut is a place of spiritual harmony evoked by light and color. He is the shaman who intervenes in human affairs when his elemental powers are needed. Russian mythology offers an analogous figure in the archetype of the Wise Old Man, a Proppian *helper*, who "appears when a hero is in desperate need of help or authoritative advice."[14] Indeed, this is the narrative function of the Eternal

Old Man in Konchalovsky's film. He stimulates erotic attachments, those urges that cross class lines, like those between kulaks (the Solomins) and poor peasants (the Ustyuzhanins), and cannot be foresworn. He shelters and heals those wounded by the world. Alerted by Taya, who had been swimming naked in a pool with swans, the Eternal Old Man comes to succor the unconscious Alexei she has discovered on the bank. The subsequent sequence, shot in long takes, shows Alexei's reawakening in the Eternal Old Man's hut and begins with a close shot of a honeycomb and a book on a table, the intimacy of the place beautifully expressed by source lighting. A seer, the Eternal Old Man is also aware of the dangers of malignant places. He stands watch over the way to the Devil's Mane—the malevolent, extra-worldly place where Nikolai and Alexei go to explore for oil and become lost in its miasmic swampland.

The most obvious manifestation of mythical opposition that operates at the level of the scenario occurs when *Siberiade*'s narrative, with its grand generational structure, is interrupted six times by montage sequences compiled from documentary footage from Soviet films representing six epochs: World War I and the Leninist intervention; the death of Lenin and the beginning of the Stalinist era; the evolution of Soviet life and the rise of Nazism; World War II and the joy of victory; postwar Soviet reconstruction and development; and a final coda of images of Soviet progress and the happiness of Soviet citizenry. Taken together, the sequences appear to give a kaleidoscopic version of the kind of official history of the party that Stalin authorized in his reductive 1938 "Short Course." What we can say for now is that *Siberiade*'s montage sequences stand in rhetorical opposition to the techniques of the film's central narrative: they employ radically different modes of representation.

Looking briefly at some of the elements of opposition, we see that in the montage sequences, the rapid-fire editing hyperbolizes the already frenetic style of Soviet documentaries and newsreels of the 1920s. Moreover, the shots are radically heterogeneous. The first montage sequence, for example, which represents events from the beginning of the century to the October Revolution, juxtaposes the following motifs, often repeated in variations: masses of people running; bells tolling; trains departing; waving handkerchiefs; explosions; soldiers on the battlefield; officers reviewing the troops; the tsar kissing a crucifix; downed soldiers; street demonstrations; Lenin gesticulating; the toppling of an imperial statue. These brief fragments do not produce a comprehensible narrative of space/time and can be understood only as a historical collage in which narration is sacrificed to the hysteria of montage. It is as if Sergei Eisenstein's dream of a symbolic language of images had derailed into utter incoherence. We quickly come to understand that this is Konchalovsky in the mode of parody.

The style of the film's principal narrative, on the other hand, contrasts at every level with the edited newsreel footage. The images are in color and the chromatic effects are unusually sophisticated and self-conscious. In contrast to the irrational space of montage, Konchalovsky shows us an enveloping natural world that penetrates even into interior spaces. While frequently full of metaphorical meanings, the visual imagery strikes us first by its phenomenological richness. Long takes predominate as does the sense of a coherent development in space and time. The epic narrative focuses on a few central protagonists, who exist as much as psychic incarnations as historical actors: they embody the action. If the effect of the montage sequences is jittery and ostensibly conceptual, the narrative discourse is dilatory, sensuous, and subjective. The "meaning" of the montage sequences takes place (if it does at all) in the mind of the spectator, who assembles the fragments into a discourse about events. The narrative sequences invite the spectator to enter a sensory world where objects and characters assume the density of the real.

AESTHETICS OF MYTHOLOGICAL SPACES

Konchalosky's approach in *Siberiade* can be seen in two elements of style that are closely allied. The first is his self-conscious aesthetics; the second is the metaphoric dimension he evokes in various elements of narrative and mise-en-scène. Regarding the first, I have already mentioned Konchalovsky's use of color. While this is particularly evident in the juxtaposition he establishes between the often saturated color of scenes set in and around the village of Elan and the use of sepia for the documentary passages, it also occurs in scenes in which Nikolai and

Alexei, and then Alexei alone, penetrate into the sinister world of the Devil's Mane. In general, Konchalovsky's palette is impressionistic in the sense that it aims at capturing, through effects of light and color, a feeling or experience rather than producing a "naturalistic" and thus "transparent" effect.

Consider the following example. Rodion, Kolya, and a homeless girl—the disenfranchised band of outcasts—escape from the clutches of the counterrevolutionary Solomins and are momentarily swept by winds across the glacial river in a sailboat. The chromatic nuances of the gray-green ice and the gray of the sky, against which the boat seems to soar in eccentric patterns, have enormous graphic power and immediately suggest the metaphoric resonance of the image: the exhilaration of freedom but also its constraints, expressed in the limited horizon and falling snow. The aesthetic experience is here allied to the mythic. The scene gives us an "auratic" perception, as Benjamin would have it: we are momentarily liberated from the inhibitions of narrative and encounter directly this free-flowing imagery in which we apprehend, as Joseph Mali says, "a deeper temporal and spatial dimension."[15]

The mythical dimension of *Siberiade* resides in the resonance Konchalovsky evokes between what is represented on the screen as occurring in the narrative present and what historian Carlo Ginzberg describes as the "unfathomable experience that humanity has symbolically expressed for millenia through myths, fables, rituals and ecstasies."[16] The forward movement of action—like the causal chain of history—is arrested by the awareness that such movement, which appears to be linear, is actually circular, that is, repetitive. On the simplest iconographical level, there is the repetition of motifs, very often underscored by nearly identical framing. For example, the repeated images of bright yellow chicks on a table in a somber interior, an apparently gratuitous detail of setting whose emphatic presence belies any narrative function. Or the shots of the village gate—a human artifact hewn by unknown hands—that links Elan with its immemorial past and that the reckless Alexei bulldozes as he reenters Elan to bring the villagers into the modern world. "Why, for all of us," T. S. Eliot asks in *The Use of Poetry and the Use of Criticism*, "out of all that we have heard, seen, felt in a lifetime do certain images recur, charged with emotion rather than others?"[17]

Siberiade is full of narrative repetition as well. The synopsis of the plot already reveals the reiterative structure of the film: each new generation replays, with variation, the conflicts of the previous one. On the level of the sequence, it is easy to show how actions by different characters mirror each other across the text. Consider for example the way departures from Elan are framed and ritualized. The revolutionary Rodion attempts to escape through a blinding snowstorm from the village gate to the river's edge, the symbolic quality of the scene underscored by the absence of ambient noise and the haunting choral melody that is a major musical leitmotif in the film. This same trajectory, framed in long shot, will be taken by Anastasia as she runs to join Kolya on the river; by Alexei as a child as he flees Spiridon, his father's murderer; and by the adolescent Alexei as he joins the new recruits embarking for the front. Through repetition, the mythical figure of departure—leaving and returning to Elan are the great hinges of *Siberiade*'s dramaturgy—emerges from the impressionistic depiction of place and action.

Reiteration lends, then, a sense of ritual to the film's narrative and suggests an elemental correspondence underlying the characters' actions. While the film asserts the continuity of actions—that they take place at discrete narrative moments, anchored in the chronology of events—it also suggests that they are, at another level, simultaneous and therefore out of time. The punctual and the mythic dimensions of actions coalesce. As Mali puts it, "It is this sense of repetition and integration of the self in the larger forces of life and history, of the continuity between ancient civilizations and our own, and of the unity of all human experience that the 'mythical method' reveals."[18]

ANTHROPOMORPHIC NARRATIVE

As we have seen, Konchalovsky invests nature with powers that go well beyond the descriptive and atmospheric function of setting or its function as psychological commentary on characters. Nature acts on its own behalf in dynamic relations with the actions of characters. I call this *anthropomorphic narrative*, which makes "objects" capable of dramatic action, while reattaching human actors to the "reenchanted" world of nature they inhabit attavistically. The river in its vast expanse, for example, is not merely the location where the comings and goings of the film's heroes take place. It is, first, a highly charged symbolic presence, repeatedly evoked in extreme long shot and from an extreme high angle that emphasizes its power. Second, the river assumes the role of helper, abetting narrative action by providing a space of transitions: it permits communication between the isolated village and the modern world and therefore invites the encounter between the forces of "history" and the archaic world of the Siberian hinterlands. Third, it is a *subject* of action. It *pushes* both Nikolai and his son Alexei, adrift in its waters, toward the center of the revolutionary movement. Finally, it is one of the objects of the heroes' quest: both Alexei and Philip, despite their commitment to industrial development, struggle to preserve the waterway from annihilation. Danger appears most forcefully when the ritual cycle of events is broken in part 4 by Philip Solomin, now a Soviet bureaucrat, who arrives, not by boat but by helicopter. Here the river loses its dynamism: it does not act, but is acted upon. Philip's comrade looks down at the seemingly endless landscape that is scheduled to be inundated for a massive hydroelectric project and says, "How can anyone live in these backwaters? In this hole." And indeed, landing at Elan, they discover a dying village inhabited by a few old men and women, a broken gate, and a cemetery.

In the mythic world that Konchalovsky evokes, dynamic nature continually reasserts itself. The symbolic center of resistance is the Devil's Mane, where the discourses of reason and the fantasy of human mastery over nature and history have no hold. It is the site where the basic structures of identity—psychological and social—come undone. Two journeys toward this unreachable place are undertaken in the film. In the first, Nikolai and his son Alexei penetrate the spectral marshes— where Nikolai believes there are large oil resources to be tapped—but are overwhelmed by the dark landscape. They sit together on a fallen log. Alexei wants to return but his father responds that he needs "to find the Devil's Mane personally" and that he will go on by himself. The Devil's Mane is the site of the irrational and the place where ghosts are encountered. A mysterious figure emerges in the toxic mist. Nikolai runs after him but takes fright. Weeping, he says they will never reach the Devil's Mane. He tosses his cigarette into the swamp, which bursts into flames. The sequence is shot in black and white but the flames are yellow and repeat the motif of the conflagration, which opened and will close the film.

The second journey (shot in greenish sepia) is undertaken by the now-grown Alexei. The fervent champion of Stalinist positivism drives a tank down the plank road constructed by his mystical grandfather, dislodging and crushing the tree trunks as he goes. He meets the Eternal Old Man and asks him how far it is to the Devil's Mane. "No one knows for sure" is the reply. Alexei continues into the swamp, leaving fallen trees in the wake of his powerful machine, which is brought to an abrupt halt in a mud hole. The proletarian hero becomes literally bogged down in the primordial quagmire. He looks up and sees the abandoned drillers' cabin, now inundated by the swamp: "So that's where they drilled," Alexei says, recalling his father's earlier prospection. He wades to the shack and enters. A poster of Stalin still hangs on the door; refuse floats around the table where he goes to sit. A dolly-in to Alexei's head on the table suggests the subjectivity of his experience: unsettling noises; moving shadows beyond the window; a hand on his shoulder. Another hand appears on the windowpane (a distorted version of the film's choral motif is heard), and Alexei calls out, "Pa! Pa!" as he did earlier in the film after his father's murder. He rips apart the door and Stalin's poster, exits, and calls again after a retreating figure who is swallowed in the mist. Alexei, who has fallen into a hole in the water, goes under. The next sequence (in color) begins in a cabin where Alexei lifts up his head from the table. Has this all been a dream?

OBJECTS MAY RETURN OUR LOOK

Now I would like to focus on an extensive episode from *Siberiade* that has a distinct mythological character: the sequences that conclude the first half of the film and recount Alexei's return from the battlefields of the Second World War. They are seven in number: (1) In a no-go zone, Alexei wanders among the derelicts and detritus of war and discovers the wounded Philip. (2) Alexei drags Philip's inert body through the dangers of the battlefield in search of safety; a rain of bullets forces Alexei to take shelter. (3) Still dragging Philip, Alexei collapses onto a dune of sand and discovers a line of tanks, passing behind him; he calls out, "Our guys!" and dissolves in tears. (4) Philip is recognized by Soviet brass, and Alexei, his savior, is recognized as a national hero. (5) A documentary sequence condenses the events of the Soviet military struggle and the homecoming of the heroic soldiers. (6) Alexei is returning from the front aboard a train where couples are dancing in a box car; still a bit shell-shocked he declares that he believes a beautiful new life is beginning. (7) In a series of tracking shots, we see Taya walking to her familiar lookout point over the river, holding a rolled newspaper in her hand (announcing the end of the war?) and watching longingly for a sign of Alexei's return.

In the following analysis, I will return to Walter Benjamin's concept of the aura and attempt to show that these sequences can be regarded as *illuminations* (except for the documentary sequence, which reprises the mode of representation I discussed earlier in this essay). In Benjamin's work, illuminations are representations that retain something of the mythological; that is, they have the qualities of ancient stories in which the human and the natural are equal animate forces. Material objects may be imbued with an aura when they speak to us about experience—when, as Benjamin puts it, what we are looking at has the capacity of returning our look. Objects are no longer the passive signifiers of place and context or tools of narrative; they act directly on human protagonists. The activation of this relationship concerns both the subject who operates within the narrative and us as spectators-subjects who are implicated in what we see (and hear).

These kinds of exchanges have nothing to do with intellection: we do not stand outside and observe such objects; we move toward them as they move toward us. As Benjamin contends, this affinity between the subject and the object retains something of the magical: Alexei, our protagonist, moves within a living world that acts upon him. We as spectators approach the boundary that traditional historiography erects between our experience in the present and the experience of others in the past, which it postulates as inaccessible. Momentarily, it seems, we may cross over. It is as if we, like Alexei, are entering a no-go zone beckoned by a "primordial longing," a surge of empathy.

Benjamin was a great modernist and a great admirer of Baudelaire, from whom he borrowed the notion of *correspondence*: the discovery of echoes of the nearly forgotten past in phenomena in the modern world. Baudelaire was not a late Romantic attempting to rehabilitate archaic myths; he saw the mission of the modernist to discover mythopoeic images in modern Paris: "to extract from fashion whatever element it may contain of poetry within history, to distill the eternal from the transitory."[19]

In Baudelaire's nineteenth-century Paris, urbanization had alienated the masses from nature and from the past—from an experience of wholeness—and, as Benjamin contends, this dislocation "had rendered all meanings temporal and conjectural, 'cultural' rather than 'natural.'" This newfound relativism, however, allowed Baudelaire (and other "realistic modernists") to invest myth with "new relevant meanings."[20] He could discern "the archaic in the anarchic, the eternal in the phenomenal," as Benjamin would uncover emanations of the past in the nineteenth-century steel-and-glass arcades of Paris. The modernist is called on to negotiate between the historical and the mythological, between the rational and the legendary.

While inaccessible to the intellect, the reality of the past is unmistakably present in "material objects (or in the sensation which such an object arouses in us)," and it may be "rejuvenated." The meanings stirred up by this "eternal restoration" are not transcendent (standing above, like the historian in relation to the narrative he or she constructs); they are immanent (they operate from *within* the object and its relation to the subject who perceives it). Myth is capable of reinvesting the object with a *frisson* that quickens what appeared as inert. On the basis of the distinction between transcendent and immanent meaning, we can differentiate between a discursive memory that regulates and dominates and a participatory memory that permits the (at least momentary) communication between subject and object. Benjamin asserts that discursive memory is destructive because it "reduces the scope for the play of the imagination."[21] It responds to the call of rational consciousness, assigns a remembered event to its place in a chronology, and establishes the causal links between one event and the others that come before or after it. Memories are thus tamed, and their orderliness sets up a resistance to the "shock" of immediate recollection. Discursive memory subjects experience to psychological discipline: it explains events in terms of the rational structures of human motivation. Older forms of storytelling, Benjamin insists, avoid this kind of interpretation and therefore retain their openness to the sharing of experience:

> There is nothing that commends a story to memory more effectively than that chaste compactness which precludes psychological analysis. And the more natural the process by which the storyteller forgoes psychological shading, the greater becomes the story's claim to a place in the memory of the listener, the more completely is it integrated into his own experience, the greater will be his inclination to repeat it to someone else.[22]

Historiography, on the other hand, demands explanation: "The historian is bound to explain in one way or another the happenings with which he deals; under no circumstances can he content himself with displaying them as models of the course of the world."[23]

As I have argued, the thematic center of *Siberiade* is the opposition Konchalovsky sets up between the mythological, linked to a primordial experience that predates rationalist history, and the implacable logic of the Stalinist narrative of revolutionary positivism. Stalinism offers a vision of progress from which human experience has been largely evacuated and in which nature is meaningful only insofar as it can be made to serve a triumphant technology. It is a world without empathy in which human protagonists are reduced to instruments in the advance toward socialism.

To measure the depth of this devaluation of the human, we need only remember the ferocity with which Stalin in the 1930s eradicated by the millions the so-called enemies of the proletariat, including the peasantry in Ukraine whose living traditions presumably threatened the progress of the revolution and who acted, the party asserted, in the interest of the class enemy by depriving the urban centers of the grain they produced. Archaic modes of understanding were viciously repressed, to be replaced by ideological abstractions that had no root in the traditions of the majority of the population. As Joseph Mali points out, the Acéphal group of intellectuals, including Georges Bataille and Roger Caillois, founded its critique of Communism on its "failure to appreciate, let alone create, the sacred in modern life."[24]

Instead they argued for the "rediscovery of primordial longings" and an alternative model of human experience in which "the conflicts of the individual condition [are] transposed to the social dimension." Obviously, the positions of the Acéphal group, with which Benjamin, the paradoxical Marxist, sympathized, stood in opposition to the materialist analysis of history.

THE *NOSTOI*: ALEXEI'S RETURN

In the sequences I call "Alexei's Return," *Siberiade*'s narrative echoes with textual references. Alexei's wandering among the ravages of war, for example, reprises scenes from nineteenth- and twentieth-century novels. Think of Tolstoy's Pierre at the battle of Borodino in *War and Peace* or Stendhal's Fabrice at the battle of Waterloo in *The Charterhouse of Parma*, to cite the obvious examples, or, more recently, the Stalingrad of Vasily Grossman's *Life and Fate* or Vietnam in Karl Marlantes's *Matterhorn*, not to mention the place that such scenes have had in the genre of the war film. Perhaps the most significant references *Siberiade* evokes, however, are to ancient stories, in particular the *nostoi*, the Greek narratives of the heroes' return from the Trojan war, notably in the Homeric epics. Like *The Odyssey*, this episode of Alexei's return in *Siberiade* recounts the homecoming from a war that has profoundly transformed the course of history and has reaffirmed a national identity.

It is important to interject here that *Siberiade*'s references to the *nostoi* have an often ironic character, based on a certain (often playful) disparity between the old "model" and the new narrative. Consider the discrepancies. Alexei is not a consecrated if beleaguered heroic figure; he is a courageous but naive foot soldier. He returns home (eventually) from a great, historic war. If the Trojan War was the "big bang" of Mediterranean culture, the Second World War can be seen as the transformative moment of the second half of the "short twentieth century" (1914–1990), which satisfied some of the Soviet Union's imperial ambitions and initiated its postwar boom in industrial and technological development.

Moreover, Alexei does not return to noble Ithaca, a seat of power, but to his isolated Siberian village, Elan, nearly deserted of life. His faithful

Penelope, Taya, waits on the bluff above the river watching for an approaching boat. Odysseus, beset as he is by diverse peripeteia, tells the tale of a voyage that takes ten years. Alexei's return takes twenty years, but in contrast to *The Odyssey*, these years are not recounted. We know only from the montage sequence that precedes Alexei's "homecoming" that the Soviet Union has undertaken massive industrial projects and that the homeward-bound war hero has expressed his enthusiasm for the "new life." When he arrives, Alexei is on a mission to prospect for oil, and he does not even recognize the woman who has put her life on hold for him. Contemptuous of the past, he drives his tractor through the ancient gate of Elan, then jumps down to allow the machine to plow ahead, scattering the terrified remnants of the village population. Alexei does not come to restore order and claim his heritage; he comes to extinguish tradition and bring the Siberian hinterland into the Soviet orbit and the modern world. Or so he thinks.

Konchalovsky's version of the triumphant soldier's homecoming is complex and reveals a deep ambivalence about the Soviet narrative. Alexei is at once a personal and a collective figure whose experience of reality recalls what Benjamin calls the *auratic*: "Experience of the aura thus rests on the transposition of a response common in human relationships to the relationship between the inanimate or natural object and man."[25] As we have seen, this relationship in *Siberiade* is *dialogic*: the nonhuman "speaks" in its own voice (as the sisters weep in the forest near Elan) and engages with its discursive (human) partner. There is a distance—and a vis-à-vis—between Alexei's subjectivity and the world that impinges upon him. The world is alive, expressive, infused with striking imagery while it displays toward Alexei an aggressive indifference. We as spectators are disconcerted by this unexpected mode of representation in which the usual relationship between characters and environment is disrupted. Our experience is close to what Freud calls the uncanny: what appears to be familiar—in this case, familiar representations of war—suddenly strikes us as freakish. Insensible objects seem to quicken and assume the ability to "return our look."

In the first three sequences of the return, narrative loosens its grip on the order of shots and allows for a dilation of time that revives in the images all their poetic power. The human protagonists—Alexei and

Philip—appear within a landscape that overrides its function as mere setting for events; indeed, landscape is itself fully an actor. Its mists control what is visible, and its desolate marshland is the active signifier of war's desolation as much as the monstrous derelicts—airplanes, tanks, trucks, bunkers—that protrude from it. Time seems to slow to a phenomenological pace—the time it takes, for the characters but also for the viewer, to be absorbed into the evolving scene. Long takes allow us to explore compositions that poetic expressionism transfigures: we are immersed in a sensate, yet symbolic world. Time validates space. This is particularly noteworthy in the "empty" shots in which the human actors exit the frame and leave us to contemplate what could have appeared as mere background.

Take, for instance, the first shot of sequence 1, in which we see a watery landscape in extreme long shot; a signpost tilting in the water identifies the scene in Russian and German as a "no-go zone." The figure of Alexei materializes as if ex nihilo: he appears in the extreme depth of a misty background, treading water, and gradually emerges from obscurity as he approaches the camera. He is surrounded by abandoned vehicles and objects—tanks, trucks, floating barrels of oil—and the bodies of fallen soldiers. He searches among the detritus looking for objects of value and finds a canteen of water, with which he will soon succor the wounded Philip. The second shot is a close-up of Alexei's distraught face and expresses his traumatized response to war's devastation. However, this alternation of scale—longer shots of Alexei among the ravages of war and closer shots that focus on his subjective state—is not analytically edited through the coded scheme of point of view (who is looking, what he or she is looking at) and is not therefore organized psychologically as stimulus that provokes a response.

There is only one extended point of view series in these sequences, and it has the symbolic function of associating Alexei with the collective experience of war. He is an individual but stands for others. That is, he becomes a communal, and therefore historical, figure. The series unfolds in the following manner. (1) Alexei, having taken cover from a barrage of gunfire, is shown in medium shot, rising to a sitting position; a jet of oil surges from a leaking barrel in the foreground. Alexei, looking down, discovers photos floating in the water and picks them up. (2) We see, in close-up, the photos of a woman and a couple held in his hands. (3) We return to Alexei as in the first shot, staring intently off screen beyond the camera. (4) A medium shot shows us the disconcerting image of a seated but dead soldier, oil surging from a barrel onto his chest. (5) We return to Alexei, as in the first and third shots. He holds his gaze, looks down at the soldier's abandoned weapons and belongings, then leans forward as if to return the photos to the fallen soldier; he hesitates, then places them inside his own shirt. Alexei thus assumes the burden of the suffering of others.

His heroic assumption of responsibility is most hauntingly represented in the images where we see the struggling Alexei dragging the wounded Philip on a blanket. The sequence begins with two shots of landscape: the first, the quiet image of waves hitting a beach; the second, an expressionistic image of the field of war, in which we see a plane with its nose in the water and its fuselage and tail sticking nearly perpendicularly into the air. Alexei then appears in a long shot as a figure tightly framed by disabled vehicles. We next see him in the background of an extremely long shot as he moves toward the foreground; his face, distorted by effort, becomes increasingly visible and we hear him muttering desperately to himself. He nearly grazes the camera as he disappears to the right. Then the camera slowly zooms out to frame an abandoned tank and trucks bogged down in the sludge. It is an unusually long take, an emphatic moment that shows a field emptied of human actors. The inanimate has repossessed the space of the image. If landscape literally frames the action of the sequence, it does not function simply to establish the scene or contextualize events. It has its own authority and seems to operate with indifference to the plight of the characters. It is simply and emphatically there.

The sequences representing Alexei's return are the first that take place outside of the village of Elan and in the grand theater of historical action, previously glimpsed only at a remove from the outer reaches of Siberia. Sepia tinting sets these sequences apart from the film's other narrative sequences. It suggests an equivalency between Alexei's experience of war and the film's documentary sequences, all tinted in sepia; the technique, not without irony, "historicizes" Alexei's return. Indeed, the sepia tones are matched in the following documentary sequence that represents the military campaign against the German invasion, elliptically represented, and the jubilation of citizenry at the victorious outcome of the war. A great deal, of course, separates the techniques of representation employed. More than compressed, the Soviet-style montage reduces representation to emblematic imagery. How is it possible to read the documentary sequence of this episode as anything but a conflation of disparate events that erases any sense of the experience of war in time and space? The documentary sequence is followed by a final scene in sepia set onboard a train: the melancholic Alexei, isolated from dancing couples, is framed in the doorway of a cattle car. He says, to those around him but without great conviction, that a beautiful new life is beginning.

A last comment. Against Konchalovsky's treatment of the ravages of war, Alexei's strangely dispirited statement about a new beginning rings hollow. But the hero's return, in Stalinist representation, is obligatorily jubilant. Victory is the triumph that makes an end not only of war but also of human suffering. There is no post-traumatic syndrome, no period of adjustment. Authors' deviations from the set piece of the triumphant homecoming were severely punished by the censors. For instance, in Andrey Platonov's superb and wrenching story entitled "The Return" (1946), the apprehensive Captain Ivanov delays his homecoming for a brief affair with a nurse. When he does reunite with his family, he sees himself as a stranger to his wife and children, and the estrangement produced by four years of absence nearly breaks his marriage apart. The story was subjected to severe political criticism, and Platonov was thereafter unable to publish any new work.

How are we to interpret the mythological narratives of *Siberiade* in the context of the complacent world of Brezhnev's Soviet Union, where the routine of state domination carries on in its empty decadence ten years before everything will collapse? What belief in the dramatic, pseudo-mythic history of the revolutionary advance toward socialism could continue to resonate with the Soviet public? And yet *Siberiade* was seen by 100 million in the Soviet Union before it was withdrawn from circulation, perhaps because of Konchalovsky's flirtation with the West (he would make his next film in the United States). Or was it because of the political ambiguities that lie not far below the surface of the film? If *Siberiade* does not directly contest Stalinist history, it does radically shift its narrative point of view. It valorizes a mythological tradition that Communism came to destroy but that stubbornly continues to assert itself. It seems to say that technological "progress" is not a substitute for the soul of a community.

In *Siberiade*'s last sequence, Philip Solomin, the enlightened bureaucrat, returns to Elan and its burning oil and gas field. In the village cemetery he has ordered demolished, where men run to save geese covered with burning oil, Philip is reunited with all the ghosts of the past whom he encloses in tender embraces. These otherworldly reunions are followed by documentary images of Soviet joy at their technological triumphs.

But is the New Socialist Man able to slough off what remains at the core of his being—the spectral past, the ancient stories, the forgotten intimacy with nature? Have the forces of nature been defeated? Have the forests been stripped of their primeval authority? Has the standoff between tradition and progress—so beautifully summarized in the shot in part 3 that begins with a close-up of the Eternal Old Man and pans up to show a towering derrick—been resolved in favor of a triumphant materialism? To go further, have the rational organization of industry and agriculture, the mechanisms of the dictatorship of the proletariat, and the "scientific" view of history in which the goal always justifies the means revolutionized the relationship that humans have to the world and to each other? Has Stalinist positivism eradicated the mystery of the world and the deeper yearnings of its inhabitants?

Walter Benjamin was particularly conscious of this dilemma of history, caught as he was in his own life by the same historical turmoil that *Siberiade* evokes. Indeed, the figures of myth that Konchalovsky sets in opposition recall Benjamin's famous meditation on Paul Klee's "Angelus Novus," in which he interprets the painting as an allegory of the angel of history. The angel's posture reveals all the anguish of witnessing the human "wreckage" strewn in the wake of events and the desire to arrest the inexorable flight to the future and restore life in its wholeness:

> His face is turned to the past, where *we* perceive a chain of events, *he* sees one single catastrophe which keeps piling wreckage upon wreckage and hurls it in front of his feet. The angel would like to stay, awaken the dead, and make whole what has been smashed. But a storm is blowing from Paradise: it has got caught in his wings with such violence that

the angel can no longer close them. This storm irresistibly propels him into the future to which his back is turned, while the pile of debris before him grows skyward. This storm is what we call progress.[26]

As I have attempted to show, *Siberiade* is both history and myth. Myth, Joseph Mali argues, becomes particularly significant in periods of turmoil—like wars and revolutions—when it is called upon to stabilize a society through "some dramatic reactivation of its original motivations."[27] Mythic narratives often focus on critical moments in the history of a community, that help to define its identity in the present. Should we understand the Brezhnev era not as a period of outward turmoil but a period of disquieting stasis where we perhaps can hear the *groanings* of a civilization faced with an unnerving future? I would argue that this is the case for *Siberiade*—and, as we will see, for Larissa Shepitko's *The Ascent*. Both films express the will to revise the unacceptable, that is, the failed vision of Stalinist history. Both express the need for a dramatic reactivation of the past. Clearly, nothing in these revisions does away with revolutionary heroes—we continue to identify with their energy, their instinctive humanism, and their self-sacrifice. Alexei burns with the fire that explodes at the end of *Siberiade*: it is his apotheosis and his gift to the future.

4

LARISA SHEPITKO'S
THE ASCENT

If we want to destroy religion and are conscious that this has to be done, since communism and religion are incompatible, then, in place of religion we must give the people not less than religion but more than religion. The soul of contemporary man is organized in such a way that if faith is removed from it, it will be completely overturned.

–ANDREY PLATONOV, "ABOUT LOVE"

MONUMENTS AND KITSCH

In Soviet visual space beginning in the 1930s, Stalin's representation was ubiquitous, invading both public and private spheres. Hyperbolized images and statues of the Father dominated parade grounds. Monumental spectacles in which human figures were reduced to dots forming the hammer and cycle or spelling out the name of the Master gave symbolic expression to the relationship between the party and the masses. Architectural settings were designed to frame heroic figures, like the bronze statues that stare at passengers from niches in the Revolution Square metro station in Moscow, or the lofty pedestal of Lenin's mausoleum where socialism triumphs over death. Stalin's dynamism could be seen, metaphorically, in his image hurtling through space on the front of locomotives. At the opposite end of the scale, Stalin's portrait was omnipresent in domestic interiors, where sentimentality replaced monumentalism. Stalinism was infatuated with kitsch, which is the other side of death, as Saul Friedländer observes in his analysis of Hitler's Germany. Pictorial motifs endlessly visualized slogans like "Thank You, Comrade Stalin, for Our Happy Childhood," and the Father's hagiographic image could be found endlessly repeated on tapestries, patchworks, and tea services. It was a kind of iconological exchange in which sacred monuments, rituals, and icons were transmogrified into their revolutionary equivalents, just as the decorative impulse in domestic interiors was transformed by its new didactic function.

Rhetorical inflation characterized all public discourse: everything was larger than life. The awesome stature of revolutionary heroes, the omniscient wisdom of party leaders, the perfidy of class enemies—all became actors in the histrionic allegories of Soviet life. Indeed, Stalin (like Hitler) was master of a political mise-en-scène that dealt in rhetorical posturing, not political realities. Institutions themselves were vacant imitations of democratic forms. In the following passage from *Everything Flows*, Vasily Grossman captures the theatrical character of the regime that makes a mockery of the values it presumably espouses:

> The freedom that had been done away with became an adornment of the state—but not, in fact, a useless adornment. This dead freedom became the lead actor in a piece of theater on a gigantic scale. The state without freedom created a mock parliament; it created mock elections, mock trade unions, a mock society, and a mockery of social life.[1]

We have seen how in *Siberiade* a counter-mythology, based in an older iconography, can generate another dimension of human history and question the assumptions of the myths of "scientific" socialism. In contrast to the epic design of *Siberiade*, Larisa Shepitko's *The Ascent* (1977) is, narratively, a much less ambitious work, but it is no less iconoclastic. While it speaks about the activities of Soviet partisans operating in German-occupied territory in Belarus during the Second World War—certainly one of the grand themes of Soviet historiography—the film eschews monumentalism and makes no attempt to represent the period in a comprehensive fashion. The film adopts, rather, a micro-historical scale: it depicts a very short span of time—two days and two nights—although there are few specific indicators of the passage of time. Shepitko seems to turn her back on the causal structure of large-scale events and, in particular, on the Manichaean struggle that pits Soviet heroism against the doomed forces of fascism. Indeed, she has no truck with dramatic inflation or revolutionary typologies of characters.

Her ambition is, rather, to imagine the psychological and spiritual dimensions—the motivational factors—that make of one partisan a patriotic hero and of another a quisling.

SYNOPSIS

The film, shot in black and white, begins, as it were, ex nihilo. In the first sequence we see nearly abstract shots of snowy landscapes—a village in the distance, some power poles—and the off-screen noise of machine guns. Dark figures emerge from a depression in the snow, like apparitions, forming sharp graphic contrasts with the landscape's whiteness.

These are partisans fleeing German fire. Several are killed. They stop exhausted in the forest and discuss plans for reaching the partisan encampment of Dubovoi. The leader suggests that one of the band, Rybak, go to a nearby farm and bring back food. A second partisan, Sotnikov, volunteers to accompany him.

In an elliptical sequence, Rybak and Sotnikov make their way across snowy landscapes toward the farm; Sotnikov, the weaker of the two, is unable to keep pace. The two partisans discover the burned-out farm, clothes still hanging on the line. Rybak proposes going on alone, but Sotnikov follows him wheezing.

Arriving in a village, Rybak confronts the village headman in his house about his collaboration with the Germans and, gun in hand, takes him outside. We hear a gunshot, then Rybak reenters, a slaughtered lamb over his shoulder.

The two partisans encounter Germans in a horse-drawn sled, who fire at them, wounding Sotnikov. Rybak flees to the woods with the lamb on his shoulder. Sotnikov attempts suicide using his rifle. Rybak takes courage, returns and rescues him by pushing him to safety. Rybak leaves Sotnikov to scout for shelter. He returns and says there is a cabin nearby.

At the cabin, Rybak and Sotnikov find an apprehensive mother and her children. As a German patrol approaches, the two men hide in the rafters. Sotnikov sneezes, revealing their hiding place; Rybak panics. The two partisans are taken prisoners along with the mother, who is forced to leave her children behind. Rybak is still in a state of panic while Sotnikov shows courage in defending the mother from harassment by the Germans.

Once inside the German fortress, Sotnikov is taken to the office of the Russian inquisitor, Portnov, in the service of the occupying German forces. Portnov is cruel and perverse and tortures Sotnikov, who refuses to give up any information. Visibly shaken, Rybak is brought in next. Giving way to fear, he quickly capitulates. Portnov offers him a post as a policeman.

In the basement where the prisoners are being held, Sotnikov confronts Rybak over his agreement to collaborate with the Germans. The village head man is brought in and some time later a young girl who refused to reveal who had been hiding her. Sotnikov offers to take all the blame and die for the others. In the morning, the basement door opens to reveal armed guards. Sotnikov proclaims that he alone is guilty and should alone be executed. Portnov dismisses his attempt at self-sacrifice.

The prisoners ascend a hill accompanied by guards and Rybak, who is now a policeman in the service of the Germans. A road covered in snow rises; at the top dark figures appear to be waiting. As they climb, the prisoners discover the scaffold and hanging nooses. Sotnikov consoles the condemned and exchanges looks with a young child. The execution takes place. As Rybak descends toward the fort, an old woman calls out to him: "Judas!"

Back at the fort, Rybak imagines the perils of an attempted escape. After the gate is locked, he looks into the blackness framed by the basement doors. He goes into the WC where he fails in his attempt to commit suicide by hanging himself from a rafter. We see the distraught Rybak's face in several extended close-ups. The initial view of the ascent is repeated, now empty. Then the shots of snowy landscapes that opened the film are reprised, and the film's action is thus circumscribed.

NARRATIVE SCALE

The Ascent is not at all characteristic of the serious historical film. As I sought to show in *Writing History in Film*, by the very concrete nature of its images, film is not a "natural" vehicle of historic discourse. Images do not have the discursive eloquence of verbal language, and they have to work to produce the large-scale figures of historical narration: historical actors who stand for social groups, not individuals; historical space whose references are conceptual, not concrete and immediate; and historical actions that are rarely confined to singular moments but tend to "leap" through space and time at the behest of historical causality. To perform its work, the historical film needs to call into question "the singular, linear, apparently self-sufficient cinematic narrative of historical events";[2] it needs to create, by one means or another, the equivalent of the voice of historical narration.

In its dominant mode, this narration takes the form of the voiceover commentary; language reasserts itself and anchors the polysemic image to its verbal discourse. However, many scholars and filmmakers propose more innovative approaches. Natalie Zemon Davis, for example, argues for *reflexive* strategies that disrupt the "transparency" of cinematic narration and represent the past in more complex ways. Robert Rosenstone proposes experimental kinds of filmmaking, "works that are analytic, unemotional, distanced, multicausal; historical worlds that are expressionist, surrealist, disjunctive, postmodern; histories that don't just show the past but also talk about how and what it means to the filmmaker (or to us) today."[3] For my part, I have argued that historical film stages an analogy between the real past and its representation and that this analogy relies on basic rhetorical figures like metaphor, irony, and synecdoche. Rhetoric regulates narrative and tames the unruly, equivocal cinematic signifier.

At first glance, Shepitko seems to fly in the face of such commitments and strategies. No voiceover controls the film's historical meaning. Characters are not social types; they are not primarily defined by their *participatory belonging*, nor are their deeds exemplary of broader historical actions. Moreover, they perform their acts in a space/time that eschews historical abstraction. Indeed, by framing the narrative the way she does, Shepitko excludes the contextualization—the web of historical actions and circumstances—that is the hallmark of historiographic representation. It is significant, for example, that she shapes events as if they were cut out of the natural rather than the historical world. The film opens and closes with shots of snowy landscapes; the characters appear and disappear as if called into being, not by historical circumstances, but by the act of narration.

Historical narratives, as French historian Paul Veyne describes them, are "itineraries" marked out across a vast field of objective historical facts: "In short, the eventworthy field does not comprise spots to be visited and would be called events; an event is not a being, but an intersection of possible itineraries."[4] Shepitko clearly does not trace out itineraries establishing the necessary links between historical facts; she is not drawn to such large-scale figures and the critical distance they entail. *The Ascent* provides us, rather, with "spots to be visited": actions taking place in a circumscribed and concrete space and time that recalls the unified mode of Greek tragedy. Indeed, at every moment we feel the pressure of the film's dramatic and emotional concentration. These are actions we can measure out with our eyes and our human sense of the passage of time, as we do in a certain kind of fiction film. Her characters are not social constructs but individuals, subjected to extreme circumstances and depicted in deeply psychological terms, who act in a space that is concrete and proximate. This work of focalization means that every aspect of mise-en-scène is invested with significance. Shepitko values the descriptive detail, the specificity of a gesture, and the spare bit of dialogue, all of which are at once verisimilar and charged with auratic undertones. In short, the film embraces a phenomenological realism and an emotional intensity that historians find inadmissible in the representation of the past. The actions that *The Ascent* narrates belong to the mode of "being," in Veyne's formulation, not to constructed abstraction.

The Ascent is a deeply experimental film, but it is not at all disjointed or postmodern. It does not indulge in effects of distance, it does not create a fragmented world or call into question its own representations, and it does not equivocate about characters. Quite the contrary, it draws us into fully described situations, constructs a sequence of suspenseful action, and imposes an intimacy with its protagonists that calls on the most emotional kind of identification. Shepitko's characters are fleshly and enigmatic, excessive compared to the historical character who exists principally as the embodiment of historical action. They do not dissolve into the anonymity imposed by the analytic categories common to the social sciences. Rather, they possess complex inner lives. They exist in a world of sensation, touching (and touched by) the environment that envelops them.

The Ascent is not, therefore, a sweeping grand narrative; it does not set out to represent the entirety of the historical event of the resistance to the German invasion of Soviet territory or to define an abstract idea like the Soviet Nation. Although a deeply poetic film, it makes no use of the easy rhetoric of the synecdoche—that pervasive figure of the historical film that suggests that what we see in the image is a fragmentary stand-in for a higher historical meaning. On the contrary, *The Ascent* produces a modest narrative that takes place in the space of two days and is represented as a simple linear progression. There are no flashbacks or parallel actions. Indeed, the film's events appear to have no antecedents and do not suggest their extension into the future. With no back story, the characters exist only in the moment and in the immediate circumstances they encounter.

When we measure the screen time (one hour and fifty-one minutes) against the story time (approximately forty-eight hours), we realize that the film is not as elliptical as typical history films. Most sequences are *scenes* in the sense that their running time and their story time are identical. Shepitko's predilection for long takes further intensifies the film's strong *degree of presence*, to use the notion Ann Rigney develops in *The Rhetoric of Historical Representation*.[5] Although we may feel that the resistance was experienced in much the same way on other battlefields of the war, the film makes no effort to suggest generalization: the action the film represents is to be taken for what it is.

I do not mean to suggest that Shepitko the author is eclipsed behind *The Ascent*'s powerful diegetic effects. As we will see, she is a strong subjective presence in the film who asserts herself in the manner of the graphic artist. We see her "hand" everywhere: in the composition of the image, in the evocative use of lighting, in the expressionistic choice of camera angles, in the predilection for close-ups.

CLOSE TO THE FACE, CLOSE TO THE BODY

As I noted, time is foreshortened in *The Ascent*, but space is equally so. The camera stays close to the body and, especially, to the face. It is difficult to recall any film since Dreyer's *Passion of Joan of Arc* that is so intensely focused on the human face as a terrain to be explored. The first example we encounter in the film is striking. In the third sequence, the exhausted band of partisans, whom we have seen in long shot as dark figures against immense snowy landscapes, drops to the ground for a brief respite in their flight from the Germans. Without regard for contextualizing longer shots, the film moves to giving us portraits in close-ups and extreme close-ups. The camera thus focalizes on faces of characters who have not yet been individualized in the narrative. This is a moment of arrested action: the partisans are engaged in breathlessly eating their rations of grain. Thus the close shots are not part of a psychological chain of action or reaction; they have, instead, a certain descriptive autonomy, although we continue to feel the weight of the characters' predicament. The lingering camera shows the partisans' faces in their extraordinary particularity: weathered physiognomies, expressive facial gestures, textures of the skin—all lent spiritual depth by the play of light and shadow.

In the film's action scenes, contextualizing long shots are also rare. The camera tends to stay close to the characters' bodies, which, this closeness suggests, are vulnerable and prey to terrible contingencies. Consider, for example, the sequences in which Sotnikov and Rybak are attacked by fire from Germans on a horse-drawn sled. Sotnikov is wounded and down, while Rybak escapes toward the forest with the lamb on his back. The camera stays close to Sotnikov as he hopelessly defends himself. In despair he attempts suicide: we watch in uncomfortable proximity as Sotnikov desperately maneuvers to position his rifle across his body to fire the fatal shot. He struggles and fails. When Rybak, having plucked up his courage, comes to rescue Sotnikov, we are positioned on a level with and very close to Rybak's body as he literally pushes the inert Sotnikov through the resistant snow. The effect is visceral: the nearness to the struggling Rybak and his burden, intensified by the nearness of the sound, provokes a sensation of anxiety in the spectator.

The Ascent thus does not proceed in the classic manner through the easy technique of analytic editing, which gives the pat answer to a question briefly asked. Shepitko prefers longer takes in which we engage in extended observation of faces, poses, and gestures. Shot duration thus poses the enigma: How are we to read this image? This does not mean that Shepitko avoids editing patterns such as point of view. Indeed, the emphasis the film places on characters' point of view further accentuates their developing emotional states. This is particularly striking in the point of view series where Sotnikov appears to undergo a spiritual transformation. Rybak has left his wounded companion prostrate in the snow to go in search of shelter. A tightly framed and extended close-up of Sotnikov's face emphasizes his staring eyes. Are they focused on an object or on an internal experience? This moment of *reticence*, to use Roland Barthes's notion, delays the resolution of the enigma. Eventually, the object of his gaze appears in a reverse angle: it is the pattern of snow-covered branches near his face. As we return to the mesmerized Sotnikov's point of view, we see him striking the branches with a stick and watching the snow that falls from them. This *fascination*— with all the force of the word's archaic meaning—calls into question any obvious reading of the moment.

I do not mean to suggest that the images are at all static. On the contrary, the prolonged shots allow us to observe shifts in expression or posture that will determine the course of the narrative. Longer takes do not undercut the capacity to create meaning through the juxtaposition of shots; rather, they tend to intensify our sensitivity to the complexity of relationships such editing suggests.

Lighting is a compositional element, which, like close framing, may focus the spectator's eye on significant aspects of a scene. Although references to painterly effects in film are sometimes overblown, they are entirely justified with regard to *The Ascent*. Particularly striking is the frequent use of chiaroscuro—the strong contrast between light and dark areas of the image—reminiscent of the tenebrism developed by Caravaggio. The theatrical deployment of light and shadow is everywhere in evidence in *The Ascent*, but it is startling in the sequences shot in interiors: the zone of shadows deepens, and shafts of light transfigure the subjects, as if under divine scrutiny. In Shepitko's compositions, light throws the human body, particularly the face, into relief: what is brightly lit is acutely observed. And these graphic illuminations, like those in religious painting, serve to transforms the material into the transcendent.

In certain sequences, the intensely illuminated faces and bodies contrast with metaphysical darkness, evincing the emotional and spiritual states of the characters. The stylistic effect heightens the images' empathetic function: we are drawn to *feel with* the characters. The most gripping example of this compositional work is the long sequence that takes place in the basement prison where the condemned await execution on the following morning. It is the proverbial night of the soul during which the protagonists will be tested and their weakness or righteousness revealed. Rybak (the craven), Sotnikov (the enlightened), the young mother (the virtuous but fearful), the headman (the self-justifying), and the young girl (the innocently courageous) are engulfed in shadows while intense beams of light illuminate their features. The close-ups and extreme-close-ups that focus on Sotnikov arc particularly lengthy: he is the spiritual center. For example, after Sotnikov announces that he will take all the blame for the group's presumed crimes and thus save the others, he is seen in an unusually composed shot: the back of his head occupies the immediate foreground while beyond him his fellow prisoners are grouped in a circle around him. The reverse-angle shot shows the object of their adoration: Sotnikov's brightly lit face in center frame; as the camera tracks in, the light on his face intensifies.

A TRANSGRESSIVE PARABLE

If *The Ascent* eschews the modes of representation typical of the history film, it also dissents from another set of principles—those that regulate Stalinist representations of history. Socialist realist narratives conceive characters as examples of their social categories with the inherent traits that the class struggle assigns them. Heroic protagonists are always exemplary, models whose actions are meant to be replicated by succeeding generations. They are transparent figures in parables that moralize human events. If *The Ascent* has a parabolic structure, it is not that of socialist realism. It does retain the primary ethical dimension of characters and their rise toward consciousness, but morality and self-awareness are not defined by the Marxist-Leninist "text": they come from within. There is no father figure who points the son toward his ineluctable destiny. *The Ascent* does not allow its protagonists to take their place in a positive vision of history. In terms of socialist history, Rybak and Sotnikov are failures. They do not complete their task. Instead, they are thwarted from bringing their comrades the food that would have enabled the partisans to reach their goal and continue the struggle for liberation of the Motherland. Moreover, they join a cohort of victims, submit to their oppressors, and die tragically or survive ignominiously. In other words, they exist in a complex world of experience that eschews the easy rhetoric of the fable.

The film's narrative hinges on parallel but opposite trajectories for its central protagonists. Sotnikov is sickly and unsuited to heroic action but proves himself capable of great internal strength; Rybak is physically strong and impatient with others' infirmities, but under the menace of death gives in to moral cowardice. We see this, for example, in the parallel sequences in which Sotnikov and then Rybak are subjected to interrogation by the sadistic collaborator Portnov. As Shepitko's framing of the action reveals, Sotnikov rejects the submissive position. The inquisition begins with a shot of Sotnikov's back that blocks our view of Portnov, who is presumably in a position of power. After he has been tortured, Sotnikov opens his eyes, and we see Portnov standing above him looking rattled. A series of reverse-angle close shots establishes Sotnikov's unflinching resolve (his staring eyes) and Portnov's inability to sustain his gaze. In the parallel sequence, Rybak's interrogation is staged very differently. The relationship of power between interrogator and victim is the reverse. We see Rybak enter Portnov's office in a wider shot; he is smaller in the frame, and we see in the same shot the scrubwoman cleaning up the last traces of Sotnikov's torture. Portnov, in total control, simply asks Rybak the existential question, "Do you want to live?" and Rybak begins giving up information. In the following sequence Sotnikov asks Rybak, "Did you stand up to it?" and Rybak replies that one has to know how to "play the Germans."

AN ARCHAIC ICONOGRAPHY

The Ascent thus plays on the ironic inversion of the socialist realist typology of heroes of the Great Patriotic War. The embodiment of resistance is not the impetuous and combative hero. Rather, it is the meditative figure of self-sacrifice who refuses to betray the resistance or himself. In *The Ascent* there is no victory in the world of material action: the protagonists do not become minor saints in a Stalinist narrative. Victory comes through transcendence: rising above the worldly, it takes the form of spiritual redemption. The saintly Sotnikov does not follow in the path of a father figure, according to the central myth that Stalinism sought to construct. He undergoes a spiritual transformation, what the film represents as an imitation of Christ, according to St. Augustine's exhortation: "Thou wouldst perhaps be ashamed to imitate a lowly man; then at any rate imitate the lowly God."[6] The Christ-like Sotnikov attempts to take upon himself the sins of the others. *The Ascent* thus taps into a much older mythology, with deep roots in the Soviet Republics' collective consciousness, particularly among the disparaged class of the peasantry.

The parallels between *The Ascent*'s narrative and the life of Christ, particularly as it is represented in Western painting, become most apparent in the depiction of the ascent that brings us to the narrative climax: the hanging of the prisoners. This is unmistakably a dramatic restaging of the crucifixion where the culminating events of the Passion of Christ are brought to mind, irradiating the events the film recounts. *The Ascent* draws on "the great 'storehouse' of those images and symbols without which there is no 'great tradition' transmitted from generation to generation."[7] The film's narrative imitates the events of the Passion, but, what is perhaps more important, it appropriates the iconography of its depiction in Western art.

Consider how the sequence of the ascent develops visually. The stationary long shot that begins the sequence of the ascent gives us a view of a snow-covered road climbing a hill. On one side, village buildings; on the other, an expanse of snowy landscape. The prisoners and guards, seen from behind, emerge into the bottom of the frame, beginning their ascent; at the top of the rise in the distant background we see dark figures waiting for them. Two succeeding long shots show us a straggling group of villagers walking behind the condemned and a high-angle view of a snowy landscape with a mutilated tree. Two close-ups of the desperate Rybak, now a collaborator, are interpolated in the long shots: in pleading tones he tells Sotnikov of his plan to escape and continue the resistance.

In the fourth long shot, we see the faces of the prisoners emerging from the bottom of the frame; as they approach, they are caught in a medium close shot. A reverse-angle shot establishes the object of their point of view: an iron gate from which nooses hang. Several closer shots show groups of German officers hanging around. One of them informs Portnov that the commandant is not pleased with the turnout. Men arrive to put logs in place, on which the condemned will stand so their heads reach the nooses. In the complex series of shots that follows, Sotnikov performs a set of gestures that reveal his humility and compassion: he asks forgiveness of the mother who is to be hanged with him because his sneeze caused her downfall; he comforts and embraces the condemned; he asks Rybak to help him mount the log; in a ninety-degree angle long shot of the gallows, we see Rybak clutching at the stump on which Sotnikov stands and in a later shot grasping at his coat; Sotnikov exchanges looks and a smile with a young boy who is weeping. As Sotnikov is hanged, his face falls toward the camera and there follow two extended reaction shots: the young boy who is wiping his tears away; Portnov, the fallen, who cannot avert his eyes and smiles bitterly.

It takes little exegesis to link the elements of this scene to the Passion of Christ in Western iconography. The hill that ascends; the gallows shot at a low angle that suggests its symbolic relationship to the cross; the painful ascent of the condemned; the Germans loitering about the site like Roman soldiers at the crucifixion—we take the elements of this scene as an analogy to the depiction of Golgotha, the hillock outside the walls of Jerusalem where Christ was crucified. The iconographic motifs suggest Sotnikov's apotheosis: he becomes a preternatural, charismatic figure who acknowledges his faults and transfixes those who observe his suffering. He is the Agnus Dei *qui tollis peccata mundi*, whose sympathetic exchange with a child, figure of innocence before the Fall, confirms. His magnetism draws the look of the rueful Portnov, irretrievably fallen. Rybak, whom an old woman will shortly call "Judas," stands at the foot of the scaffold as the tortured figure of betrayal.

REIMAGINING SOCIALISM

In *The Ascent*, Shepitko takes up one of the crucial events—and one of the most mythologized—of Soviet history: the Great Patriotic War against the German invasion of Soviet territory. How are we to interpret Shepitko's gesture of casting the film's story in the ethical and religious terms we have just discussed? It is clearly a radical departure from the narrative of the war authorized by Soviet socialist realism. Even in the late Brezhnev period, the antifascist heroism of the Soviet people under the leadership of dauntless Stalin kept its sacral character. Stalin's betrayals (like those documented in *Katyn*) and his strategic errors were yet to be subjected to scrutiny by Soviet historians. The official narrative of the Great Patriotic War was untouchable, as it remains to a large extent today. In order to understand the boldness of Shepitko's revisionism, it is worth tracing the development of Soviet nationalist ideology.

The 1930s had seen the emergence of the notion of "socialism in one country," the Stalinist line that justified abandoning the central Marxist idea that revolution would take place only as a concerted international movement. As Arthur Koestler documents in *Darkness at Noon*, his novel about the Stalinist purges at the end of the 1930s, it became the duty of Communist Parties outside the Soviet Union to sacrifice the interests of their own working classes in order to help Stalin build Soviet industries. In the context of this refurbished national ideology, the Master became the symbolic embodiment of the revolutionary movement and epitomized the "superstitious worship of authority" that Marx had decried. Stalin had a model close at hand. In *Imagined Communities* cultural historian Benedict Anderson argues that the Communist regime quickly moved its capital to Moscow and occupied "the ancient citadel of Czarist power." Despite its putative intention of revolutionizing consciousness, the regime understood the expediency of bowing to an autocratic ideology and embracing what had come before: "such leaderships come easily to adopt the putative *nationalnost* of the older dynasts *and* the dynastic state."[8] Thus the socialist state sought its authority "in a territorial and social space inherited from the prerevolutionary past."[9] "It was the old Tsarist Empire," as historian Eric Hobsbawn puts it, "under new management."[10]

Socialism in one country was thus a retreat from Marxist internationalism and required a distinctly anti-Marxist ideology. Under the existential threat posed by the Nazi invasion of the Soviet Union, which ended Stalin's brief but unholy alliance with Hitler, it was all the more crucial to maintain national solidarity. This was not self-evident given the immense geographic expanses and ethnic diversity of the Soviet Union. Many citizens of the outlying republics knew little of the Russian metropole, except through the apparatuses of the Stalinist state, and could not be expected to have, instinctively, the sense of belonging that a foundational mythology provides. As novelist Vasily Grossman argues, Stalin chose this moment of grand pathos to "proclaim openly his ideology of State nationalism."[11] Russia was no longer "the first among equals" in relation to the other republics that, with it, made up the Union: it was, as Benedict Anderson asserts, the Motherland, in whose defense the masses, bound by this "deep, horizontal kinship" could be mobilized.[12]

The Soviet state thought it could imagine the nation as an organized community, inhabiting a common territory, only through the efforts of state propaganda and the tireless pedagogical campaigns intended to inculcate patriotism. Was this sufficient to motivate the selfless actions the Soviet people took in their own defense? They acted most certainly out of self-defensive fear, but, as *The Ascent* suggests, heroic action was also motivated by impulses that were more positively human. Grossman in his monumental novel *Life and Fate* describes the impact of national consciousness at a time when the heroic resistance at Stalingrad that succeeded in encircling the German armies offered the only point of light in the darkness of the occupation: "National consciousness is a powerful and splendid force at a time of disaster. It is splendid not because it is nationalist but because it is human. It is a manifestation of human dignity, human love of freedom, human faith in what is good."[13]

MONUMENTS OF FORGETTING

Speaking about the German drive for expiation of its crimes through the proliferation of commemorative monuments, Andreas Huyssen illuminates the underlying paradox of places of memory: "The more monuments there are, the more the past becomes invisible, the easier it is to forget: redemption, thus, through forgetting."[14] The impulse to erect monuments raises several kinds of suspicions about monumental art in the twentieth century, and as Huyssen points out, modernism, followed by postmodernism, was intransigent in its critique of the monumental:

> The monumental is aesthetically suspect because it is tied to nineteenth-century bad taste, to kitsch, and to mass culture. It is politically suspect because it is seen as representative of nineteenth-century nationalisms and of twentieth-century totalitarianisms. It is socially suspect because it is the privileged mode of expression of mass movement and mass politics. It is ethically suspect because in its preference for bigness it indulges in the larger-than-human, in the attempt to overwhelm the individual spectator. It is psychoanalytically suspect because it is tied to narcissistic delusion of grandeur and to imaginary wholeness.[15]

Stalin's monumental ambitions were not without parallel to those of Nazi architect Albert Speer, who intended the monuments of the Third Reich to survive, even after the demise of the fascist state, in the undiminished visibility of their ruins. As Huyssen puts it, "It was the last stage of Romanticism of ruins in which an originally melancholy and contemplative impulse was transformed into an imperialist project of conquering time and space."[16]

In the postwar period, the Soviet state manufactured memorials of gigantic proportions. Obelisks and towering bronze-cast statues of heroic Soviet soldiers were enclosed in elaborate architectural settings—closed spaces set off from the traffic of ordinary life. The theme of Mother Motherland was particularly prevalent: giant statues of the Mother, further elevated by enormous pedestals, dominated often complex sculptural ensembles and stood guard over the remains of soldiers interred in mausoleums at her feet. Mother Motherland at Kiev was sixty-two meters tall, but The Motherland Calls, commemorating the Battle of Stalingrad, measured eighty-seven meters and was declared the largest statue in the world in 1967.

These were aggressively antimodernist shrines, both grandiose and sentimentalized, which addressed a public whose identity was as monolithic as the art. It is an art that overwhelms, indeed terrorizes, the observer, while indulging in monstrous kitschiness. The monuments' proportions extinguish any possibility of personal identification with the object or any emotion other than awe. These are conspicuously symbolic constructions that have no inner life and therefore allow for none in the observer. They curb any urge to relive the realities of the Second World War, submerging them in a sterile triumphalism. They crush the deeper emotional truths of national patriotism that emerge from obscure, immemorial traditions, presumably made obsolete by the Soviet revolution. Stalinist art is implacably positivist: these monumental representations of heroic figures and events mark out the unstoppable advance of socialism, reducing the experience of the past to a numbing teleology. Stalinist art stifles the imagination. It tolerates no experimentation it deems deviant. It requires the artist to eliminate everything that cannot be taken in at a glance so that visual texts become immediately "readable," according to a shared key to symbolic representations. Soviet art must be utterly unambiguous, its interpretation served up in advance.

Such tributes were conceived as *places of memory*, to use historian Pierre Nora's term. It is helpful, in analyzing the special character of Stalinist monumentalism, to recall how Nora parses the multiple features of the word "place." First, the place must have a *material* (but not necessarily topographical) existence: for example, the presence of monuments to the dead of World War I in virtually every French village. Second, the place must be *functional* in the sense that the vestiges of the past it collects and displays are part of a social effort to transmit and reactivate memories, as in public holidays like Martin Luther King Day or pilgrimage sites like the Vietnam Memorial in Washington, D.C. Third, the place must have a symbolic aura that resonates in the public imagination, be a site that organizes and condenses the public's emotional and ideological experience of the past. Finally, Nora argues, a place of memory is constituted through a collective "will to remember," the desire to "stop time, to inhibit forgetting, to fix a state of things, to immortalize death, and to materialize the immaterial."[17] Without this elemental motivation, historical memorials are inorganic and irrelevant to public life. One can stop the process of forgetting—stop death—only if what one wills to remember is a still living memory.

Stalinist memorials certainly exist concretely; more than that, they exhibit themselves ostentatiously. They were designed to provoke in the spectator a resurgence of patriotic feeling, largely overborne by the monuments' numbing hyperbole. Do Stalinist memorials have an *aura*? What emanates from them has little to do with the spirit—the breeze or breath of the Greek root of the word; their blatancy thwarts rather than organizes public emotion. Finally and most tellingly, Stalinist monuments do not embody a collective will to remember; they do not "materialize the immaterial." They cannot "immortalize death" because, paradoxically, only monuments alive in the shared memory of a group can stop time. What Stalinist monuments express is, as Huyssen observes, "narcissistic delusions of grandeur" and "imaginary wholeness."

After the Soviet state fell of its own weight, the fate of Stalinist monuments, especially those representing the pantheon of the Communist leaders, is illuminating. In Eastern Europe in particular, they were torn down in acts of public violence or they remained as derelicts in public spaces where they lost their ritual function. Some of them are now collected together in the outdoor Szobor Museum in Budapest, removed from the sphere of civic life and haphazardly arranged.

In the Brezhnev era, Stalinist monuments survived as whited sepulchers: anachronistic representations sustained by the bureaucratic policies of the ruling elite. Resistance to new forms of public art and new ideas was not just imposed by the state; it reflected the complacency shared by the general population. As Eric Hobsbawn observes, for Soviet citizens the Brezhnev years were the "best times they and their parents, or even grandparents, had ever known."[18] It was an era of comfortable demoralization. It is not difficult to imagine the alienation the artistic elite experienced faced with the inflated rhetoric and banalities of socialist realism in the late 1970s and the world-weary passivity of the Soviet public.

In this context, Shepitko's *The Ascent* is a transgressive work committed to a particular kind of social endeavor: reawakening a shared experience of the past and reinvesting it with a vital energy that decades of stolid representations had repressed. Like all the films in this study, *The Ascent* is intent on recovering the psychological dimension of history. We should remember that in 1976 the events of World War II and the mass struggle against the Nazi occupation were part of the living memory of a substantial portion of the Soviet public. With *The Ascent* we are in the domain of collective memory. The term has become quite nebulous in critical practice, but I refer here to the concept of collective memory developed by philosopher Paul Ricoeur, who has traced its development in philosophical and sociological terms in his *Memory, History, Forgetting.*

Ricoeur anchors the notion in the work of German phenomenologist Edmund Husserl, who first theorized a collective consciousness based on "intersubjective communities of a higher order." The passage from the individual "I" to the communal "we" takes place as a process of *"social communalization."*[19] Thus, Ricoeur argues, collective memory exists thanks to an analogy with individual "mine-ness":

> It is only by analogy, and in relation to individual consciousness and its memory, that collective memory is held to be a collection of traces left by events that have affected the course of history of the groups concerned, and that it is accorded the power to place on stage these common memories, on the occasion of holidays, rites, and public celebrations.[20]

It is precisely this kind of affective community, with its shared memories and common experience, that *The Ascent* aims to regenerate. We should keep in mind Ricoeur's point that collective memory exists by analogy with individual memory. Collective memory must ultimately refer back to those atoms of experience so compelling represented in Shepitko's film: very real human bodies exposed to mortal dangers, individual minds tested by devastating circumstances, and individual souls engaged in a transcendent drama that demands excruciating choices. These are the materials of historical memory.

SPEAKING ABOUT THE HUMAN EXPERIENCE OF HISTORY

Frank Ankersmit argues that historical representation is intended to "compensate for the absence of the past itself": "The real thing is not, or is no longer available to us, and something else is given to us in order to replace it."[21] Moreover, Ankersmit observes, history is not a science of logical propositions in which words designate things in the world, in this case historical events, with the (presumed) transparency characteristic of the natural sciences. Rather, it sets up a relationship between two things: the events that have transpired in the past and the representation that the historian constructs of them. Writing history is not, then, a question of a studied imitation in which the historical text mimics events through their exact description, according to a logical order the historian has discerned as already existing in the historical field he or she is investigating. Historical narrative is a textual construction that has a looser relationship to past reality that Ankersmit formulates as *being about*. Moreover, as Walter Benjamin maintains, mimesis operates according to an exchange in which past experience imbues its representation with some of its vital force. This analysis is equally valid for audiovisual representations: images and sounds, which are of course always directly related to the "reality" out of which they are produced, also stand as a replacement for a reality that no longer exists. This is true whether the images and sounds are historical "documents" or they are constructed using the resources of mise-en-scène. We are speaking here of course of serious representations of history, in which the distinction between "fictional" and "factual" modes loses much of its pertinence.

Following this analysis, we can assert that *The Ascent* has a well-defined historical objective: it *speaks about* the human experience of the Great Patriotic War. That the film anchors this experience in the bodies and the inner lives of its protagonists, that it draws on narrative modes derived from fiction, or that it has recourse to an "archaic" mythology and to "retrograde" iconographical traditions does not in the least undercut its historical character. Rather, I would argue, Shepitko uses these strategies to step outside the imperatives of Stalinist history and dissent from its forbidding, and often murderous, teleology. She steps outside Stalin's Machiavellianism that held that revolutionary goals justify any means whatever: human masses could be sacrificed— millions of them—to the "objective" needs of the party. *The Ascent* circumvents such ideological imperatives and restores a "regressive" humanism in which the physical and moral sacrifice of the individual reclaims its precedence and its historic value. *The Ascent* is, as Constantin Parvulescu and Robert Rosenstone would have it, counterhegemonic.

Against Stalinism, Shepitko poses a view of history in which the human has not been sacrificed to a notion of social destiny. Historic actors take on the features of the ordinarily human in ways that solicit the spectator's identification. They are individuals with complex internal lives. They are not actors in the moralistic melodrama that state ideology imposed on representations of the war. They act out of solidarity with other victims in concrete moments. They react against the threat of oblivion—the fate the film materializes in the ever-present snow that blows even through the window of the prison and into its existential darkness. The characters are defined by overwhelming circumstances, but the courageous are capable of acting against their own self-interest. They are capable of reflection, of making personal decisions, of assuming their freedom, of transcending tragedy through self-sacrifice.

In his novel/essay *Everything Flows*, Vasily Grossman has given one of the most telling analyses of the impact of coercive state policies on the Soviet population and the Soviet intelligentsia. At the beginning of the novel, the central protagonist, Ivan Grigoryevich, has just been released from a gulag after thirty years of incarceration. He returns to St. Petersburg, now Leningrad, which should hold the memories of his years as a student there. He finds the city utterly changed. In the manner of Rip van Winkle, Ivan observes the strangeness of the cityscape and its inhabitants: "People's faces had changed a great deal. Visible and invisible ties had been broken—broken by time, by the mass deportations after the assassination of Kirov, by the snows and dust of Kazakhstan, by the devastating years of the siege; Ivan Grigoryevich was alone; he was a stranger."[22]

Grossman's allusions may not have the same resonance for contemporary audiences—Kirov, who was the key figure in the opposition to Stalin's progressive seizure of ultimate state power, was probably assassinated by the NKVD, an event which Stalin seized upon to begin extensive purges within the party; the steppes of Kazakhstan were the site of several gulag concentration camps; the siege refers to the Nazi offensive against Leningrad—but what is clear is the depth of change. At the same time, though, as Grossman observes, state control under Stalin perpetuated tsarist power over all of society and penetrated into every aspect of Soviet life, with devastating effects:

> No power in the world was vaster than the power he [Peter the Great] had gathered to himself and to which he had given expression—the majestic power of the wondrous State. This power had grown and grown. It now

reigned over fields and factories, over the writing desks of poets and scholars, over sites where new canals and dams were being built, over quarries, sawmills and timber forests; it was able, in its great might, to control both the vastness of space and the secret depth of the hearts of enchanted human beings, who willingly offered up to it the gift of their freedom, even of their wish for freedom.[23]

I would argue that it is important to see Shepitko's *The Ascent* against the background of this inculcated submissiveness which Grossman describes not so long before the film was made. *The Ascent* expresses the need for higher metaphysical truths than those carried by Stalinist narratives. In a more heroic age—that of the struggle against Nazism in particular—such narratives doubtless retained their power to stir the collective imagination. In the complacent Brezhnev era, however, they were for ordinary Soviet citizens more likely a matter of lip service, inured as those citizens were to a life controlled by the ubiquitous bureaucracy. Shepitko's film is a provocation. It is a dramatic reactivation in which Soviet mythology is turned on its head. The impetuous young proletarian hero has been displaced by a figure from another mythology: the unshakable spiritual moralist who leads the way toward death and transcendence.

5

PATRICIO GUZMÁN'S *NOSTALGIA FOR THE LIGHT*

Objectively, of course, the various ecosystems that sustain life on the planet proceed independently of human agency, just as they operated before the hectic ascendancy of Homo sapiens. *But it is also true that it is difficult to think of a single such natural system that has not, for better or worse, been substantially modified by human culture. Nor is this simply the work of the industrial centuries. It has been happening since the days of ancient Mesopotamia. It is coeval with writing, with the entirety of our social existence. And it is this irreversibly modified world, from the polar caps to the equatorial forest, that is all the nature we have.*

—SIMON SCHAMA, *LANDSCAPE AND MEMORY*

DESOLATION AND MEMORY

Nostalgia for the Light (2010) takes place in an exceptional landscape: the vast Atacama Desert in Chile. As an image shows us early in Patricio Guzmán's film, the Atacama can be seen from space as a singular brown patch because, his voiceover explains, it contains absolutely no humidity, and, as a result, harbors no animal or vegetable life of any kind. One would assume that such a desolate landscape would be the last place on earth in which to recover human memory. Yet, as *Nostalgia for the Light* makes clear, it is a privileged location for such recovery. Aridity stops the ravages of time and makes the past more accessible than elsewhere. It mummifies human remains and preserves textiles of pre-Columbian peoples, a godsend to the archaeologists who study them. It conserves the buildings and artifacts of nineteenth-century mining operations where Indian workers lived in conditions of virtual slavery. At night the dryness of the air brings the observer close to the firmament where "the secrets of the sky . . . fall upon us, like translucent rain." Consequently, the Atacama houses the largest and most powerful observatories in the world, by means of which astronomers recover another kind of history: the past of the galaxies, the still vibrant energy of the Big Bang.

Historian and filmmaker Guzmán comes to the desert for yet another reason. He is searching for the traces of a more recent history, those of the military coup d'état of 1973 and its brutal aftermath. The abandoned barracks where miners had been housed were at that point transformed into a concentration camp, where many of dictator Augusto Pinochet's "disappeared" waited for death. Thereafter, the widows, mothers, and sisters of murdered victims—the women of Calama—came to the desert to search for the scattered remains of their loved ones. Some are still searching.

As Guzmán made clear in his interview with Rob White, in Chile history has never caught up with memory. The Pinochet regime imposed rigorous censorship on political speech and was never called to account for its murderous acts. "Pinochet governed with terror," Guzmán tells us. "No professor could make a reference to the coup in a classroom. It's an extraordinarily strange thing because Chile was a very cultured and sophisticated country. All culture disappeared. . . . There was like a freezing, a paralysis."[1] The prohibition was perpetuated after Pinochet's fall from power in 1981 through a politics of denial on the part of subsequent governments, fearful of confronting a historical reality that might stir up nasty memories, and the rightward turn of a once socially committed Catholic Church. It was better, it seemed, to promote a soothing forgetfulness, and certainly more prudent.

In his film *Chile, Obstinate Memory* (1997), Guzmán documents his long-delayed return to his homeland after years of exile and his often frustrated search for the traces of Chile's traumatic past. He brought with him his documentary trilogy, *The Battle of Chile*, which he saw as an instrument for combatting Chile's political quietism. The final sequence of *Chile, Obstinate Memory* shows the reaction of a young audience to a projection of the third part of the *The Battle of Chile*: shots of weeping faces overcome by the revelation of the past so long held in check. The sustained pathos of the sequence measures what is for Guzmán the impact of still unreleased repression in Chilean culture.

There is no doubt that the longing that Guzmán expresses in *Nostalgia for the Light* is intensified by his status as an exile and his long absence from Chile. After the coup d'état he was threatened with execution and detained inside the infamous national stadium. At his release, Guzmán fled first to Cuba, taking the footage for *The Battle of Chile* with him, as the Cubans offered to support the production of what was to become a five-hour documentary. From there, he immigrated to Spain and finally to France. Like other members of the Chilean diaspora of intellectuals and artists, Guzmán was profoundly marked by the experience of exile. Even when it became "safe" to return to Chile well after the end of the Pinochet regime, Guzmán could not adjust to a culture of historical denial. The homecoming in Guzmán's case was particularly painful. Chile was still unrecognizable for him, as *Chile, Obstinate Memory* makes clear. The unacceptable present was elided with the even more unacceptable past. It is understandable that Guzmán, and many of his protagonists in *Nostalgia for the Light*, yearn for the sense of wholeness they can locate only in the pretraumatic past.

At its release, *Nostalgia for the Light* provoked something of a scandal in militant circles. Was this poetic film an evasion of responsibility, even a betrayal of the Marxist ambitions of South American political cinema? Indeed, *Nostalgia for the Light* is not a discursive film in the usual sense and does not take explicit political positions or recommend specific action. Although Guzmán amply demonstrates his commitment to historical memory, as the following analyses will show, his approach is both intimate and imagistic. He wants to *touch* the process of memory, its insistent demands but also its divagations and irrational desires. It is not just the memory of others that Guzmán elicits; it is his own. Indeed, the lyricism of *Nostalgia for the Light* takes root in Guzmán's own subjectivity. The historical horizon the film evokes cannot be separated from the filmmaker's own memories of the period of innocence before Chile took the road toward socialism and was brutally punished by the coup d'état.

In his autobiographical remarks, Guzmán describes how he evolved personally and professionally in the years of exile. He underwent a ten-year period of silence in which he felt himself incapable of making films. When he began working again, it was, he affirms, as if he had not aged at all but took up filmmaking with renewed vigor. Guzmán speaks in similar terms about the general hiatus he perceives between the 1970s, in which he produced *The Battle of Chile*, and the more postmodern concerns of his current work beginning in 1990s, the period in which he produced films that were perceived as less political.

Guzmán has always been an intuitive filmmaker, searching for what was not apparent: the energy that flows below what can be objectively perceived. As Jorge Ruffinelli puts it, Guzmán wanted to film "invisible acts," the substrata of events. However, his approach to the representation of memory in *Nostalgia for the Light* suggests a radical personal transformation in which the act of remembering prevails over every aspect of life and consciousness. Memory incorporates all—the bodily, the metaphysical, the material, the historical, the cosmic. As the filmmaker describes the experience, the boundaries of his ego dissolve, as does the difference between past and present:

> I think that life is memory, everything is memory. There is no present time and everything in life is remembering. I think memory encompasses all life, and all the mind. I'm not simply me—I'm my father and all that came before me, who are millions. *Nostalgia for the Light* sprung from this concept. It involves body and soul but also matter, the earth, the cosmos, all combined.[2]

NOSTALGIA: THE FILM BEGINS

No establishing shot, no narrator's voice, indeed no other frame of reference, prepares us for the first images and sounds that appear. Mysterious mechanisms, a curving track, the grating sound of an approaching "vehicle," rotating wheels, a telescope, then the film's title followed by multiple images of celestial bodies in space. No clue as to where we are, in what context the film begins. From the images of archaic mechanisms, we turn to what appear as nostalgic images of a domestic interior: flickering shadows, a close shot of a curtained window through which we see trees, then a broader view of a kitchen.

The voiceover then manifests itself: "The German telescope that I've seen once again after so many years is still working in Santiago, Chile. I owe my passion for astronomy to it. These objects [referencing the sequence of shots of interiors: shadows on an old carpet, a plate and napkin on a table] could have come from my childhood home, to remind me of that far off moment when one thinks one has left childhood behind." Thus, after an initial delay, Patricio Guzmán asserts himself as the film's controlling subject. However, his is not the neutral voice of classic documentary; rather, he infuses the images and sounds with personal experience. I begin with myself, he in essence tells us, thus casting aside the "objectivity" that his historical subject matter might seem to dictate. This is what I called, in reference to Wajda's *Katyn, autobiographical affect*; it will pervade not only Guzmán's personal reminiscences but the entire body of the film.

What is striking in this prologue is that the interchange between images and sounds on the one hand and the voiceover on the other is not at all exegetic. The words do not explicate, nor do the images and sounds illustrate. The textual elements are more autonomous and their relationship more ambiguous. Images of a domestic interior remind Guzmán of his childhood, but they also bring to mind a period of historical innocence: the relative serenity of Chile before the turbulent period of attacks against Salvador Allende's Popular Unity government and *la via chilena al socialismo* (the Chilean road to socialism), the military coup d'état, followed by the Pinochet dictatorship and the campaign of terror in which thousands became *desaparecidos* (the disappeared). The nostalgia of the film's title suggests the kind of yearning for something lost that cannot be directly expressed in language, whether verbal or audiovisual, but reemerges ineffably as sensation and mood. Frank Ankersmit argues that mood resonates in the subject of experience without the subject being aware of an object of his or her mood. These are transitory states of mind in which the subject is not as yet separated from the object: "moods and feelings are objectless; they can even be said to precede the differentiation between self and the world, between subject and object."[3]

Svetlana Boym contends that nostalgia exists as the irrational juncture of an absent space (the home that has been lost) and the contemporary space of our daily experience. Using a cinematic metaphor, she suggests that nostalgia is like the superimposition of two images: they cannot be separated without breaking apart the meaning their combination expresses. While nostalgia implies the irrational presence of two spaces, the longing the subject feels is not so much for a place as for a time:

> At first glance, nostalgia is a longing for a place, but actually it is a yearning for a different time—the time of our childhood, the slower rhythms of our dreams. In a broader sense, nostalgia is rebellion against the modern idea of time, the time of history and progress. The nostalgic desires to obliterate history and turn it into private or collective mythology, to revisit time like space, refusing to surrender to the irreversibility of time that plagues the human condition.[4]

Indeed, the dominant theme of *Nostalgia for the Light* is the (often tragic) struggle against the irreversibility of time.

In Boym's typology, Guzmán's film belongs to *reflective*, rather than *restorative*, nostalgia. Guzmán is not interested in the "reconstruction of the lost home," the *nostos*. He is focused on the *algia*, the painful longing: "Reflective nostalgia does not follow a single plot but explores ways of inhabiting many places at once and imagining different time zones; it loves details, not symbols."[5] Indeed, as we will see, *Nostalgia for the Light* brings together "narratives" from different times—from the cosmic to the contemporary—that are rooted in the same space, the landscape of the Atacama. Moreover, Guzmán avoids the symbolic because that figurative operation closes off experience by subsuming it under abstract and intractable meanings. He delights in the detail, that free agent open to associations whose meaning is, at least temporarily, suspended.

AGAINST DISCOURSE

Recovery of the living past is not a product of cognition; it cannot come from an interpretation of the past through the analysis of documents and their logical concatenation. Nor can it result from rhetorical eloquence, the power to persuade through the vivid (and calculated)

expression of thought and emotion. The place where the encounter between past and present may be enacted cannot be described in terms
of style or content; it belongs to the more amorphous sphere of sensation. "As soon as content, or form and style enter the scene," Ankersmit
argues, "a temporal 'heaviness' inevitably enters the scene favoring
either the past (object) or the present (subject)—and the doors between
past and present will then silently but irrevocably be closed."[6] The recovery that *Nostalgia for the Light* seeks is an *experience of history*, like
the experiences I have described in the preceding chapters. However, it
takes root in a landscape that seems to escape from Shama's notion of
our irreversibly modified worlds. The Atacama is not evidently "coeval
with writing": the traces of social existence one finds there are sparse
and incongruous. They resist writing, if we understand writing as the
discursive act that makes sense of the world.

Although historical experience—unlike childbirth—cannot be in-
duced, historians may avoid or delay closing the door between past and
present. They may refuse to confine representations to the categories
of analysis historical method imposes on inchoate traces of the past.
They may stand outside the "prison-house of language," in particular
the narrative and rhetorical structures that shape historical meanings.
For Hayden White, historians choose first of all a rhetorical *trope* that
will determine *in advance* the shape of a piece of history. In a previous
work, I described that moment in the following terms:

> White's theory of historical rhetoric concerns the initial stage in the de-
> velopment of a historical narrative when the historian draws the funda-
> mental contours of his work. He adopts the word *prefiguration* for this
> moment of the genesis of discourse. To represent "what really hap-
> pened," the historian must first prefigure the field of historical events.[7]

In adopting the narrative "genre" (a key notion that White applies to
historiography) in terms of which a set of "event-worthy" material is to
be understood, historians choose ipso facto to include those elements
that conform to the meanings the genre imposes and exclude what they
see as extraneous. Embedded in the narrative line, "facts" lose their experiential character and become elements in a discourse of signs. It is
the framework—constructionist, deconstructionist, or other—that wins

out. The danger is that historical representation may endlessly reflect, not the reality of the past, but the organized mind of the researcher (a component of the institution of historiography, as Foucault would have it). On the other hand, as I have been proposing, there are approaches that allow for much more "play," where the conceptual framework is kept in abeyance. These approaches do not prefigure the field of the past and therefore do not shut themselves off from the terror or the ecstatic pleasures provoked by unmediated experience.

BREAKING OUT OF THE PRISON-HOUSE OF LANGUAGE

As any viewer immediately understands, language in *Nostalgia for the Light* has nothing to do with the pragmatic discourse of historians. The voiceover, as I have already observed, eschews interpretation; it is not a gloss of the images, although it retains the power of language to organize. Like the images, language also undergoes an aesthetic transformation. It is, to borrow the literary term, *poetic* language, if we understand poetry as conveying "heightened forms of perception, experience, meaning, or consciousness in heightened language."[8] Poetry is the language of experience in the sense that it involves a post-ponement of meaning (the shut-off valve of experience).

Consider, for example, a passage from the closing moment of the film, described in example 5.1. The language is perhaps the most "con-clusive" of the film in that it generalizes about the experiences the film has represented. Yet observe how Guzmán exploits all the resonance and ambiguity of metaphor in the interchange between the visual and the verbal.

In this passage, Guzmán sets up a comparison between the enormity of the problems of Chilean history and the immensity of the cosmos. The difference in scale of these two objects is held in check by the metaphor the text develops: the child's marbles, which evoke Chile's period of innocence, are posited as equivalents of cosmic spheres. Whence the poetic figure: "each of us could carry the entire universe in the depths of our pockets." Part of the poetry of this verbal text has to do with the figurative ambiguity of the images that accompany it. The

EXAMPLE 5.1
COSMIC MARBLES

IMAGE	VOICEOVER
1. Marbles on a light blue back-ground (the camera pans).	Compared with the immensity of the cosmos, the problems of the Chilean people might seem insignificant. But if we laid them out on a table, they would be as vast as a galaxy. Whilst making this film, looking back, I found in these marbles the innocence of the Chile of my childhood. Back then . . .
2. Close-up of a sphere (a cosmic body?).	. . . each of us could carry the entire cosmic universe . . .
3. A second sphere.	. . . in the depths of our pockets.
4. Extreme long shots of the lights of Santiago (the camera pans).	I am convinced that memory has a gravitational force. It is constantly attracting us. Those who have a memory are able to live in the fragile present moment. Those who have none don't live anywhere.
5. City lights.	Each night, slowly, impassively, the center of the galaxy passes over Santiago.

textual metaphor I have just described, for example, is expressed visually by the uncertain status of the spheres in shots 2 and 3: Are these objects marbles or celestial bodies? While the comparison is quite "irrational," it allows us to conceive that memories have "gravitational force" and that they are the (paradoxical) basis for living in the "fragile present."

The frequent offset between the voiceover and the image is highly significant in Guzmán's film. The voiceover and the image frequently "talk about" apparently different things, yet their juxtaposition asks the viewer to hold them together by understanding their relationship in poetic, not literal terms. In a manner that mirrors the passage I just cited, the film's prologue links Chile's historic innocence, expressed in

EXAMPLE 5.2
A SHATTERED PEACE

IMAGE	VOICEOVER
1. A coverlet on a bed, with patterns of light.	At that time, Chile was a haven of peace isolated from the world.
2. Patterns of light on floorboards.	Santiago slept in the foothills of the Cordillera . . .
3. An arbor seen through a window framed by a crocheted panel.	. . . detached from the rest of the world.
4. A stained glass window, a piece of pottery on its sill.	Nothing ever happened.
5. A tree blows in the wind against a house painted in bright blues and yellows.	The presidents of the Republic walked unescorted through the streets.

the voiceover, to the nostalgic images of a domestic interior, like that of his own childhood.

As shown in example 5.2, this passage from the prologue creates a mood of nostalgic serenity about the past and its wistful images remain open to the associations the spectator may bring to them. There are, however, many moments in *Nostalgia for the Light* that are more radically dissociated from any structure, narrative or figurative, and offer the spectator no obvious way to anchor images and sounds in an act of comprehension. There is no specific context linking what we perceive to a sequencing of events. There is no language, even poetic, to intervene. There is no rhetoric—no comparisons, no metaphors, no figurative framework—to blunt the images' irrational juxtaposition. Meaning is more than postponed; it is deflected. The representations given are just there. Consider this short sequence:

1. A shot of the sky dissolves into a rock formation, set off by the white of salt deposits.

2. A lateral pan to the right reveals a mummified arm and hand stretching diagonally across the screen. (Do we retrospectively identify the "rock" of shot 1 as the body's shoulder emerging from the desert floor?)

3. A second pan right moves across a red woven textile, then reveals a skull with hair.

4. Shot 3 dissolves into a shot of cosmic swirls in outer space, then a second, under which we hear the sound of thunder.

Many sequences in *Nostalgia for the Light*, like this one, seem to be engrossed in contemplation. Prolonged long shots appear as fascinated by the massive forms of the white observatories set in the desert landscape or against the radiant sky. Other sequences fixate on the mechanical operation of the observatories whose movements set up patterns that are nearly abstract. Most striking perhaps are the recurring images of cosmic phenomena whose otherworldly forms and colors transfix the gaze. As in all aesthetic experience, there is an initial phase of contemplation in which the viewer is absorbed by the art object, *undergoes* the object. He or she "understands" it, in the sense of taking it in, before beginning to analyze the work in detail or contextualizing it using the intellectual tools of social or art history. Aesthetic experience is direct and immediate. Cognition has not yet taken over and imposed the separation between subject and object. At moments like those I have described, Guzmán leaves us in suspension in front of the object and, to a certain extent, this suspension will not be entirely resolved, or, better, will be resolved, to a certain extent, in ways we could not have anticipated.

As we know, image and sound discourses, even those that are tightly controlled, are vulnerable to slipping into the pre-logical regions of the unconscious and the unintended. Guzmán does nothing to prevent such slippage; indeed, he willfully preserves the intractability of the image, its resistance to set meanings, and he calls on the poetic potential of language to subvert its own transparency. Moreover, he seems intent on protecting the authenticity of experience by frequently undercutting the logical links between shots or between what the voice evokes and what the image shows. He also delays making connections between the spheres of experience he is investigating. Indeed, Guzmán insists on their heterogeneity: What does the search for bone fragments in the desert have to do with the history of the night skies? In a similar way, Guzmán has suppressed the role of narrative at the level of the large "scenario" of the film. *Nostalgia for the Light* does away with chronological and causal connections so that the film's "episodes" are strangely autonomous and indeed out of time. It is, I would argue, Guzmán's intuition that the "protective shell of narrative" needs to be stripped away for other kinds of experience to become available and other methods of holding them together to emerge.

In general, *Nostalgia for the Light*, like other films in this study, works through a process of *dissociation*: Guzmán's text suppresses the logical links between images or between images and sounds. The film's disjunctive style deprives us of the usual narrative and psychological mechanisms—the associations we are programmed to discern in the chain of images and sounds. First, it *atomizes* our experience, compelling us to "read" the images differently. We become acutely aware of the *aesthetic* dimension of the image or of the effect produced by the juxtaposition of image and sound. This is the moment of fascination and contemplation, a "static" moment in which we suspend, however briefly, the attention we pay to the film's unfolding. Second, dissociation calls nonetheless for a resolution. The text is, after all, not meaningless. If the associations we feel compelled to make cannot be located on the surface, they must lie somewhere underneath, in a kind of textual unconscious, so to speak. We become aware of these correspondences not through deliberation but through the poetic effects that Guzmán's film promotes at every moment.

Paradoxically, Guzmán, as we will now see, does feel a need not only for moments of explication—his own, of course, however impressionistic they may be—but also for the interpretations he will solicit from the unusual sensibilities of two scientists.

ARTICULATING VOICES

The Atacama is an enigma. Is this desert—a place of passage for thousands of years—an exceptional ecosystem where the human submits to rather than shapes the landscape? Paradoxically, it is both an inhospitable space where human culture has never taken root and an exceptional archive where traces of history have accumulated. But what is the relationship between all these disparate historic presences that come together there? It is a central question that Guzmán's film addresses. How is it possible to bind things together, to produce an understanding of the different layers of history deposited there as if by happenstance?

Three voices take charge of this mission. The first is Guzmán's voiceover, as the passages from the film cited above make clear. The other voices belong to two scientists who work in the Atacama. The first is an astronomer, the second an archaeologist; both appear directly on camera as Guzmán interviews them. He has clearly prepared them for their task: to reflect on the special character of the Atacama and the relationship between the two sciences practiced there, but also the relationship between scientific research and the search that widows, mothers, and sisters engage in to recover something of their lost loved ones. Such reflections are clearly speculative, and the scientists' musings often take on a poetic character, particularly in relation to the images. Against images of overlapping rocky plates in the desert, then a time-lapse shot of a starry sky above mountains, the archaeologist asks why two different kinds of scientists who study two different kinds of objects work side by side in the desert:

> Why are some places more suitable for this study of the past? Why are there archeologists and astronomers in the same place? The answer is simple, the past is more accessible [here] than elsewhere. The translucency of the sky is, for the archeologists of space, what the dry climate is for us. It facilitates our access to evidence of the past.

For his part, Gaspar Galaz, the young astronomer, suggests that all research has a point in common: its objects are always in the past. The light of galaxies that reaches across time, the geological strata that represent the hardened layers of the past, the objects and documents preserved by intention or by chance, the mental and material objects that memory saves from oblivion. Indeed, he asserts, all of life experience takes place in the past, including the conversation he is having with Guzmán. Everything that one experiences is always at a remove, even the flash that separates stimulus and perception caused by the speed of light. Guzmán's voiceover asks, "So we don't see things at the very instant that we look at them," to which Galaz replies: "No, that's the trap. The present doesn't exist. The only present that might exist is the one in my mind. It's the closest we come to the absolute present. . . . And not even then!"

Astronomer, geologist, archaeologist, and historian are then all students of the past—at varying degrees of remove. In conversation with the archaeologist, Guzmán points out that it is recent history, whose traces we would expect to find in more detail, that has received the least scrutiny. Recalling the recent past is perilous because it has the power to disrupt the present. Dangerous memories threaten to lift unspoken prohibitions and endanger institutions whose function is to keep the public order. Denial is, as we know, a defense mechanism that applies not only to individuals but to societies. It creates zones of anxiety and blocks the public understanding of events. Without representation, experience cannot be clarified nor can the public grasp its affective significance.

The passage sketched out in example 5.3 evokes a particular zone of social anxiety: the exploitation of Indian labor in the nineteenth century, a piece of labor history that has been blocked out by deliberate negligence. As Guzmán's and his interlocutor's comments suggest, this is the historiography of avoidance that responds to direct political censorship or to the (more subtle but nonetheless effective) academic constraints on what constitutes an appropriate (or indeed fundable) subject of historical investigation. Here as elsewhere, a rich field of historical experience is left fallow.

In this montage, the photographs are enigmatic, fragments of time and space recorded in detail and excerpted from a field of unexamined historical traces. We are convinced of their authenticity, their quality of *having-been-there* that Roland Barthes ascribes to the referential power of the photographic image. Irrefutable vestiges of past experience, they hang suspended in time, artifacts of experience we are in no position to understand. We are unable to identify the human figures the images preserve in such phenomenal detail. We know little of their social circumstances. We cannot recognize the kinds of labor the images document nor in whose interest the images were taken. As the archaeologist's remarks make clear, historical discourse has made no attempt to organize the field and give it narrative coherence. And yet the images persist—like many of the traces Guzmán documents in his film—and resist the political forces that would consign them to oblivion. If there

EXAMPLE 5.3
HISTORICAL TRACES

IMAGE	VOICE
1. A medium close shot of the archaeologist.	Voiceover: Yet this country has not yet considered its past. It is held in the grasp of the coup d'état, which seems to immobilize it. Archaeologist: This is the paradox that concerns you most. . . . It's worthy of your concern.
2. The first in a series of black and white photos of documentary scenes from the nineteenth and early twentieth centuries: a huge crowd in the street, assembled in front of a building.	We've hidden away our nearest past.
3. Return to the medium close shot of the archaeologist.	It's a huge paradox. We know hardly anything about the nineteenth century.
4. Photo 2: a mining operation.	How many secrets are we keeping about the nineteenth century!
5. Photo 3: drilling equipment and two workers.	[*No voiceover.*]
6. Return to the medium close shot of the archaeologist.	We have never acknowledged that we marginalized our Indians. It's practically a state secret.
7. Photo 4: Indian workers.	We've done nothing to try to understand . . .
8. Return to the archaeologist.	. . . why in the nineteenth century staggering economic phenomena such as saltpeter appeared yet today there is nothing left.
9. Photo 5: two locomotives and six workers.	[*No voiceover.*]
10. Photo 6: two laborers drilling.	We've kept our recent past hidden.
11. Photo 7: a room full of men dressed in white and wearing caps.	We've concealed it.
12. Photo 8: Indian workers.	We avoid looking at this recent history.
13. Return to medium close of the archaeologist.	It's as if this history might accuse us.

is an underlying poetic figure in *Nostalgia for the Light*, it is certainly this irony: that the jagged edges of memory—like the hand emerging from the sand at the gravesite discovered during the filming—may protrude even from a politically regulated silence.

In cases where there is no historiographic memory, the task of preserving memory devolves to the individual witnesses who resist the soporific effects of deliberate indifference. Memory is then marginalized because its witnesses are isolated voices expressing their opposition to official history and its painful omissions. As we have seen, the opening sequences of *Nostalgia for the Light* are autobiographical references to Guzmán's own childhood—a time of peaceful "slumber" from which he is awakened by "a revolutionary tide [that] swept us to the center of the world." Among the film's protagonists are survivors of Pinochet's murderous regime, who struggle, against implacable opposition, to drag their past into the present.

Memory is framed by Guzmán's voiceover, which presents Luis, a member of the group of Pinochet's prisoners who were also star gazers: "He wasn't able to escape, but, by communicating with the stars, he managed to preserve his inner freedom. He remembers traces that have been erased, electric cables, watchtowers. Luis is a transmitter of history." Miguel, an architect, preserved the memory of the architectural space of the camp. The voiceover, set against images of Miguel's drawings, remarks: "When the military saw the published drawings of the camps which they had dismantled, they were dumbstruck." In his apartment Miguel demonstrates how he paced off the dimensions of buildings and open areas. At the end of the sequence, we see Miguel and his wife from behind as they move along a stone walkway, and then a second shot from behind the couple shows them seated on a bench. The voiceover comments: "Miguel and his wife are for me a metaphor of Chile. He is remembering, whilst Anita is forgetting as she has Alzheimer's disease."

THE WOMEN OF CALAMA

In his novel *Austerlitz* W. G. Sebald describes the obsessional search for the past, in this case the character Austerlitz's search for memories of his parents, both of whom were deported by the Nazis. He attempts to recover the image of his mother in a propaganda film produced by the Germans on the Theresienstadt camp where she was interned, finally isolating a frame from the film in the background of which he sees a woman's face that corresponds to his "faint memories."[9] Or in Paris he imagines his father at Drancy, the notorious transfer camp, "still in his good suit and his black velour hat, calm and upright among all those frightened people."[10] Many of us, Austerlitz affirms, have a rendezvous with the past in which an unexpected recognition places us outside of time:

> Or I felt . . . as if my father were still in Paris and just waiting, so to speak, for a good opportunity to reveal himself. Such ideas infallibly come to me in places which have more of the past about them than the present. For instance, if I am walking through the city and look into one of those quiet courtyards where nothing has changed for decades, I feel, almost physically, the current of time slowing down in the gravitational field of oblivion.[11]

Austerlitz continues to speculate: "And might it not be . . . that we also have appointments to keep in the past, in what has gone before and is for the most part extinguished, and must go there in search of places and people who have some connection to us on the far side of time, so to speak?"[12]

As we have seen, Guzmán considers the Atacama as a privileged site of such encounters with the past whose purpose is indeed to place us out of time. Perhaps the most poignant figures of memory are the women who still come to the desert in search of some vestige of victims' remains that Pinochet made every effort to unearth and dispose of. They come to a potential site of memory that revives in them the (impossible) hope of recovery. They do not simply want remains; they want resurrection—the ability to relive what has been lost. What is striking is the psychological reiteration of a cycle that can end only in surrender or death: the auspicious mood of the women's arrival in the desert is followed by their grinding search for remains and finally their capitulation to despair. As we see a series of shots of a woman with a shovel in hand, the voiceover explains: "The women of Calama

EXAMPLE 5.4
FRAGMENTS OF MEMORY

IMAGE	VOICE
1. Close-up of Vicky Saavedra. As she speaks of the pieces of her brother's skull, she demonstrates their location on her own head.	Voiceover: What did you find of your brother finally? Saavedra: A foot. It was still in his shoe. Some of his teeth. I found part of his forehead, his nose, nearly all of the left side of his skull. The bit behind the ear with a bullet mark. The bullet came out here. That shows he was shot from below. . . . They finished him off with a bullet to the forehead.
2. Medium close shot of Saavedra.	I remember his tender expression and this was all that remained . . . a few teeth and bits of bone. And a foot. Our final moment together . . .
3. A photo labeled "Jose Saavedra Gonzalez" against the desert floor.	. . . was when his foot was at my house. When the mass grave was discovered, I knew it was his shoe and his foot.
4. Return to medium close shot of Saavedra.	That night I got up and went to stroke his foot.

searched for twenty-eight years, until 2002. Some of them continue to search as victims are still being found." The woman identified as Vicky Saavedra appears in close-up (see example 5.4), and Guzmán interviews her off-camera (he never appears visually in the film):

The theme of failed recovery is again manifest in Guzmán's interview with Violeta Berrios (see example 5.5). Here the retrieval of remains provokes Berrios's tragic ambivalence—"I want them so much/I don't want them." She is suspended between the need to search and the fear that what she finds will put an end to the unconscious desire for resurrection.

The landscape of the Atacama is the film's setting, the space that gives access to the traces of history that the various protagonists seek

EXAMPLE 5.5
THE IMPOSSIBLE DESIRE OF BEING

IMAGE	VOICE
Violeta Berrios in medium shot.	Voiceover: Some people may wonder why she wants bones. Berrios: But I want them so much! When they found Mario's jawbone, I told them I didn't want it. I told Dr. Patricia Hernandez, "I want him whole. They took him away whole, I don't want a piece of him!"

to recover. In the film's construction, it is also the ground against which the diverse human activities the film depicts take on form and meaning: it is, for example, the "natural" context within which the interviews with Vicky and Violeta are shot. They are "set against" the desert, this agent/actor that takes on multiple roles. In its immensity it "belittles" the search for bodies. For example, we see the following representation of Vicky's search: (a) a medium shot of Vicky, turned three-quarters away from the camera; (b) an extreme long shot of her tiny figure dwarfed by an expanse of rocky desert in the foreground and a background made up of the rounded forms of mountains set against the sky; (c) a return to a medium shot of Vicky; (d) a close-up of Vicky's face looking down at the earth; and (e) another extreme long shot of a woman walking away from the camera toward distant mountains. The voiceover begins, "The women of Calama searched for twenty-eight years . . . ," and the image gives us a close-up of Vicky's lower legs walking in the desert and then a close-up of her against the sky.

In this alternation of scales, the desert comments, with indifferent irony, on Vicky's futile action. Later in the film, one striking image presents the irony in emblematic form: the shot is immense, the visual field divided between the darkened earth and the luminous sky at dusk, and at the center between the two cosmic elements, the tiny silhouette of the figure of the searcher. When Violeta's description of her relationship to her brother's remains reaches its most intense moment ("I don't want to die before I find him"), three shots of empty desert landscape interrupt the interview, as if to allow Violeta to recover her composure.

HISTORY HAS BECOME PRIVATIZED

Nostalgia for the Light, as I hope I have shown, is a complex text made up of fragments of experience, held together by an audiovisual "language" that rejects the usual tools of discourse. The film's author does not attempt to take up the position of the historian capable of grasping events retrospectively as complete and meaningful. He does not integrate moments of experience into a coherent narrative; indeed, the film's editing eschews the principles of continuity. Even the thematic strands— the history of Pinochet's victims, the history of pre-Columbian peoples or of nineteenth-century Indian labor, and the history of the universe— are broken up by a textual alternation that undercuts the sense of cohesion. The experiences the film evokes remain, as it were, in suspension, while, beneath the surface, an emergent system of associations takes the place of a structured discourse. Thus *Nostalgia for the Light* confronts the spectator with an apparently disorderly succession of images and sounds. Absent the usual structures of understanding, the film calls on the spectator's intuitive responses: he or she suspends the need for interpretation in favor of the *perception* of the audiovisual object and the currents of meaning it can produce.

In *Nostalgia for the Light*, we contemplate the puzzle of a past that has come apart in pieces. Guzmán's approach is not without parallels to movements in contemporary historiography, in particular those that question the classical notion that the past can be understood, globally and retrospectively, as the complex relationship between events held together in a "synoptic gaze," the scientific equivalent of God's knowledge of the world. The assumption in classical historiography is that all significant events can be integrated into an overarching narrative that determines, according to the historical method, their place and importance.

Contemporary historiography, Ankersmit observes, is considerably less confident about the organization of time and causality and the hierarchy it imposes. As the large-scale object of history disintegrates, so does history as a collective enterprise.

> The disintegration of the past as a unity in itself, however complex, thus prompted the dissolution of the quasi-collective knowing subject as embodied by the discipline. Ontological disintegration was followed by epistemological disintegration. This loss of clarity and of an organizing center from which we can grasp and act on the world is generally seen as a loss of bearing, as a loss of utopia in political thought, and of our capacity to distinguish between the important and unimportant, the relevant and the irrelevant."[13]

As the synoptic position crumbles, many historians seek refuge in the indisputable material traces of a past, carefully circumscribed in the specificity of a place and time. In short, history has been "privatized": it belongs to the individual researcher and the field he or she sets out to explore. Historiography is thus atomized, so to speak, and the historian, relieved of at least some of history's cognitive baggage, recovers something of his or her subjectivity. The Atacama, as it is represented in *Nostalgia for the Light*, can be compared to such a historical field. If the film's themes move among radically different periods of time, they are geographically enclosed. This unforgiving landscape sharpens our perceptions of the historical traces to be found there and provides the space of their convergence. It is a bulwark against the ominous process of forgetting.

NOSTALGIA AND THE FOLDS OF MEMORY

I do not mean to suggest that in *Nostalgia for the Light* Guzmán functions as the historian sifting and evaluating the traces of a vanished world. He is, after all, a nostalgic who, above all, "yearns to be at home in the world." As Guzmán meditates on history, the nostalgic material he exposes to view "mirrors the melancholic landscape" of his own mind. He indulges in what Boym calls the "sensual delight in the textures of time." He savors images redolent of the past and revels in fusing seemingly incompatible scales of time, investing the most immediate of human experiences with a cosmic dimension.

In "A Berlin Chronicle" Walter Benjamin describes how he might conceive of the personal memories of his youth as a "system of signs" that makes "a colorful show" against the gray background of a map of central Berlin: houses of friends, meeting halls for the Youth Movement, brothels, and cafés, constituting intense splashes of remembered experience.[14] Acknowledging his debt to Marcel Proust, Benjamin recalls the French writer's notion of memory, both momentous and urgent, in which what "began so playfully became awesomely serious." Benjamin's metaphor for the retrieval of the past is evocative. It is like a closed fan that can be slowly unfurled: "He who has once begun to open the fan of memory, never comes to the end of its segments. No image satisfies him, for he has seen it can be unfolded, and only in its folds does the truth reside." What is powerful in memory exists in the smallest detail and "that which [remembrance] encounters in these microcosms grows ever mightier."[15]

Guzmán's references to the worlds of the Atacama involve a good deal of play—the kind of serious play Benjamin observes in Proust. Benjamin's metaphor of the "fan of memory" is quite apt to describe the textual appearance of *Nostalgia for the Light*, particularly if one imagines a fan of painted scenes visible only as pictorial fragments at the edge of each fold. The partially unfolded fan (the film) is not a representation in the sense that it fulfills our desire for meaning: to see the whole of it—the truth—and therefore understand how each shiver of experience is to be held in the mind. Indeed, what kind of global "truth" could the film reveal? It is not bound together as fragments of memory of a single individual, Guzmán. His memories—unlike Benjamin's memories of Berlin—constitute only one element of a complex text. Many sequences represent fragments of experience from other individuals, rendered through Guzmán's probing mise-en-scène and empathetic camera. What the film represents is something like collective memory, which has historical scale but can be conceived only by analogy with individual memory. The assumption is that memories are generated as shared experience and that there is an underlying affinity tying together the film's protagonists in their struggle against forgetting. From this implicit solidarity the film's political character emerges.

Guzmán seizes on the shattered fragments of memory—the fragile moorings that attach the present to the past. At the same time, he recognizes that the world he knew—the Chile of his childhood—has been subjected to a historical disaster that can never be repaired. In *Nostalgia for the Light* Guzmán undertakes a work of mourning in which he contemplates the pain of his loss and the pain of others, for many of whom grief is still at the edge of denial. What Violeta Berrios and Vicky Saavedra experience is a *desire of being*, to have again what they once had. This desire is of course irrational, a protest against the irreversibility of time. At the same time, their obstinate refusal to "move on" is a political offense. Official history does not countenance memories that do not fit within the narrative authorized by the state. Indeed, Guzmán's memories, those of the people he interviews, and those implicit in the documents he brings to light have all been marginalized. They are the unwanted expression of a past that power pushes toward forgetfulness and society stigmatizes as excess. But Guzmán insists that memory is a field of resistance. "I am convinced that memory has a gravitational force," the filmmaker observes in the final moments of his film, as the impassive galaxies so close to us in the Atacama pass over Santiago's night sky.

6

RITHY PANH'S *S-21: THE KHMER ROUGE KILLING MACHINE*

Only one judgment is passed on the executioner—from looking at his victim as other than human, he ceases to be human himself. He executes the human being inside his own self; he is his own executioner. But—no matter how hard the executioner tries to kill him—his victim remains a human being forever.

—VASILY GROSSMAN, *EVERYTHING FLOWS*

RITHY PANH'S *S-21: The Khmer Rouge Killing Machine* (2003) addresses the Cambodian genocide more than twenty-five years after the Communist Party of Democratic Kampuchea (CPDK) took power in 1975 after a five-year civil war and more than twenty years after the CPDK was swept from power by the Vietnamese army in 1979. There has been no rush to judge the iniquities of the Khmer Rouge regime. Indeed, as Rithy Panh points out in his autobiographical work, *The Elimination*, justice was neither swift nor truly punitive: many Khmer Rouge officials continued for years after the collapse of the regime to exercise their functions in government. Although operating on the fringes of Cambodia, Pol Pot clung to power and benefitted from at least nominal recognition by the United Nations until 1991! The head of the Khmer Rouge police, the notorious Duch, responsible for the butchery described in *S-21*, was brought to trial only beginning in 2010. To this day, only a few of the Khmer Rouge responsible for genocidal atrocities have been judged, and most remain free.

Before addressing Panh's work, it is important to retrace the history of Stalinist terror as it develops its particularly virulent strains in Asia.

REVOLUTIONARY TERROR MOVES EAST

One of the major inspirations for this book is historian Timothy Snyder's *Bloodlands: Europe Between Hitler and Stalin* (2010), a study of those areas of Eastern Europe between Berlin and Moscow that were ravaged by the Nazis and the Soviet Union and where the majority of European Jewry lived. What is particularly impressive in this groundbreaking account is not just the systematic analysis and the compelling documentation, often based on the testimony of victims. It is also the resolve Snyder shows in exposing the parallel realities of Hitler's and Stalin's territorial ambitions and the massacres they carried out, on their own populations and those they conquered, to further their ends. The Nazis and the Soviets used remarkably similar methods.

In terms of numbers, starvation was their most important instrument of extermination, pioneered by Stalin as he deprived Ukrainian "kulaks" (in reality, most were simple peasants) of all the grain they produced. Five million people died between 1930 and 1933 as a result of Soviet agricultural policy. Indeed, in times of peace, the Soviets outperformed the Nazis as agents of death. The next most lethal method was mass shootings over trenches; those depicted by Wajda in *Katyn* were typical of Soviet war crimes against POWs (see chapter 1). As Snyder points out, the startling truth is that the majority of European Jewry perished well before the Nazis began mass gassing in extermination camps like Auschwitz, Belzec, or Sobibor. Ironically, much of Holocaust studies has focused on the work camps and their *univers concentrationaire* precisely because being sent to a concentration camp was not necessarily a death sentence, and many victims survived to bear witness to what they experienced.

East European archives only gradually began to open after the fall of the Soviet Bloc, and until very recently it was not possible to give accurate estimations of the numbers of civilians who died in the Soviet gulag. In his article, "Hitler vs. Stalin: Who Was Worse?" Snyder affirms that Stalin—though his crimes were horrific—was responsible for fewer noncombatant deaths than previously thought: "Judging from the Soviet records we now have, the number of people who died in the Gulag between 1933 and 1945, while both Stalin and Hitler were in power, was on the order of a million, perhaps a bit more."[1]

Despite the enormity of Stalin's crimes, there has never been the equivalent of the Nuremberg trials for Soviet crimes against humanity. Such trials were obviously not possible during the Soviet period, and, despite the opening of Soviet archives, admissions of crimes seem unlikely under the Putin regime. Moreover, there has long existed a taboo in the West against exposing the facts of Stalinist atrocities. The indelible stain attached to any collaboration with the Nazi regime does not extend to associations with the murderous Soviet state, or those of other Communist regimes like Mao's China. Sartre famously argued that intellectuals should keep quiet about the Soviet camps for fear of demoralizing Billancourt, that is, Western Europe's working class. As historian Tony Judt remarks, Sartre, the great moralist, made a decision "not to think of those crimes in ethical terms, or at least in a language that would engage his own ethical commitment."[2]

This *bad faith* was all too widespread in the West long after revelations of Stalinist crimes could no longer be ignored. In France governments of the Left have included the French Communist Party without any fear of stigmatization, under Mitterand, for example. Whereas intellectuals have been publicly shamed for associations with Nazism (Martin Heidegger, Paul de Man), there was no shame involved in such associations with Stalinism, for example in Pablo Neruda's writing a eulogy to Stalin at his death. In the Soviet Union, traces of a shameful past were eradicated (Khrushchev had the gulags bulldozed). There is no public monument to the victims or museum of the gulag in Russia, nor has there been any campaign since 1989 analogous to denazification in Germany after 1945. Monuments to Lenin still have a place of honor in public spaces in Russia. Stalin remains a folk hero in his native Georgia even among some Georgians who acknowledge his crimes. Similarly, Maoist imagery reemerges in public spaces in China.

In his foreword to the English-language edition of *The Black Book of Communism*, historian Martin Malia calls Communism's campaigns of terror "the most colossal case of political carnage in history": according to the work's authors, 85 to 100 million victims were killed in the interest of various Communist regimes. Even if we take account of recently reduced estimates of Soviet crimes against civilians, the number remains stunning. Malia contends that *The Black Book*'s sober accounting of Communist crimes and criminality place several points beyond dispute, among them: that the initial phase of Soviet Communism was not benign; indeed, it was the Leninist conception of a party dictatorship, even if it was proposed as expedient and temporary, that was at the root of the policy to eradicate all "class enemies," especially among the peasantry; that the regime's brutality could not be explained through reference to the violent heritage of tsarist Russia; that it was, rather, the "deliberate policy of a new revolutionary order" that eclipsed anything from the past; and that violence "escalates as the movement goes East" where "the leap from the kingdom of necessity to the kingdom of freedom" was considerably more problematic.[3] Moreover, the lineage of Communism—from Stalin to Mao, Ho, Kim Il-Sung, and Pol Pot—is also indisputable: each successor receives from his predecessor material support, the basic elements of party dogma, and, perhaps most important, schooling in methods for eradicating the regime's enemies. Pol Pot just took things further: "By the time the logic of revolutionary extremism reaches Cambodia, communist ideological purposes have merged with Nazi collective categories."[4]

As Snyder observes, both Nazism and Stalinism proposed utopian visions of their conquests: "Stalin's utopia was to collectivize the Soviet Union in nine to twelve weeks; Hitler's was to conquer the Soviet Union in the same span of time."[5] Each "utopia" was controverted by reality, but then "implemented as mass murder": "In both collectivization and the Final Solution, mass sacrifice was needed to protect a leader from the unthinkability of error."[6] Stalin accused the kulaks, the Ukrainians, and the Poles. Hitler accused the Jews. In Cambodia, Pol Pot accused the "New People," the presumed remnants of Lon Nol's bourgeois regime. His utopia was a coerced rural socialism where doctors became peasants and peasants, with their innate practical gifts, became "doctors." In order to destroy capitalism, it was sufficient to forcibly evacuate the cities and to place the evacuees in such terrible conditions that they would die from starvation, overwork, and disease. The Khmer Rouge's perceived enemies—the educated and mercantile classes that presumably resisted socialist revolution—could simply be shot.

Rithy Panh documents this social catastrophe and its human consequences in his book *The Elimination*, which includes much autobiographical material. In a matter of days, 40 percent of the Cambodian population was driven from the cities into the countryside. The revolutionaries had no plan for the dispossessed—the so-called "New People": "There was no overall plan. No organization. No dispositions had been made to guide, feed, care for, or lodge those thousands and thousands of people."[7] Panh's narrative describes in excruciating detail how nearly his entire extended family died as a result of the Khmer Rouge's fanatic policies.

The Khmer Rouge's political actions are summarized in the montage that opens Panh's *S-21: The Khmer Rouge Killing Machine*. It contains the only archival footage in the film and represents the revolutionary transformation of Cambodia that the Khmer Rouge accomplished in a matter of weeks.

1. The first shot is a pan of Phnom Penh showing buildings with people on balconies, street scenes full of the movement of cars and people.

2. Shots 2 through 8 show Khmer Rouge soldiers and leaders in different locations in the city; the last in the sequence is a phalanx of party leaders aligned above a parapet wall shot from below. The sound track gives us revolutionary songs. A succession of intertitles encapsulates the events: "17 April 1975: Victory of the Khmers rouges." "Displaced populations/town-dwellers driven out." "Schools closed, currency abolished, religions banned." "Forced labour camps, surveillance, famine, terror, executions."

3. Shot 9 pans across empty streets in Phnom Penh where there are no signs of life: an abandoned car, a bonfire, piles of possessions left behind. On the soundtrack we hear gunshots.

4. Shot 10 contrasts with shot 9: it shows the Cambodian countryside teeming with activity as workers shoulder burdens suspended from poles. The titles translate the song we hear in the background: "Bright red blood that covers cities and plains of Kampuchea, our motherland." In shot 11 we have another view of workers, as the song continues: "Sublime blood of workers and peasants / Sublime blood of revolutionary fighting men and women." Later in the film, such revolutionary songs will emerge with chilling irony from a nocturnal long shot of the buildings of the prison called S-21, emptied of its victims.

Despite the legacy of terror, there were some significant differences between Stalin's and Pol Pot's tactics. Stalin used the Soviet show trials

(1936–1938), to wipe out all the remaining party stalwarts who had made the revolution and constituted a perceived threat to his power. Stalin's methods, so compellingly evoked in Arthur Koestler's *Darkness at Noon* (1940) and Victor Serge's *The Case of Comrade Tulayev* (1967), were the model for those used against the prisoners in Pol Pot's S-21, where party "traitors" awaited death. But there was a notable deviation: whereas the Soviet Stalinists carried out their procedures of "persuasion" in secret and, when successful, made public spectacle of the accused and the crimes to which they had confessed, Pol Pot insisted on absolute secrecy in everything. The party interdicted all communication between the prison and the outside world, between guards and prisoners, and among the prisoners. No outsider was to know the conditions under which prisoners were held or the methods of interrogation and torture being used. Executions were to be totally clandestine. Execution was a forgone conclusion for all prisoners because death sealed the lips of those who confessed to crimes against the party. The extensive prison archives were to remain inaccessible, except, one can speculate, for the historians who would eventually use the material as a basis for the history of the heroic defense of the Angkar (the Party of Democratic Kampuchea).

POL POT'S TOTAL INSTITUTION

S-21, as historian David Chandler points out in *Voices from S-21*, was an extreme example of what Erving Goffman identified as total institutions: "Their encompassing or total character is symbolized by the barrier to social intercourse with the outside and to departure that is often built right into the physical plant, such as locked doors, high walls, barbed wire, cliffs, water, forests, or moors. These establishments I am calling *total institutions*."[8] The Soviets had always been adept at secrecy: the trains with their blinds pulled down that sped through the Ukrainian countryside at the time of the great famine; the NKVD's Lubyanka prison, a transit point for one terrible destination or another, whose blind windows and silence novelist Vasily Grossman describes in *Life and Fate*; the stifling sequestration of the Siberian gulag. Secrecy was equally the aim of successive Communist regimes such as Mao's China or the state that has come the closest to an extreme total institution in itself where isolation is policy, propaganda ubiquitous, and all of life is regimented: Kim Il-Sung's North Korea.

At S-21 the prison was cut off from its environs, victims were tortured in a building separated from those where the other prisoners were held, and the executions were carried out at another site, Choeung Ek, to which the condemned were transported on trucks in the dead of night. Life—if it can be called that—in S-21 was severely regimented: for the guards, rules dictated absolute vigilance. They were to prevent any communication between prisoners, thwart all attempts at escape or suicide, and act without pity. They were not to eavesdrop on interrogations. They were forbidden to take naps, or even to sit or lean against a wall while on duty. The victims, shackled and immobilized on palettes, beaten and taunted, interrogated and tortured, suffered the loss of all ability to act or react and were reduced to objects of subjugation.

It is not difficult to trace the Khmer Rouge's Communist heritage. Pol Pot's political education began in France where he was a student in the 1950s and became a member of the French Communist Party (FCP). In this period, the FCP remained a significant political force despite De Gaulle's rise to power and retained the prestige it had gained from its role in the resistance. It also maintained very close ties with Stalin, whose campaigns of terror it had never criticized, indeed, had worked to justify. In the 1950s, the staging of other show trials in the newly formed Soviet Bloc—in Czechoslovakia and Hungary, among others—must have struck the young Pol Pot. In these tribunals, the accused were identified as agents of a foreign power and/or counterrevolutionary ("Trotskyite") conspirators. Dehumanized by Stalin's inquisitional methods, they appeared as shattered figures who had confessed their crimes. The "evidence" marshaled against them was exhaustive and irrefutable, and the guilt of the accused, determined in advance, often led swiftly to execution. Above the proceeding hung the specter of Stalin, the Master, whose paranoid fantasies the trials were fashioned to vindicate. All these elements would have their analogs in the judicial machinery of Pol Pot's S-21.

It is likely, Chandler argues, that the highly codified procedures adopted by Angkar found their way to Cambodia through the agency of a Chinese official, K'ang Sheng, the head of Mao's secret police, who had "masterminded the Chinese reeducation campaign at Yan'an in 1942 and 1943 and the sweeping purges of the 1950s."[9] Indeed, S-21 was conceived as a perverse institution of rehabilitation in which reeducation led swiftly to death. Moreover, there is evidence that K'ang Sheng "befriended Pol Pot when the latter visited Beijing in 1966"; he doubtless functioned as a mentor to the future Great Leader of Democratic Kampuchea.[10]

In 1976 the second wave of purges began at S-21. It focused not on eradicating the bourgeoisie as a class but on ferreting out bourgeois tendencies within the party itself. Hannah Arendt identified historical moments like political purges in the Stalinist mode as the dawn of pure terror: "Only after the extermination of real enemies has been completed and the hunt for 'objective' enemies begins does terror become the actual content of totalitarian regimes."[11]

It is important to emphasize this political history because the full weight of its realities is only now being acknowledged. Indeed, it is shameful to realize that intellectuals on the far Left continued to support the Khmer Rouge even after the revelations of its genocidal actions. As Panh observes, Noam Chomsky and his co-author, Edward S. Herman, in their *After the Cataclysm* (1980), scoffed at the idea that a "handful of demonic creatures," that is, the Khmer Rouge leadership, could be responsible for this strange "autogenocide."[12] If the archives of most Asian Communist regimes remain closed, those compiled by the party in Democratic Kampuchea at S-21—at least those that have been salvaged—are open. There is nowhere else in Asia anything comparable to the Tuol Sleng Museum of Genocide, now housed in the buildings of S-21 where researchers are able to work on original documents, for example through the Cornell microfilming project. This access not only permits the construction of a clear factual narrative of Pol Pot's program of terror at S-21, but also reveals in unanticipated ways signs of the human experience within the mechanisms of death.

LIFE AFTER GENOCIDE

Panh's motivation for addressing the Cambodian genocide reminds us of Wajda's in producing *Katyn*. Panh was haunted by his personal memories of genocide. He, along with his parents and sisters, was deported from Phnom Penh, and he watched helplessly as all but one of his immediate family died of exhaustion, starvation, and disease in the countryside. The orphaned Panh immigrated to France where he was granted refugee status. He hoped to "erase everything and begin again at zero," but such a withdrawal from his traumatic past proved impossible. Pahn began studying filmmaking at IDHEC (Institut des Hautes Etudes Cinématographiques) where he was driven by the idea of preparing himself to confront the experience of genocide:

> Without genocide, without wars, I would probably not have become a filmmaker. But life after genocide is a terrifying void. It is impossible to live in forgetfulness. You risk losing your soul. Day after day, I felt myself sucked into the void. As if keeping silent was capitulation, death. Contrary to what I at first thought, to relive is also to take back your memory and your ability to speak.[13]

S-21: the Khmer Rouge Killing Machine is autobiographical in the sense that the past that Panh is conjuring up has haunted his existence. In 1996, while making a film called *Bophana, a Cambodian Tragedy*, based on the case of a woman who was tortured and executed for sending love letters to her husband, Panh staged an extraordinary encounter between survivor and artist Vann Nath, who painted from memory scenes of abuse and victimization, and the guards responsible for interrogating, torturing, and executing prisoners in the death camp named S-21. In an ironic twist of history, Nath, who survived S-21 because the Khmer Rouge designated him as the prison's official painter, turned his art against those he was formerly forced to serve. It was this experience of delayed confrontation that led Panh to conceive the project that would become *S-21:The Khmer Rouge Killing Machine*. Panh writes that Vann Nath, whom he had first met at the Paris Peace Accords in 1991, would "become the central character of my work on memory during the succeeding ten years."[14]

In preparing to shoot *S-21*, Panh recruited an all-Cambodian crew. His intent was to eliminate cultural or linguistic barriers between the filmmakers and their subjects—victims or perpetrators—and promote maximum receptivity based on a shared knowledge of a common history. Panh did not intend, however, that lifting such barriers should result in an exchange between the filmmakers and their subjects. Indeed, he imposed a rigorous discipline on himself and his crew: they were not to identify with the victims or perpetrators, but to stand at an emotional distance from them. They were to be instigators prodding their subjects, not participants involved in a dialogue.

From this position, Panh becomes the film's overriding conscious-ness. He makes himself into an *instrument* of revelations through his strategic approach to the resources of documentary mise-en-scène. We will shortly look at Pahn's staging techniques in detail, but I would point out here perhaps the most powerful among them: *psychodramatic mise-en-scène.* Historiography has never seen psychology as a friend of history because it has often served to provide reductive interpretations of the motivations of historical figures. However, Panh is not interested in suggesting psychological answers to the conundrums of genocide that pass understanding. He uses psychodramatic techniques, rather, as a powerful instrument for releasing experience of the past. To use Ankersmit's metaphor: Panh "pulls the faces of the past and present together" by provoking his subjects to *actualize* what has existed only as suppressed memory.

"AT THE CROSSROADS OF THE BIOLOGICAL AND THE MENTAL"

Before beginning the analysis of *S-21*, I would like to refer to one more historian, Philippe Ariès, best known for opening up two new fields of inquiry: the history of childhood and the history of death. Ariès, asso-ciated with the Annales school, turned away from the great events and figures of political or ideological history and chose to focus on the his-tory of everyday life. He is therefore a "deviant" figure in relation to the Rankian tradition of scientific historiography: he was not content to stop at the behavioral surface of events—observing actions and orga-nizing them in causal sequences—but felt compelled to dig deeper into what we can only call collective *experience*, with its inevitable psycho-logical and symbolic dimensions. With regard to the experience of childhood and the experience of death, Ariès probed the unsettling layers of a community's shared sensibilities and attitudes—unspoken systems of symbols and values essential to a society's collective identity. What such an investigation primarily demands is not detachment but empathy and imagination because the historian must be able to work his way toward an understanding of what has been termed the "collective unconscious."

In his preface to Ariès's collected *Essais de mémoire* (1943–1983), historian Roger Chartier identifies the principles that underlie Ariès's approach to history:

> Through these texts, Ariès recalls the two convictions that have sustained his entire work. The first assigns to History an object that is familiar neither in the Maurrassian tradition [referring to Ariès's early flirtation with monarchist ideologist Charles Maurras] nor in the university curriculum: specifically, involuntary feelings, unconscious habits, secret behaviors. Far from the narration of political history, far from clear thoughts and manifest ideologies, this is a History of the "collective unconscious," or rather the "collective non-conscious," defined as the system of representation, common to all societies, which spontaneously links the gesture of the individual to the shared code and thereby delineates what it is possible to think, to say and to do.[15]

As Chartier points out, sensibilities are not determined by social and economic conditions or by ideologies: "They are to be understood at the crossroad of the biological and the mental, at the intersection of physical givens and psychic investments."[16] They have to do with the unconscious of the body—the "training" we absorb without being aware of it—and the emotions, attachments, the "natural" proclivities that operate sub rosa and yet define collective identity.

We should not forget that these physical givens and psychic investments refer first to the individual member of a society, who literally *embodies* the physical and mental dispositions of a culture. It is through the sense of "participatory belonging" that individuals, largely unconsciously, commit themselves to the "imagined community," to use historian Benedict Anderson's helpful formulation.

CULTURAL MURDER

What Rithy Panh reveals in *S-21* is the perverse attack, organized by a Communist regime and carried out by perpetrators scarcely less dehumanized than their victims, on the integrity of the body and on the personhood of individuals who find themselves cut off from the source of meaning that "tradition" has instilled within them. In *The Elimination* Panh describes this politics of denial in terms of the puritanism imposed by the party. "Nothing belonged to me, not even my nakedness," Panh remarks about this period. Indeed, he has no recollection of seeing "a bare, living body," nor does he remember seeing his own face, except as a reflection in water. The body was a forbidden site of bourgeois individuation and had to be repressed:

> Only an individual has a body. Only an individual can look out from inside his body, which he can hide, offer, share, wound, bring to orgasm. Control of bodies, control of minds: the program was clear. I was without a place, without a face, without a name, without a family. I'd been subsumed into the big, black tunic of the organization.[17]

The film gives us a terrifying picture of the process of dehumanization and cultural murder. "Enemies of the people" were arrested without charges and presumed guilty, particularly those whose "class background" condemned them in advance. Blindfolded and humiliated by guards, they were transported by truck to S-21 where they were shackled to wooden palettes, deprived of all personal possessions, nearly starved, and constantly monitored and abused by guards. They were subjected to interrogation and frequently tortured with the object of obtaining a confession for acts presumably carried out for a foreign power (the CIA, the KGB, or the Vietnamese). "The prisoners must be prepared to tell the story of their treasonous lives," former commandant Duch affirmed.[18] The delicate task was to force the accused to confess without killing them in the process because the torturers were required, on pain of death, to document the guilt of their victims. These confessions, often improbable, even ludicrous, inventions, conformed to the Stalinist genre of self-criticism. The deviant party member rewrote his or her life story from a "correct" class position, to flush out the "imperialistic habits of our hearts."

David Chandler points out that at S-21 confessions had four parts: (1) the "life story," the class background, family, and other social relations that disposed the confessor to class deviation; (2) the "political biography," the story of the confessor's treasonous acts; (3) the traitor's "plans," the detailing of other acts the confessor would have committed if he or she had not been arrested; and (4) the enumeration of the "strings of traitors," denunciations of other deviants that perpetrators extorted from their victims.[19] Once their confessions were complete, the prisoners were quickly and brutally executed. Abuse and humiliation of the body, isolation from others and any remnant of normal life, torture, forced confessions that annihilated the individual's sense of self and of belonging to a human community—these were all techniques for expunging the "physical givens and psychic investments" that underpin the "collective unconscious" that Ariès saw as the basis of communal existence. To describe this process, the commandant Duch used the word *kamtech*, devised by the Khmer Rouge, which signified "to destroy and then to erase all trace: to *reduce to dust*."[20]

The mystery of terror is how it was possible, under fascist or communist regimes, to train the torturers and executioners, bleeding the human psyche of that presumably essential feature of humanness: empathy. It is not simply that the perpetrators tortured and killed under threat of reprisals and death if they failed in their mission; they carried out orders with indifference and often with relish.

RESTAGING EXPERIENCE

The Tuol Sleng Museum is a place where written and photographic documents, many still lying uncatalogued and unexamined, hold the promise of piecing together a historical accounts of the Cambodian genocide. The documentary fragments, on the other hand, constitute, in their particularity, a field of traces capable of awakening memory in the killing machine's perpetrators and the few victims who survived. The same documents thus serve quite distinct purposes. History intends to explain events by turning documents or aspects of documents into historical facts that can be aligned on the causal chain that produces their meaning. The reactivation of memory, on the other hand, involves moving in quite the opposite direction, back toward traces as the raw elements of experience. It is this "rawness" that Panh the provocateur exploits to stage the return of the repressed.

Rithy Panh refers to S-21 the prison as a dramatic space. Indeed, the "reunion" he organizes by inviting survivors and perpetrators into that space is harrowing for his "actors." One victim, simply examining the prison façade, is overcome by tears, while the reunited perpetrators greet each other with uneasy smiles and gestures of guilty complicity. In Aristotelian terms, the mode of representation Panh adopts is theatrical rather than narrative: the characters speak in their own voices and on their own account rather than being spoken about. Panh is not present within the scene—as Claude Lanzmann or Marcel Ophuls are present in their documentaries about the Holocaust. Instead, he directs the "action" from outside: "I deliberately chose to stage this situation, by imposing on myself a moral rigor that requires that I keep the necessary distance from the witnesses and that I not let them deviate from the goal we had set."[21] He may keep the witnesses at arm's length, but his hand subjects them to an unsparing mise-en-scène. He is not interested in resolution, he is interested in exposure: How did these perpetrators function within the Khmer Rouge killing machine, how did they represent their actions to themselves, and how do they assume their responsibility when confronted with the enormity of their crimes?

The witnesses are the film's dramatis personae. Two are victims (of the approximate fourteen thousand victims, only three were still alive at the time of the filming). The film's protagonist is Vann Nath, who survived the killing machine because the commandant, the infamous Duch, valued his services as the prison's painter and enjoyed talking with him about art. Nath sees himself as an instrument of memory; he revisualizes in an expressionistic style the grotesque and violent scenes of daily life in S-21. He assumes the role of the film's moral conscience, confronting the witnesses when they obfuscate or prevaricate. The second victim, Chum Mey, who is overwhelmed by his experience and the denunciations of innocents he made under duress, survived because he was charged with repairing the typewriters essential to producing the confessions that all victims were compelled to write.

The other characters are perpetrators, among the few, at Panh's instigation, willing to face their crimes: guards, interrogators, the archivist, a prison "doctor," a driver of the trucks of death, executioners. They are reluctant to speak the unspeakable and yet feel compelled to do so out of fear of bad karma, whose symptoms—headaches, lack of appetite, insomnia—torment their bodies. Like the victims, the perpetrators are individuals. Particularly prominent among them is Him Houy, the high-ranking "chef-adjoint du Santébal" (assistant head of the DK's security police), but all of them have their scene to play. Indeed, Panh's approach is more dramatic than historical, centered on characters rather than social categories; the intent is, literally, to flesh out history. As Panh puts it, "I wanted to be able to put a name to a face. I didn't want anonymous victims or torturers with masked faces."[22]

Panh recognizes that the party developed a kind of political language, purified of human complexities and honed to its single-minded purposes. "In Khmer Rouge Marxism," he observes, "everything passes through language. Everything converges on the slogan. It's a dream of press-ganging the world, of holding it in a sentence: 'The radiant revolution shines forth in all its splendor.'"[23] Panh the *metteur en scène* is wary of speech—of learned speech that imposes itself through mindless repetition, of empty mantras invented to justify the brutal actions of genocide. The servants of death whom Panh confronts in *S-21* and who are on some level aware of their guilt since they suffer from it symptomatically, are still incapable of conceiving of their acts except in slogans. The party does not make mistakes; the arrested are (by definition) guilty; it is only a question of extracting their confessions. In his account of his interviews with the wily Commandant Duch in preparation for his documentary, *Duch: The Master of the Forges of Hell* (2011), Panh is aware of the necessity of breaking down the defensive wall of language: "The executioner never falls silent. He talks. He talks endlessly. Adds. Erases. Subtracts. Recasts. And thus he builds a history, already a legend, another reality. He hides behind speech."[24]

Faced with lies of language and lies of the body, what is required is implacable vigilance. "Of course you can always look away," Panh tells us. "Take your focus off your subject. Let it move aside, drift, disappear—a simple eye movement is enough."[25] But it is the filmmaker's obligation to resist any deviation from his goal. It is especially important to expose a particular regime of disavowal characteristic of perpetrators who are coerced into testifying about their deeds: I cannot deny that I tortured and executed my victims (the evidence is, after all, irrefutable), but I acted only because I was a hostage to the commands of the party and am therefore also myself a victim of the authoritarian state, an unwilling cog in a ruthless machine. In *S-21* the art of staging, the art of framing, and the art of editing are probative instruments, acting against such denial. They call into question the self-serving maneuvers of bad consciences.

The dramatic structures that Panh sets in motion are distinct in their methods. The first is a confrontational mode in which Nath, the interrogator, challenges the behaviors—of victim and especially perpetrators—that seek to evade and obfuscate. His instruments include documentary evidence from the S-21 archives—records of denunciations, confessions, photographs—as well as Nath's painted depiction of scenes from his own experience.

In the first organized confrontation, Nath the artist stands before his rendering of the cell where he was kept with other victims chained to palettes on the floor in symmetrical rows. The first shot is wide and sets up the face-off between Nath and the perpetrators, an awkward group aligned in depth facing the painting. The opposition is then reinforced through analytic editing. Although the victims' painted bodies are indistinguishable in their common misery, Nath identifies—humanizes—them by recounting the fate of individuals among them and describing the monstrous conditions under which they are held. The camera is close and pans between Nath's face and the painting, giving us access to his emotions and reactions. The perpetrators, on the other hand, are shown in medium shots. Their bodies are stiff and their faces inexpressive as they defend themselves against Nath's accusations. He demands, for example, what the murdered children of S-21 were guilty of. In response, the perpetrators cite the omniscience and moral authority of the party, which propounded the dogma of guilt by contagion: the collective guilt with which a father or mother could infect a whole family. A close-up of Nath's face full of anger and disgust closes the sequence.

The second method is what I have called *psychodramatic mise-en-scène*, in which the perpetrators act out moments from their lives at S-21, in the ghostly setting where their acts actually took place. Panh is quite explicit in describing how he staged a replication of the past: "And then I had the idea of taking the guard back to S21 . . . and because the guard said he worked at night, I took him there at night." Panh lit the scenes with neon because that was how the Khmer prison was lit. Place evokes memory, he contends: "I sought to create an atmosphere, which recalled the situation which the guard was actually working in."[26] Nothing can be allowed to disturb this carefully crafted illusion of presence. It is for this reason, for example, that the camera stops at the threshold of a cell and does not follow the guard into the dramatic space where he is reenacting his abuse of prisoners. It would be, Panh explains, as if the cameraman were walking over the imagined bodies of victims that the "actor" and the film's mise en scène have placed there.

This kind of staging does not engage in interrogating witnesses and challenging their bad faith, as we saw in the example of the faceoff between Nath and a group of perpetrators. It is based, rather, on a carefully planned confrontation between the present of the subject and his past, often stimulated by settings, objects ("props"), texts, and, perhaps most intimately, the replication of movements and gestures that Panh shrewdly suggests:

> Often during the filming of *S21: The Khmer Rouge Killing Machine*, I ask the "comrade guards" to "make the gestures" of the period for my camera. I specify that I'm not asking them to "act," but to "make the gestures"—a way of extending their words. If necessary they start, stop, and start again ten or twenty times. Their reflexes return; I see what really happened. Or what's impossible. The method and the truth of the extermination appear.[27]

As he explains in his interview with Joshua Oppenheimer, it was in the process of working with the guards that Panh began to realize that language was not an effective vehicle for expressing traumatic memory but that access to the past could be found through the body. "And it's then that I discovered," Panh explains, "that there was another memory, which is the bodily memory." Violence is, he asserts, quite literally *un-speakable*: "Sometimes the violence is so strong that words don't suffice to describe it. And also that violence may be so strong that the words become inaudible."[28]

In the most charged examples of psychodramatic mise-en-scène, we witness the fusion of the subject—the executioner in the present—and the object—his acts in the past—as evidenced by the resurgence of long suppressed emotion.

I will begin with examples of the impact of an object on the testimony of witnesses. The first is a shot sequence filmed with a stationary camera. By this technique, Panh maintains his distance from the witness, establishing a kind of moral detachment reflected in the scale and composition of the shot. The scene takes place in a vast empty room whose windows give onto an exterior corridor. It is shot in depth: we see debris seemingly raked into piles along the right wall, an interrogation table standing in the left middle ground, and a door situated in the far depth of the space. Seated at the table, a man, whose features distance obscures, reads from the Santebal (security police) manual on how to conduct an interrogation. While we are listening to the voice speaking about interrogation tactics reverberate in this emptiness, four other men appear in the doorway in depth carrying a large object. As the men approach, we distinguish a rudimentary chair, secured to a small platform and equipped with a belt at its base and some apparatus at the level of the sitter's head. They place the chair to the left of the table, a bit farther in the background. As the men exit, the voice addresses the question of torture: when to use it, how much, and in what spirit. In the second brief example, Panh has given to a group of guards seated on the floor of the same empty room an immense rolled-up photograph. As they unroll it, the guards identify with rapt attention the subject: it is the execution ground at Cheoung Ek where they point out the hut that functioned as a waiting room of death and the location of the trenches over which they bludgeoned their victims.

My next example is more intimate: it focuses on an individual, and the scale of shots is, in the beginning, much closer. "If you want to make a film about dignity, about memory," Pahn stipulates, "you stay very close to people."[29] The sequence begins with its stimulus: a photographic portrait of a handsome young boy in a cap with an earnest expression.

(The archives are alive, Panh tells us.) The voice off screen, which belongs to the adult looking at his own image as a child, begins its autobiographical account. A child is taken from his village, blindfolded and shackled. Terrified, he is transported by truck to an unknown location, which he comes to know as S-21. He is given work outside the prison walls raising pigs. Meanwhile he undergoes indoctrination by the Santébal security police, and, when he can be trusted, he is integrated, still a child, into the Khmer Rouge killing machine. What is particularly arresting is the emotion with which the narrator speaks, as if the distance between his present and his past were being erased in his mind.

During this narration, the images often work in counterpoint. The initial take is quite long. The camera lingers on the portrait held in the narrator's hands, then slowly pans up to a close-up of the narrator himself, visually making the liaison between past and present. The camera crosses from his face to the faces of other guards, his listeners, who are simultaneously examining archival photographs of human bodies and presumably their consciences. The narration concludes in voiceover: we are in the same visual space but at a different time. In a long take we see the narrator pacing forward and back in the empty depth of the room as if his voice no longer had an impact on his body. The image perhaps suggests that no perpetrator's narrative of persecution comes to closure, even if he is himself a victim. He is always thrown back to the repetitive obsession of the unredeemed.

My final examples follow the more classic notion of psychodrama in which the subject replicates specific actions from the past in hopes of overcoming the psychic pain they have generated. The "actor" whose actions are being restaged is the same as in the previous example— the child-become-perpetrator—but our focus is on the depiction of the daily routines he performs in subjugating the prisoners. A handheld camera has already followed other guards in their rounds as they move, rather mechanically, down the prison corridors and peer into the cells checking on their imaginary charges. But this guard is more susceptible to psychodramatic techniques and, as we see, more prone to tipping from repetitive imitation into real experience. He appears in two sequences—both shot as very long takes—that represent his daily routines.

In the first, the camera is a stationary set up in the vast room where other reconstructions have taken place. Panh and his crew keep a discreet distance from the guard—he is seen in long shot throughout the sequence—as he replicates his past actions. As the guard moves about inspecting the imaginary rows of shackled prisoners, he narrates his actions: "When on guard duty, I inspect the locks four times. I rattle the lock and the bar. I test it. All's well. I do the next row." And then: "I start the body search. I feel their pockets. I look here and there. They mustn't have a pen with which they can open their veins or hide screws or rivets they can swallow to kill themselves." At this moment there is a shift in register as the narration is mixed with direct speech: "'Sit! No one move!' Then onto this row. 'On your feet! Hands up!' I start my search." "You! Taking your shirt off? Without the guard's permission? To hang yourself by your shirt? Give me that!' I grab it and take it away." The mechanical action becomes imbued with an emotion that could come only from the past: his voice is angry as he rebukes the inmates. In his recreation, the guard is, on the one hand, the narrator, who describes his own actions as if he were observing himself and explaining his actions to others. On the other hand, he casts himself, at moments, as the character who performs them and speaks in his own voice, thus placing himself at less of a remove. This ambivalence positions the guard somewhere between representation and the recovery of experience. The latter asserts itself insistently as we can judge from the guard's mounting rage.

The second sequence takes place in the "real" space of a former cell. Everything about the mise-en-scène is different. The camera is placed in the corridor outside the cell where the action can be seen through the observation windows the guard also uses or through the entrance whose imaginary door the guard repeatedly pretends to unlock, open, then close and relock as he brings prisoners water, the "can," or a bowl of rice soup. The moving camera allows us to follow the activities within the cell in medium long shots but also gives us intimate closer shots of the guard as he observes the prisoners through the windows and threatens to beat them with a club. If the first sequence is a chilling view of violence at a distance, the second brings us into a relationship with the guard that is uncomfortably close, as if we needed to resist identifying with the perpetrator.

Panh's work in *S-21* partakes of both the theatrical and cinematic. He assembles his "cast" of actors, places them in settings, blocks their positions, suggests their movements, or allows them to improvise, and provides them with "props"—all with the intention of evoking a certain kind of "performance." The difference from staged theater is that there is no theatrical text, no prescribed narrative development, no written dialogue. And the actors do not play roles in the ordinary sense; they play themselves, as they are in the present and as they may have been in the past. Some of them play themselves openly, allowing the past to break fully into the present; others act in denial of themselves as they existed in the past; still others, gradually or abruptly, come to abandon their resistance and admit the past into awareness, theirs and ours.

In *S-21* the settings are not theatrically constructed spaces but the real space of the Khmer Rouge prison—the site of the museum of the Cambodian genocide, as well as the abandoned buildings with their prison cells and interrogation rooms where the dust and debris of the past still move in the wind and the walls are still stained with blood that diligent washing has not completely effaced. The execution ground at Choeung Ek remains unchanged except that the corpses, which lay scarcely below the surface, have been removed for decent burial. The remnants of murder and the ghosts that memory sees everywhere are still so chilling that the guilty, whom Panh brings there to bear witness, speak in hushed voices. It is a place, Panh tells us, that is still "haunted as if impregnated with the drama that unfolded there."

There are degrees of immediacy in the representations *S-21* gives us. The "coldest" moments are those in which the witnesses explain procedures, mimic mechanically their old routines, read confessions of their misdeeds, or point out, reluctantly it seems, their moral flaws. More immediate are the moments in which the witnesses face a document that accuses them, for example the mug shot of the young woman who was tortured into confessing that she betrayed the revolution by defecating in the operating room of a DK hospital. The "hottest" moments are those in which the witness loses mastery over his testimony and something in him fuses directly with the experience he thought he was simply describing.

All of these moments are meticulously prepared and shaped. It is not that Panh rehearses and blocks out the actions of his actors. On the contrary, his choice of shooting in long takes guarantees a certain freedom for the witnesses. However, he chooses the setting and the nature of the encounters he wants to film, and selects camera angles and shot scales that apply the degree of pressure that the kind of testimony and the witnesses' character demand. His mise-en-scène reposes on both first-hand experience and historical analysis. It is, on the one hand, intuitive and empathetic, and, on the other, it is intellectually tough. It is not Panh's intention to alleviate the pain of memory; there is no "cure" for the sorrows of genocide. He organizes, rather, a resurgence of living memories that block the work of forgetting and retaliate against the enormous human losses he will not leave unspoken.

7

JOSHUA OPPENHEIMER'S
THE ACT OF KILLING

The play's the thing . . .

—WILLIAM SHAKESPEARE, *HAMLET*

THE PARALLELS between Rithy Panh's *S-21* and Joshua Oppenheimer's *The Act of Killing* (2012) are striking. Both films emerge from the political history of the same global region: Cambodia in *S-21*, Indonesia in *The Act of Killing*. Both filmmakers address calamitous events that formed (and deformed) the history of a nation and remained unresolved at the opening of the twenty-first century. Both events took place in the context of the Cold War and were impacted by American foreign policy and the War in Vietnam. Both films focus on the perpetrators of mass murder: the Khmer Rouge executioners (1975–1979) in the first and members of President Suharto's death squads (1965–1966) in the second. The fact that the Cambodian genocide was carried out by rabid Communists and the Indonesian genocide by rabid anti-Communists is an irony of history. The specificities of method and ideology made little difference to the victims, and history should make no moral distinction between them. Both Panh and Oppenheimer set out to represent the techniques that totalitarian regimes used to crush any real or imagined opposition. Both express the outrage one should feel toward violence that operates with impunity and iniquities that go unpunished.

As we will see, Oppenheimer, like Panh, uses strategies of psychodramatic mise-en-scène but of a quite different sort. Panh, as a Cambodian and a victim of genocide, is an insider to the situations he evokes; he knows whereof he speaks. He casts himself as the implacable *metteur en scène* who sets the stage and directs his actors, sometimes coaxing but more often coercing revelations about the historic violence in which they are implicated. He is the film's moral compass, and he constantly punctures the perpetrators' illusions and thwarts their desire to dissimulate. Oppenheimer, on the other hand, is an outsider, an American filmmaker who sets out to study acts of violence of a particular type, at a particular historical moment, and in a particular cultural context. Indeed, his approach is genuinely ethnographic. He spent eight years researching his subject, gaining the trust of members of Suharto's death squads, and penetrating their moral universe. He is both intuitive and objective—the requisite characteristics of the ethnographic filmmaker. He collaborates with an ethnic Indonesian, whom he acknowledges as his co-director but who appears in the credits only as "Anonymous" for fear of reprisals.

HUNTING DOWN THE DEATH SQUADS

As Oppenheimer explains in an interview he gave to *Democracy Now!*'s Amy Goodman (a bonus feature in the DVD version), the title *The Act of Killing* has more than one meaning. The first reference is to the crimes committed in 1965–1966 by death squads in the wake of the coup d'état that was engineered by the Indonesian military and resulted in the overthrow of President Sukarno. These death squads, recruited from gangster milieus, executed thousands of Communists and other perceived opponents of the right-wing usurpers: liberal intellectuals, trade unionists, peasants, and the ethnic Chinese, who were all ipso facto "Communists" in the eyes of the autocratic regime that Suharto eventually imposed. The killings were abetted by a mass paramilitary organization called the Pancasila Youth, still three million strong at the time Oppenheimer shot his film. The death squads were in great measure responsible for consolidating the Suharto regime, which would rule Indonesia for more than three decades.

The acts to which the film refers were indeed momentous. Although the number of the dead cannot be easily calculated, most estimates range from five hundred thousand to a million. Physical evidence is slight; few traces of mass graves have been unearthed. But we do know the victims' bodies clogged Indonesian rivers for months. It was not possible, Oppenheimer explains, to interview victims, not only because there were so few survivors but also because they quite rightly saw the perils of testifying.[1] The gangland killers, on the other hand, were everywhere in plain sight and very loquacious. They were considered national heroes who had no need to hide their past. Oppenheimer puts it this way in his interview with Amy Goodman:

> It is as if I were in Nazi Germany forty years after the Holocaust and it's still the Third Reich, the Nazis are still in power. Official history . . . aging SS officers allowed to boast about what they've done, even encouraged to do so, so that they become these feared proxies of the state in their communities, in their regions, and also so that they can justify to themselves what they've done.

Who are these "feared proxies of the state" Oppenheimer studies in *The Act of Killing*? For the purposes of representing what has been termed the Indonesian genocide, Oppenheimer decided to focus on a single group of torturers and executioners out of the countless mass murderers he interviewed. His chosen subjects are leading members of Suharto's death squads in the city of Medan on the island of Sumatra; among them we find Anwar Congo, the charismatic gangster who becomes the film's protagonist. These perpetrators identify themselves as the "movie house gangsters" because they operated out of a movie theater where they earned money by scalping tickets, among other illicit activities. Across the street a storefront served as their office, and upstairs on the rooftop they established their killing ground. The movie house gangsters were not only ruthless killers, but also ardent cinephiles, in love with the Hollywood cinema. Hollywood provided them with their ego ideals (tough gangster figures or flinty Western heroes), the iconography of urban violence or the lawless frontier, and all the conventions associated with these and other genre styles. Most bizarrely, their cinephilia embraced the incongruous desire for pure spectacle embodied in the musical comedy.

In the opening sequences of *The Act of Killing*, shot against an urban landscape of glass fronted buildings and a revolving billboard, Oppenheimer in running titles is explicit about his approach: "When we met the killers, they proudly told us stories about what they did. To understand why, we asked them to create scenes about the killings in whatever ways they wished. The film follows that process, and documents its consequences." Is it possible, Oppenheimer's approach asks, to use the gangsters' bravado and their penchant for telling stories to create meaningful representations of the Indonesian genocide? Can the imaginary be an instrument of truth?

The second layer of meaning in the film's title, as Oppenheimer makes explicit in his interview for *Democracy Now!*, comes, then, from the verb "to act" defined as performing a role in a narrative that is usually (but not necessarily) fictional. Indeed *The Act of Killing* includes a kind of psychodynamic performance through which the actors—our coterie of gangsters—rehearse (that is, repeat), under the protective cover of fiction, the vile actions they carried out in the past. Performances of this kind involve real pleasures but also certain risks for the actors, who in this case are also the authors of their reenacted lives. Let me recall Octave Mannoni's striking formulation of the pleasures that game-based activities, indeed all fantasy, produce: "Je sais bien mais quand même." In other words, *I know very well* that what I am acting out, in my mind or on one of the many stages of the imaginary, is not real, *but all the same* what pleasure I derive from imagining it![2] However, in some circumstances, the pleasures of fiction involve risk. When Oppenheimer's actors, who are mass murderers, deal with reimagining their own past so charged with violence, there is always the danger that the protective trappings of fiction (what we know to be real) might give way. The imaginary moment of representation may collapse, and the actors may find themselves face to face with their intolerable past.

A DISPARATE TEXT

The text that Oppenheimer constructs is extraordinarily complex, as I will attempt to demonstrate in the following analysis. For the moment I would emphasize the diversity of approaches he adopts—the positions of enunciation, as theorists would term them—toward his subject.

1. There are "straight" documentary sequences in which the objective is to capture certain realities of contemporary Indonesia, in particular its political culture. Oppenheimer shows us how the instruments of repression—through the unholy complicity of government officials of the highest ranks with organized crime—operate to maintain the status quo. We see, for example, the fascistic demonstrations the Pancasila Youth engage in, and the governor of North Sumatra telling his guests at an official reception, including gangsters: "We have so many gangsters, and that's a good thing. . . . All we have to do is direct them." In these sequences Oppenheimer maintains his distance from the facts he is exposing, in the manner of political documentary.

2. Oppenheimer uses the more intimate and subjective techniques of cinema direct to penetrate into the world of the gangster. For example, we watch as Anwar Congo and the young thug Herman Koto relax in a bar with their henchmen, or we contemplate the insomniac Anwar on his bed in the dark unable to sleep. Oppenheimer also uses cinema direct's roving hand-held camera to allow us to experience moments of unrehearsed action. For example, we follow gangsters on their daily rounds and look over their shoulders, so to speak, as they fleece Chinese shopkeepers, the defenseless victims of sanctioned ethnic persecution.

3. There are sequences—or moments within sequences—that I will call "intersubjective," in which an individual subject (or group of subjects) addresses himself (themselves) directly to the filmmakers. This dialogic form, which I will discuss shortly in detail, foregrounds the relationship between the two spaces: what is before the camera and what is behind it. For example, in a bar where he has been singing with his cohort, Anwar Congo shifts his posture of enunciation to confess to the filmmakers that his bad dreams come from what he did: "Killing people who didn't want to die."

4. There are the sequences in which the gangsters reenact the history of the violence that resulted in the consolidation of Suharto's military regime in 1965–1966. These "reconstructions" adopt several modes of representation, from the minimally to the maximally "fictionalized": (a) Demonstrations of actions taken in the past are presented as such and addressed to the camera. Anwar Congo shows the filmmakers, for example, the technique of murder by garroting that avoided the messy post-execution clean-up. A complicit smile toward the

camera seems to say, "See how clever I am." (b) There are reenactments staged "on location" using nonprofessional actors, mostly the gangsters' relatives and friends. The most extensive example is the depiction of a village massacre, in which Herman Koto, a commander of the Pancasilo Youth, and a visiting government official direct the action. (c) There are two studio-shot sequences making expressionistic use of low-key lighting and analytic editing, in particular the close-up, to enhance atmospheric and psychological effects. Both restage the torture of a victim in the gangsters' office. (d) There are reenactments that are so imbued with the gangsters' fantasies that their relationship to real events is tenuous at best. In the production number set to the song "Born Free," for example, two victims in medium shot remove the garroting wire from their necks; one of them places a gold medal around Anwar's neck (he is dressed in monk's robes) and, while shaking Anwar's hand, declares: "For executing me and sending me to heaven, I thank you a thousand times, for everything."

5. Finally, there are sequences of heavily sexualized fantasy having no discernible relation to historical events. These are modeled, again at the behest of the gangsters, on the Hollywood musical number that abandons all sense of plot to indulge in gratuitous spectacle. A line of beautiful female dancers in brilliant yellow (later in brilliant red) emerges from the mouth of an enormous fish (actually a seafood restaurant) dancing in unison, albeit awkwardly; to their right sits the thuggish Herman Koto in drag—a grotesque Carmen Miranda figure who appears repeatedly as a fantastic element in many sequences.

This typology is, of course, a simplification because many sequences combine more than one type or move from one position of enunciation to another, as I will attempt to make clear in the following. The variety of types is one measure of the film's complexity. Oppenheimer does not seek to harmonize his text or allow us to indulge in the narrative pleasures of a coherent set of motivated actions unfolding in a clearly articulated space. A given sequence does not appear to follow logically from the one that precedes it, nor does it allow us to anticipate what is coming next. Indeed, Oppenheimer seems intent upon giving us an extremely fragmented depiction of the hubristic, nostalgic, yet fearful world of the aging executioners. It is a cubistic picture (if I may be allowed the comparison), in which each element seems to adopt a different point of view on the subject. Their point of convergence is not on the picture plane of the screen but in the mind of the viewer.

THE ACT OF KILLING AND THE HISTORY OF DOCUMENTARY

It is significant that Amy Goodman in the introduction to her interview with Joshua Oppenheimer asks whether *The Act of Killing* is in fact a documentary or something else (a question the edited interview does not address). She asks the question, one assumes, because of the ways in which the film blends fiction and nonfiction. Although this "hybrid" form strikes many as a contemporary phenomenon, a product of postmodernist experimentation, traditional documentary has long embraced such fictional elements as the restaging of real events for the camera. Robert Flaherty's *Nanook* (1922) inaugurates the genre by restaging events in the life of an Inuit family, events that belong to a remembered but already distant past.

Even in the history of the ethnographic film—to which I would attach *The Act of Killing*—the only subgenre of documentary that remains, one supposes, under the control of trained professionals, there has been a tendency on the part of some ethnographers to move away from the consecrated rules of scientific practice. They call into question a practice rooted in logocentrism: the notion that a scientific discourse is, by definition, verbal, and that the ethnographer is bound to subject everything he or she observes, whether directly or through audiovisual recording, to the cool objectivity of the ethnographer's language. Cinematographic images are particularly suspect because they are indeterminate, open to "irrelevant" associations, and tend to escape from the analytic categories ethnographic discourse attempts to impose on them. The classic position in ethnography was that filmed behavior is relegated to an initial stage of information gathering and therefore fated to disappear as such from the scientist's finished product. It is still heretical in certain circles to consider that a film could substitute for a verbal discourse in communicating ethnographic information. This argument holds that not only is there the inherent danger of images stirring up primary elements—suppressed thoughts, moods, and desires—but that there is also the risk that the coded language of film, forged in the crucible of fiction, can easily take over and divert audio-visual documents to its own purposes.

How, then, is it possible to say that *The Act of Killing* gives us insights into the caste of Indonesian gangsterism it claims to study when the filmmaker seems intent, not on suppressing the projective power of images, but on exploiting it. Indeed, Oppenheimer seems to abdicate his responsibility to gather and organize material by handing over to his subjects the task of representing themselves in whatever manner they see fit. He even allows them—indeed, encourages them—to give expression to the grotesque fantasies they concoct from their morbid cinephilia.

In short, Oppenheimer appears to cast himself in the role of the abettor: the skilled technician, acting under the direction of perpe-trators of mass murder and providing them with all the resources of mise-en-scène and the cinematic apparatus they need to construct a perverse history of the Indonesian genocide and thus to justify actions that are blatantly unjustifiable. By putting himself in the service of the debased figures he is studying, does Oppenheimer run the risk of debasing himself, whatever his good intentions might be? He was con-cerned enough about the ambiguous moral position he was placing himself in to consult with human rights activists in Jakarta, who en-couraged him to pursue his course so that public expression could be given to the repressed experience of ordinary Indonesians.

ANOTHER ETHNOGRAPHY

Oppenheimer's work recalls the methods of French ethnographic film-maker, Jean Rouch, whose legacy has, unfortunately, been neglected by recent Anglo-American theorists of documentary.[3] The relationship be-tween Rouch's innovative approaches and those practiced by Oppen-heimer can be specified in the following terms. First, very early in his career, Rouch suppresses the ethnographer's voiceover in his films (the incontrovertible "voice of science" that manages the images) and realizes his desire to "let things speak for themselves," albeit under very controlled conditions. Oppenheimer likewise eschews the easy power of language to organize a discourse on mass murder in Indonesia. *The Act of Killing* has only a few introductory intertitles and no voiced commentary. Like all documentary filmmakers, Oppenheimer does, of course, control a great deal through the choices he makes. He chooses where to place his camera and how long to keep it running. Out of the hundreds of subjects he interviewed, he chose to focalize his narrative around a central figure, Anwar Congo, in whom he discerns the nascent signs of pain and remorse. Through the editing process, he selects the material to be included (from the vast amount of footage he shot). He uses the editor's craft to create relationships between shots, whether reconstructing the relatively fortuitous events not staged for the camera and therefore open to chance or producing sequences in the more tightly controlled shooting conditions involving a small cast of characters. *The Act of Killing* demonstrates, once again, that meaningful juxtaposition is the major discursive instrument in the hands of the documentarist.

Second, following Rouch, Oppenheimer employs a method that critics have termed *intersubjective* mise-en-scène. He does not suppress the presence of camera and crew, using, for example, the techniques of habituation most elegantly applied by Frederick Wiseman, whereby the cinematographer and sound engineer, whose presence becomes commonplace for the participants, disappear, at least theoretically, into the ambient space of the institution he is studying. Rather, Oppenheimer sets up a dialogic relationship between the two subjects of the shoot: the filmmakers and the whole filmic apparatus on one side and the actors and extras on the other. As we will see, he even promotes the idea that the actors can cross over into the space of production in the role of scriptwriter or director of action. Oppenheimer includes an emblematic shot of Anwar Congo perched on a crane with his eye looking through the camera lens.

Although he never appears in the image, the filmmaker's voice, at moments, directly addresses the actors—and they in turn him—in the manner Claude Lanzmann uses in *Shoah*. Take the following example. Adi, the aging gangland executioner who flew in from Jakarta to participate in the shoot and who is clearly uneasy about what the film might unleash, is driving toward the airport to return to Jakarta (one has the distinct feeling he is fleeing from the trouble he foresees). At this moment he is engaged in dialogue with the one of the filmmakers, whom we hear in voice-off. In alternation, we see Adi in medium close from the passenger's position, a shot broad enough to capture his gestures of protest and defiance, and we see him framed in close-up in the rearview mirror. This latter point of view—one that Oppenheimer exploits elsewhere in the film—makes us intimately aware of Adi's facial expressions while he seems oblivious to the fact that he is being filmed. These reaction shots reveal a lot about Adi's fear and anger while the matter-of-fact tone of the voice-off prods him about his violent past: "I don't mean to make you uncomfortable, but I have to ask. By telling yourself it was 'war,' you're not haunted like Anwar. But the Geneva Conventions define what you did as 'war crimes.'"

Intersubjectivity asserts itself primarily, however, in the way the actors directly address the filmmakers, who for the most part do not overtly reciprocate. For example, Anwar Congo is so pleased with his performance in a reenacted torture scene that Oppenheimer shows him on a monitor that he exclaims: "This is great, Joshua. This is very good. I never imagined I could make something so great." One major aspect of intersubjectivity that Rouch pioneered in his ethnographic films was precisely this kind of exchange in which the participants reviewing sequences from the film comment on how the film represents them and their actions. The technique, sometimes referred to as "shared anthropology," not only empowers human subjects to take an active part in their own representation, but also provides a whole new layer of information, a strategy that Oppenheimer fully exploits in his film. To take a simple example, while examining rushes of the sequence where he demonstrates the method of strangling victims with wire to avoid the mess of blood, Anwar Congo objects to his own lack of realism: "I never wore white pants. I always wore dark colors. I look like I'm dressed for a picnic." As we will see, in *The Act of Killing* this kind of reflexive practice can lead to a self-examination of a much deeper kind.

The intersubjective character of *The Act of Killing* is also unmistakable in the foregrounding of the cinematic apparatus, a major feature of French New Wave experimentation and political modernism in the late 1960s and 1970s. Oppenheimer's subject is much more the preparation for the shoot than the presumed product, the film that the gangsters envision but that will remain forever unfinished. We see, for example, the film crew setting up the lighting for one of the studio-shot sequences. We then watch makeup artists transform Anwar's and Adi's faces into grotesque masks of suffering while the two gangsters converse in a close two-shot about the moral survival of the murderer: "Killing is the worst crime you can do. So the key is to find a way not to feel guilty." Indeed, *The Act of Killing* seems to belong at times to that new genre, "the making of," a frequent bonus feature in DVD releases of films: how the actor-screenwriters conceptualize a sequence (what they should include, what should be left out); how the actor-directors experiment with staging (whether or not to offer the victim a smoke); how the actor-filmmakers reflect after the fact on what they have produced (how effective it is as filmmaking or what impact it may have on the public). Scenes are never rendered as complete, self-sufficient pieces of narration.

Third, Jean Rouch, a major source of inspiration for the French New Wave, pushed against the boundaries that separate nonfiction from fiction. In his innovative *Moi, un noir* (1958), he encouraged his "subjects," Nigerian immigrants who had come to the Ivory Coast in search of work, to give expression to their dreams. Thus, he not only recorded the immigrants in the tribulations of their daily lives, but also documented their fantasies. Rouch's actors indulge in playful whimsy: Oumarou Ganda takes the pseudonym of Edward G. Robinson, Petit Touré calls himself Eddie Constantine, and Alassane identifies himself as Tarzan. This "ethnofiction" (as the genre was later dubbed) embraces the sort of cinematic references that will characterize *The Act of Killing*. As I attempt to show in the following analyses, it is the impulse to fictionalize that pushes the gangsters toward revelations they did not anticipate. Indeed, gratifying one's fantasies by projecting them into the public space of representation is fraught with danger.

THE FILMMAKER LIES IN WAIT

Oppenheimer's intentions and those of his gangster *metteurs en scène* are not the same. Indeed, the difference between them is the crux of meaning in *The Act of Killing*. This may seem an obvious observation, but some critics of the film cast Oppenheimer in the role of the investigator who becomes implicated in the evil he is studying, a figure familiar in literary and cinematic fiction. Many images the gangsters produce are indeed so blatantly amoral and abhorrent to humanist sensibilities that some spectators find them unwatchable. It is easy, then, to lay the responsibility for these abominations at the feet of the person who has made them possible. And indeed Oppenheimer is a facilitator, and he has run the risk of seeming to be outside the game, simply recording his gangsters' arrogant fantasies. How much more palatable such images would be if they were accompanied by the voiceover of moral outrage. But Oppenheimer obviously does not deal in the palatable. He is not interested in undercutting the power of the gangsters' representations of their own history. However the question remains: In the world of horrors that *The Act of Killing* constructs, where do we find the critical distance without which the film would lose its analytic capacity and its moral footing?

Part of the answer lies in the scandal the images provoke in us, as we watch Anwar Congo dancing the cha-cha-cha on the rooftop of death or see the complicit smile he directs at the filmmaker after his demonstration of death by strangulation. The gestures are so unseemly and delivered with such a sense of impunity that they stand as their own critique. This kind of critique depends of course on the context of reception. We know to what extent censorship conditioned the Indonesian public to passively accept their history of violence. In an interview on Indonesian television, portions of which Oppenheimer includes in *The Act of Killing*, Anwar basks in the glory of his past whose violence the newscaster refers to with utter complacency. It would of course be another matter when the completed film was shown in circles of human rights activists and to international audiences. Then the very act of exposure constituted an act of judgment. One is stunned to learn that the gangsters, except for the more worldly Adi, who realized what they were in for, were taken aback, indeed quite hurt, by the film's reception outside Indonesia's zones of censorship.

Perhaps more important, critical distance comes into play in Oppenheimer's sensitivity to moments when something untoward is about to take place. Something cracks in the process of filming the sequences the gangsters have elaborated, and an unscripted moment—a reality of one sort or another—intrudes. Such moments are of course common in the production of any film. This is when the director calls out "Cut!" so that the diegetic effects he or she is seeking to produce can be preserved. All can be repaired on the editing table. Oppenheimer, on the other hand, keeps the camera rolling when representation fractures, and he has not the least intention of correcting such "mistakes" on the editing table. He is not interested in maintaining clear continuity and producing the unproblematic narrative the gangsters have conceived. Rather, he lies in wait for the unanticipated, for latent realities, suppressed but tenacious, that call out for expression. It is important to recall that Oppenheimer, after eight years of investigation and shooting, chose to center his film on Anwar Congo. He "lingered" with him because he saw that in Anwar, contrary to the hardened shells of the other gangsters he interviewed, pain was close to the surface.

A particularly striking example of Oppenheimer's strategy can be seen in a pair of sequences in *The Act of Killing* that "mirror" each other across more than an hour of the text and represent two different stages in Anwar Congo's psychological evolution and self-awareness. Both are shot in studio and reenact, in the style of film noir, the torture and execution of one of the gangsters' victims. In this controlled environment, Oppenheimer exploits the full potential of multiple cameras capable of producing the psychological effects typical of analytic editing. The cut to the close-up from the medium shot is repeatedly used. In the first sequence, which occurs twenty-eight minutes into the film, Anwar and Herman play members of the gang. Herman wields a knife; Anwar torments the victim with the offer of a "neo-colonialist" cigar. The close-ups focus on Anwar, not on the anonymous victim. Anwar is totally at ease in his role. He helps tie the victim to a table, then in medium shot crawls into the dark space under the table to secure the garroting wire around his neck. As he emerges, he feels enough in charge to halt the shooting because he hears from off-screen the muezzin's call to prayer: "Hold on, Joshua. It's evening prayers." Oppenheimer, ever watchful, keeps his camera running as the sounds of daily devotion invade the space where violent men seek the representation of their violent acts. The irony, to which the gangsters seem impervious, intensifies as the actors wait to return to their work and talk scornfully about human rights. Caught in close-up, Anwar paces as he expresses his pride in being a "free man," the Dutch expression that designates the gangster. "Back then there were no human rights," he continues. "There are people like me everywhere in the world." The last shots shows Anwar and Herman seated near the window, fanning themselves with their hats in the intolerable heat.

Inexplicably, in the second sequence, which occurs an hour and forty minutes into the film, Anwar is cast in the role of the victim of torture. Surely this reversal of positions was engineered by Oppenheimer because this is precisely what he wants Anwar to experience. Will playing the role generate a moment of empathy? He must have known that at this point in Anwar's development, the gangster might respond to the stimulus.

The sequence is preceded by an extended close-up of Anwar in a rear-view mirror, from the surreptitious point of view I previously described. Slowly opening and closing his eyes, he is clearly under the sway of a disturbing emotion. On the set, Anwar receives the final touches of the makeup that creates his bloody face. This sequence itself, like the first, is analytically edited, and plays out in the same chiaroscuro lighting. Again Oppenheimer employs an alternation between medium and close shots: the former frame Anwar in a chair surrounded by his tormentors; the latter are close-ups of Anwar's face in which we begin to detect real feelings emerging from the mechanics of play acting. The victim is no longer anonymous: he is at once Anwar the real gangster and the bigshot Communist Anwar plays. We are now focused on the victim's reactions, particularly in close-up.

At first, Anwar appears to be in control. He says to Herman: "Hit the table to frighten me." Herman complies, threatens Anwar with a knife to his throat, then ties a blindfold across his eyes. At this moment the close-up on Anwar's face is disquieting. Herman places the garroting wire around Anwar's neck and steps back to increase the tension. Anwar begins to gurgle to feign strangulation, and then something untoward occurs. In medium shot, we see Anwar raise his right hand, presumably tied behind his back, to the level of his leg where it appears to shake uncontrollably. Herman is unnerved: "Are you alright?" he asks as he loosens the wire. Anwar responds, "I can't do that again." A voice cries "Cut!" but the camera continues to roll as we watch Anwar slowly blowing air in and out in an attempt to recover self-control. The regrettable omission of footage in the theatrical cut that we see in the director's cut is the more gradual build in tension in this sequence as Anwar slowly comes unglued. The wire is stretched around his neck twice, not once, and the close-ups of Anwar's reactions to the menace of torture are more frequent and more prolonged.

SCREENING OUT HISTORY

The sudden transition from fictional reenactment to real experience is, Oppenheimer tells us, the objective of the strategy he developed for the film. As he reveals in his interview for *Democracy Now!*, Anwar and his colleagues, given carte blanche to reenact events in whatever manner they chose, began to embellish scenes, giving them an increasingly surreal character, "which I filmed because they were allegories for a system of impunity." Allegories, however, are symbolic structures intended to stand for hidden moral and political meanings (etymologically, "allegory" is "other speaking"). There is, in this sense, nothing allegorical about what Oppenheimer captures on camera. Through the gangsters' extravagant burlesque we are probing the dark underbelly of their unconscionable violence.

Although the political dimension of *The Act of Killing* is front and center in the film and in the filmmaker's discourse about his film, this is only part of what Oppenheimer is really after. He wants to know the gangster from the inside, and to do so means breaking through the killer's hardened defenses. How terrifying is it to realize that Anwar and his cohorts would leave the movie house where they had seen an Elvis Presley musical, dance across the street to their office, climb the stairs to the roof garden where, still under the sway of the musical's ebullient mood, they would proceed to execute their victims? How wrenching is it to see Anwar, having just given a demonstration of how to perform a bloodless execution, dance the cha cha cha with such heartless indifference in that morbid location? How disconcerting is it to watch Anwar's reflection in the mirror of a salon where he is having his hair dyed blithely talk about how life—his ruthless life of violence—imitates art: "I was influenced by stars like Marlon Brando, Al Pacino [in obvious reference to *The Godfather*]. Those were my favorites. And Westerns with John Wayne."

Imitations of this kind combine the real and the imaginary in a manner characteristic of metaphoric figures, fusing the two terms of the comparison. It is as if the gangster were saying, "In life, I performed this real act of murder, but I assumed, at the very moment of the act, the fabricated identity of a fictional character." Not only does the imaginary embellish the real; it also helps defend the murderer against the real experience of his acts. In the reenactments they produce for *The Act of Killing*, the gangsters engage in exactly this kind of metaphoric play: the cinematic screen—with its fictional characters, locations, and actions—functions as a screen in the psychological sense. It shields the players from the perils of memory—the kind of involuntary memory that threatens to precipitate them into an unbearable experience of the past. They adopt the trappings of cinematic fiction in the Hollywood manner. Certain genres obviously appeal to them. The fantastical costumes, saturated colors, and choreographed movements of the musical create moments of pure denial and self-aggrandizement. The sordid locales, the slouched hat brims and trench coats, and low-key lighting of the film-noir gangster film allow them to reenact a scene of torture within the protective structures of that kind of fiction.

The "first-line" *metteurs en scène*—the gangsters who are responsible for restaging their own actions—*hyperbolize* every element of mise-en-scène. Musical numbers, for example, are not just abstracted from the film's narration; they appear as free-standing oneiric spectacle, self-indulgent fantasies fixated on the display of the female body. As I mentioned earlier, the gigantic fish on the banks of a river disgorges a line of beautiful women dressed in yellow satin and dancing, not without a certain self-conscious awkwardness, in the manner of, say, nightclub scenes in Douglas Sirk's *Imitation of Life*. Without, of course, Sirk's dark irony. In another sequence, the film's central gangster figure, Anwar Congo, appears in apotheosis (he is costumed in monk's robes) in the exotic setting of a waterfall and palm trees, where he is surrounded by beautiful women dressed in red and white gowns as we hear strains of "Born Free."

Perhaps the most uncanny representation of gangster violence takes on the genre conventions of the Western. Consider the following brief sequence:

1. A close-up shows Anwar wearing a cowboy hat. He puts a retainer in his mouth, and we wait as he clicks it in place.

2. In medium shot, a dresser adjusts Anwar's costume. Anwar's voiceover begins: "What's clear is no film has ever used our method."

3. A long shot frames Anwar swinging a lasso and Herman in drag (the dominant color is turquoise). The landscape emulates the Western's expansive grasslands with mountains in the background.

4. A medium shot shows Anwar on horseback as the voiceover continues: "We can attract a huge audience!"

5. A medium long shot shows Herman in white pants and a black brassiere. Anwar pursues his commentary: "Humor, it's a must!"

6. A close-up shows Herman in drag being coiffed by a hairdresser, and in the background cattle stand behind barbed wire.

7. A long shot frames Herman in drag with a multicolored umbrella seated on a cart drawn by an ox.

8. A medium shot shows Herman tossing the umbrella, shouting, "Fuck this umbrella!" The voiceover continues: "Herman's trapped. He should scream, 'Leave me alone! Stop! Stop!'"

9. A medium shot reveals Anwar directing the action, the crew in the background: "Meanwhile, the three of us scream, 'You Communist bitch!' (Anwar spits). Keep attacking her."

10. In medium shot, Herman in drag is being pursued by a lascivious cowboy: "I'm gonna rape you! I'm gonna kill you!" He slaps "her" to the ground and blood appears on "her" face.

11. Again in medium shot, the cowboy slaps Herman's naked fat belly and derides him: "How long have you been pregnant? You'll give birth to a Communist!"

12. An axis match of the previous shot shows a wider view. Voiceover: "But if the audience is tense the whole time with nothing to entertain them, it will never work." The cowboy grabs Herman's breast.

It is difficult to imagine a representation of real events as bizarre, as dissonant as this sequence. The humor of parody, as Anwar self-consciously acknowledges, is intended to deflate the meaning of violent acts. The grotesque as a hyperbolic mode of representation subverts the audience's ability to identify with characters and recognize their suffering. The whole "method" whose originality Anwar extolls consists in blending the incompatible: the reference to sinister acts of violence by which thousands were brutalized and murdered and the representation they are given in a kind of sneering reflexivity. In addition, there is the reflexive character the sequence openly displays through Anwar's commentary on method and on the action he is directing.

LATENT ANXIETY SURFACES

We should not be surprised to discover that in a community that has never officially recognized its history of genocide, never acknowledged its victims, indeed has never permitted any public representation of Indonesians' historical experience of violence, fear lies very close to the surface. Indonesians, including the gangsters' family, friends, and neighbors, are reluctant to play the part of the victims in reenactments, as if this fictional association might put them at risk. Anwar's neighbor Suryono asks the gangsters to include in their film the story of his stepfather, murdered in the systematic purge of the ethnic Chinese who were considered, ipso facto, Communists. In the massive expulsion of "enemies" of the state, Suryono's stepfather was called out of the house one night and disappeared, his body discovered under an oil drum. "We [the other members of the family] were dumped in a shantytown at the edge of the jungle," the stepson continues. The gangsters, made visibly uncomfortable by Suryono's narrative, respond: "We can't include every story or the film will never end."

In a subsequent sequence, Suryono has agreed to play the part of the victim to be tortured. It is simply a rehearsal in which the gangsters reconstruct aspects of their sadistic methods: the glass of water they force on the victim, the cigarette they offer, the blindfold intended to terrorize. Oppenheimer's camera fixes the victim in close-up, tied in a chair, as one gangster says, "Ask him again about his activities." Suryono is visibly shaken, breaks into tears, and sobs as he begs for mercy. His face contorts, he drools, snot running from his nostrils, as another gangster asks, "Should we kill him?" Oppenheimer interpolates between the close-ups of Suryono shots of the reactions of the gangsters, particularly Anwar, who appear dumbfounded by the raw emotion they have provoked.

Something similar occurs, but on a much grander scale, when the gangsters stage the massacre of the residents of Kampung Kolam, in the set of village huts constructed amid a forest of decapitated palm trees. The Indonesian Deputy Minister of Youth and Sports, Sakhyan Asmara, arrives and embraces Anwar: "Wow! All the killers are here!" Standing imposingly atop his jeep, he is there to encourage the actors: "Just improvise and express your anger." The first take begins. We see Anwar in close-up egging on his actors: "Take no prisoners! Destroy them all!" We see Pancasila Youth with torches about to attack and hear a voice from off-screen urging, "Chop off their heads! Burn them! Kill them all!" A medium shot reveals the Minister of Youth who is clearly taken aback, and then Herman intervenes shouting, "Cut! Cut! Cut!" The minister cautions the cast and crew, "We shouldn't look brutal, like we want to drink people's blood. That's dangerous for our organization's image."

A brief interlude occurs: in a long take we see Anwar lying in bed in the dark unable to sleep while in the background images of a boxing match flicker on a television screen.

Oppenheimer presents the massacre as a montage sequence, a succession of rapidly cut images, many overlaid with images of fire. The Pancasila Youth drag their victims across the ground, attack a defenseless man, raise a helpless young boy above their heads, terrify a young girl, their machetes poised in the air, and so forth. Eventually we hear "Cut! Cut! Cut!" as a long shot frames members of the youth brigade standing above the amassed bodies of their victims. The bodies start to rise, some smiling, others clearly in shock. The histrionics of the scenes of mayhem, fired up by Herman and Pancasila commandos, have had their effect: many participants—for the most part relatives or neighbors of the gangsters—are overcome by their own, presumably feigned emotions. A voice calls for water. A close shot shows us three children weeping. In long shot we see an old woman prostrate and stunned. A member of the Pancasila Youth comes to comfort her, blowing air across her face and hair. A two-shot shows us Herman helplessly trying to console a young girl who is weeping uncontrollably: "Febby, your acting was great. But stop crying. You're embarrassing me. Film stars only cry for a moment."

MURDER WILL OUT

In a static sequence-shot, Oppenheimer frames Anwar and Herman in relaxed poses (Anwar with one leg crossed, Herman eating a banana) as Anwar the theorist discourses on violent action in films and audience response:

> Why do people watch James Bond? To see action. Why do people watch films about Nazis? To see power and sadism! We can do that! We can make something even more sadistic than what you see in movies about Nazis. . . . Because there's never been a movie where heads get chopped off—because I did it in real life!

Not everything can be contained, even circumscribed by the conventions of genre. The extra twist in Anwar's self-portrait as the sadistic killer is that he is not just an actor, he "did it in real life." Oppenheimer intuits in Anwar a yearning to break through his ego defenses. With the proper preparation by Oppenheimer the analyst (to speak in Freudian terms), Anwar the patient will succumb to his own desire to express (in the literal meaning of the word) what he has so long pushed back into his unconscious mind. He will then confront the reality of his own acts, and experience them as a living part of his being. We have already seen how cracks can appear in the logical structures of representation when Anwar the perpetrator assumes the position of the victim.

Oppenheimer is obviously eager at moments to get Anwar alone, to isolate him from the bravado and banter of his cohorts, so that he can probe feelings that would otherwise remain dormant. In a haunting sequence, apparently shot at Anwar's instigation, Oppenheimer films his subject as he travels by train to a location in the countryside, the site of an atrocity he committed that has deeply disturbed him. As the camera shifts between shots of the countryside taken from the train and a medium shot of Anwar seated in the railway car, we hear him explain the pull of this particular place: "Why am I coming to this place? Because it affected me deeply. Because the method of killing was very different. Is it because I've been telling you my story so honestly? Or maybe the vengeance of the dead? I remember I said, 'Get out of the car.'"

The imagery changes radically: we see a sky, blue with dusk, and the flight of countless birds. In voice-off, Anwar continues: "He asked, 'Where are you taking me?' Soon he refused to keep walking. . . . I saw Roshiman bringing me a machete." A medium close shot reveals Anwar in his haunted site, obscurely lit, his back against the trunk of a tree. He continues the narrative: "Spontaneously, I walked over to him and cut his head off. [He imitates the gesture of the coup de grâce.] My friends didn't want to look. They ran back to the car. And I heard this sound. [Anwar gurgles.] His body had fallen down and the eyes in his head were still open." Anwar looks up, his own eyes shining in the light. Now the camera frames Anwar in long shot as he lifts himself up. "On the way home, I kept thinking, why didn't I close his eyes? All I could think about was why I didn't close his eyes?" The camera shifts back to the medium close shot that frames Anwar as he stretches out his hand. "And that is the source of all my nightmares. I'm always gazed at by those eyes I didn't close." The sequence closes with a shot repeating the motif of bird flights against the night sky.

In this sequence, Anwar exposes himself in the most intimate manner. Oppenheimer is careful to suggest how privileged the moment is, how confidential. He uses the two shots of dusk and flying birds to set the scene off from the brightly lit shots of green landscapes over which Anwar's dark narration begins. We recognize this framing device because the filmmaker has used it before to emphasize the urban context within which the action takes place: deserted cityscapes redolent of moral emptiness or architectural spaces alive with jarring movement and reflective surfaces. In the darkness of this place, a deep correspondence emerges. Anwar's face strives toward the light, resonating with the spiritual intensity we attach to chiaroscuro lighting. Oppenheimer is careful not to cut into this moment of exposure. There are only three shots—the central one, a long shot, creating momentary relief from the pathos of the two closer shots. (Even more affecting, the director's cut includes more continuous and longer takes.) Otherwise,

Oppenheimer allows Anwar to narrate his experience uninterrupted by the tools of cinematic representation. In the manner of a Rossellini faced with a revelatory moment, Oppenheimer respects the integrity of the event. He is aware that in this isolated and fleeting moment his camera is watching someone being possessed by the past.

THINGS FALL APART

The Act of Killing is, among many other things, the study of a man who, under the pressure of memory, is increasingly unable to hold it together. In a sequence near the end of the film, Anwar once again loses his balance. The sequence is very simply structured as a point of view series, an alternation between shots of the person looking and shots of what he is looking at. It opens with a close-up of Anwar, dressed with his usual flamboyance and seated in an equally flamboyant throne-like chair. The camera, implacable instrument of analysis, records in intimate detail the emotions that cross his face.

The sequence unfolds in absolute continuity but the continuous take of Anwar in close-up is broken by seven shots of a television monitor showing moments from the sequence of torture in which he plays the part of the victim. During these moments, Anwar's commentary and exchanges with the filmmaker are heard off-screen. In the first shot Anwar says, "You know the scene where I'm strangled with wire? Please put it on." He lights a cigarette. While an image of his bloodied head appears on the monitor, we hear off-screen Anwar calling his grandson: "Yan? I want him to watch this." We return to the close-up of Anwar: "Yan, come see grandpa beaten up and bleeding." Anwar gets up and exits the frame. While he is gone, we continue to stare at the baroque ornamentation of the chair.

Anwar reenters the frame and gathers his two sleepy grandsons on his lap. Anwar asks the filmmakers to turn up the volume and is unresponsive to the voice from off-screen: "But this is too violent, Anwar. Are you sure?" The point of view series continues, the dark spectrum of the scene of torture contrasting with the brightly lit, saturated colors that show Anwar and his grandsons. Anwar reassures his grandsons that "this is only a film," but is overtaken by the realism of his own performance. He smiles broadly as he says, "It's so sad, isn't it? That's your grandpa. That's your grandpa being beaten up by the fat guy. Grandpa's head is smashed." The children look dazed, and Yan giggles. Anwar kisses one grandson, and the children leave the frame.

Alone again on screen and confronted with his suffering image, Anwar's face turns serious; he winces and half closes his eyes. "Did the people I tortured feel the way I do here?" he asks. We see Anwar the actor threatened with a knife. "I can feel what the people I tortured felt." In close-up again, Anwar gestures with his hands as if he were trying to grasp something. "Because my dignity has been destroyed." He glances off-screen: ". . . and then fear comes, right then and there. All the terror suddenly possesses my body. It surrounded me and possessed me." A voice from off-screen tells him: "Actually, the people you tortured felt far worse (Anwar looks stunned) because you know it's only a film. They knew they were being killed." Anwar replies: "But I can feel it, Josh (his face contorts and his eyes tear up). Really I can feel it. Or have I sinned? Is it all coming back to me? I really hope it won't. I don't want it to, Josh." Anwar shakes his head as if to rid himself of a vision.

I have cited this sequence in considerable detail because it illustrates how it is that the past can come to inhabit the present. As we have seen in other films in this study, this often occurs as a sudden and highly charged moment of recognition. As he calls for the torture scene to be replayed, Anwar surely remembers the emotions his role-playing evoked in him at the time and how risky reviewing the footage may be for his psychological defenses. He calls for his grandson Yan. We know from the sequence in which Anwar asks Yan to apologize to a duckling whose leg the child has broken, that his love for his grandchildren is his connection with lost innocence, just as in *S-21* we first see the torturer Him Houy in the heart of his family caressing his naked baby son on his lap while complaining of insomnia and headaches. Anwar has—and not unwittingly—staged his own moment of revelation.

Yan and his brother are narrative *helpers*: they bring pressure to bear on their grandfather's latent feelings and thus push him toward recognition. Anwar's awareness seems to vacillate. On the one hand, he is defensive—"this is only a film"; on the other hand, these bloody images are his and simultaneously the images of his countless victims.

Anwar the spectator, Anwar the actor, and Anwar the character are engaged in a devastating movement of identification. He holds it together until his grandsons leave. Then he evokes his state of mind and asks the questions that can lead only to painful disclosures. If he can conceive of his own suffering when he acts out the position of the other, his victim, then he can conceive of the suffering he has caused others in real life. The contract of fiction—this is only a representation and therefore I am not in danger—is broken. We hear Anwar's stunned voice ("Is it all coming back to me?"), acknowledging that he is pulling together the face of the past and the face of the present, as Frank Ankersmit so eloquently put it. And we see the transmutation in Anwar's face and in his desperate gestures—in the nonverbal signs of a devastating recognition.

It is not at all surprising that this sequence is followed by the haunting episode that closes the film. In long shot we see Anwar, dressed in a mustard yellow suit, approach the entrance of what once was the gangster's office, now a boutique. The camera follows him as he crosses the salesroom, lined with handbags suspended from rods. We see Anwar in medium shot as he crosses the storeroom, where stacks of bags in plastic line the floor. In long shot we see him begin to climb the stairway. On the rooftop, two very long takes in medium shot show Anwar reacting to what he sees and remembers. The camera shadows his movements and pauses as he does for long moments of silent reflection. Anwar acknowledges, "This is where we tortured and killed the people we captured." A long pause follows. "I know it was wrong—but I had to do it," he confesses—*almost* confesses, since the murders were somehow beyond his control. He paces, then begins to retch. He leans over a long basin and continues to retch. The camera gives him no quarter as it continues to roll.

A second long take shows Anwar seated on the edge of the basin. He picks up a length of wire, a piece of wood attached at the end. We recognize the wire: he left it there after he demonstrated his strangulation technique early in the film. "This is . . . one of the easiest ways to take a human life. And this (lifting up a gunny sack) was used to take away the human being we killed. Because without this . . . maybe people would know." He begins to retch again, spits, wipes his mouth, and then stares into space for a long moment. A long shot frames Anwar's diminished figure in the rooftop doorway as he slowly begins to descend the stairs. A deep shot of the salesroom frames Anwar in the background as he pauses at the door, then exits and turns left. The static, empty shot is held for a very long moment, and the only action we see and hear is the traffic passing in the street.

Very little explication is needed to understand the import of this sequence. Oppenheimer's camera is a moral force that traps Anwar in this sinister confessional. The ironic rows of handbags under florescent lighting deflate any pretension of grandeur. The penitent's climb toward the place of his ordeal and his descent as a diminished human figure have strong mythological resonance. The verbal confession of wrongdoing he makes on the rooftop is inept and incommensurate with the crimes he is charged with. The dry retching, which Oppenheimer records unmercifully, is a much more potent avowal. Anwar's body would purge itself of its sickness of the soul but to no avail. Re-experiencing the past does not promise resolution. Whatever his fantasies propose, Anwar's victims will never thank him for executing them and sending them to heaven.

KNOW THYSELF

As Arthur Danto reminds us, Aristotle, in *The Poetics*, gave us a stunning insight into the psychological dimension of mimetic representations: "The sight of certain things gives us pain, but we enjoy looking at the most exact imitations of them, whether the forms of animals which we greatly despise or of corpses."[4] Pleasure depends, of course, on the sort of contractual guarantee that spectacle offers, as psychoanalyst Octave Mannoni describes in his brilliant analysis of theatrical illusion: "When the curtain rises, it is the imaginary powers of the Ego which are at once liberated and organized—dominated by the spectacle."[5] But as we have seen in *The Act of Killing*, things are much less clear when the "master of the game"—Anwar Congo—is telling his own terrifying story, no matter what distance he attempts to take from his harrowing past. Although he seems less vulnerable the more fantastical the spectacle he imagines, irony, humor, and all the trappings of mise en scène are ultimately not enough to protect him from the sinister "real things" he attempts to transfigure. A feigned corpse can without warning become a real corpse, or at least the living memory of a real corpse. Indeed, we have witnessed the chilling moments when Anwar falls from the realm of the imaginary into the realm of the real, as he does so painfully in the last sequence of the film. His exit from the rooftop killing field and from the film is full of existential pain and suggests that the dangerous game he is now fated to play is far from over.

It is worth following a bit further Danto's analysis of mirror theories of mimetic representation in "Works of Art and Mere Real Things." Plato's Socrates confirms (with what touch of irony, we're not sure) the metaphor of representation as "a mirror held up to nature," the prevalent conception of the mimetic arts in the ancient world. If the theory has not survived unscathed, Danto turns our attention to one "asymmetrical" feature of mirrors to which "Socrates was curiously insensitive" and which opens up, he amply demonstrates, a richer analytic perspective. "There are things," he observes, "we may see in [mirrors] we cannot see without them, namely ourselves,"[6] in particular, I would add, those areas of the physical self—the face and the gesturing body— that are, we suppose, most expressive of our inner beings. It appears that, for the ancients, the myth of Narcissus stood as the first model of likeness as representation. Narcissus falls into a state of rapture upon seeing his own reflection on the surface of a spring. Faced with an irresistible object—another reality—he can see but not touch, Narcissus becomes aware that the image he has so intensely cathected is his own and dies of thwarted love. Self-knowledge, Danto tells us, led to this "epistemological suicide to be taken seriously by those who suppose 'know thyself,' Socrates' celebrated cognitive imperative, can be pursued with impunity."[7]

The "hero" of *The Act of Killing*, Anwar Congo, is a Narcissus-like figure. He falls under the spell of his own image—not a reflection given in reality but a self-presentation he carefully constructs for his own pleasure. In "life," he is an incurable dandy, an exhibitionist obsessed with his appearance. He dyes his hair, sports flashy clothes, choreographs his movements, observes himself in mirrors, and controls the settings in which he exhibits himself. Recall, for example, the sequence in which Anwar relives, on video, the moments in which he, the perpetrator, plays the role of the victim of violence—a dangerous substitution, as we saw. He is posed on a throne-like chair, calls his grandsons to watch the footage on his lap, and glibly compliments the realism of his own performance, in the manner of the child-like "Look at me, look at me!" It is a moment of fascinated self-absorption that leads to an unexpected turn of the screw. Anwar comes to an awareness, through role reversal, of the unbearable suffering he has caused others: I have felt what they felt, he confidently asserts. This is not a moment of true empathy, we immediately realize, because Anwar remains narcissistically fixated on his own feigned emotions. It takes the voice of "Joshua"—Oppenheimer speaking to him from off-screen—to alert him to the difference between the suffering one may experience *as if* one were dying and the suffering of those who *know* they are dying.

This brings us to a second mirror theory of mimetic representation, which Danto ascribes to Shakespeare, or rather to one of Shakespeare's characters. "Hamlet," Danto tells us, "made a far deeper use of the metaphor: mirrors and then, by generalization, artworks, rather than giving us back what we can already know without benefit of them, serve instead as instruments of self-revelation."[8] In *Hamlet*, Hamlet the prince, haunted by his father's ghost, devises a strategy for confronting Claudius, the usurper king, who has murdered his father and married his mother. He stages a play, *The Death of Gonzago*, whose plot and characters hold up a mirror to the king's murderous acts. Claudius, the spectator of dramatic actions that too closely resemble his own, comes face to face with the representation of his crimes in a moment of recognition that is complex in structure. As Danto puts it, at this moment of revelation, Claudius "perceives that Hamlet knows that Claudius knows that Hamlet knows the shameful truths."[9]

Danto "updates" this reflexive mechanism of recognition by suggesting that its structure is Sartrian in character. Sartre proposed the distinction between the *Pour-soi* (the knowledge one has of one's conscious states) and the *Pour-autrui* (the recognition of oneself as the object of the gaze of other people): "It comes as an unforeseeable metaphysical surprise, accordingly, that the *Pour-soi* realizes that it has another mode of being altogether, that *it* is an object for others." It is through the other that the subject can conceive of itself as an *object*:

"it comes to the recognition that it has, as it were, an outside and an inside, whereas the *Pour-soi* alone would be "metaphysically sideless.""[10]

This kind of "marvelous coentrapment of consciousness" has an even more complex structure in *The Act of Killing*. Unlike, Claudius, Anwar Congo has not concealed the murderous acts he has committed. Indeed, he appears devoid of shame and delights in demonstrating—representing—them for others in often playful guises. Until his encounter with Oppenheimer, the Other for Anwar was the iniquitous culture of the Indonesian government and its ruling cliques. His "inside" has been comfortingly validated by his "outside." He basks in his well-earned celebrity as an anti-Communist hero: killing "Communists" is not after all a crime. He is only symptomatically aware that his psychic equilibrium is an illusion and that the guilt he represses is working its way toward consciousness. For his part, Oppenheimer does not play the game of *metteur en scène* in the manner of Hamlet. His strategy is to conceal his status as an (oppositional) Other: he plays along, appearing to collude with Anwar. All the while Oppenheimer the provocateur pushes Anwar toward the moral awareness he senses is welling up within his being and that can only be expressed through the visceral response of his body.

There is then a basic discrepancy between the two collaborators' intentions and the different eyes they cast on the representations they "co-author." There are in effect two "plays": the one Anwar believes he is constructing and the one Oppenheimer delivers to us as spectators. The fact that Anwar's accounts of events are distorted by fantasy and bent to the conventions of the Hollywood cinema serves to stave off recognition—his, not ours. Such is the function of "humor" in such representations, as Anwar the theorist makes explicit in commenting on his method for "directing" the film's Western sequence. The mirror is warped. The distortion, carefully nurtured by Anwar as metteur en scène, delays the moment of self-revelation: the recognition not only of the nature of his acts but also their meaning that imperils his soul. It is the "guileless" Oppenheimer, so patient and yet so vigilant, who stages the moment of revelation.

As the film ends, we are left with the feeling that Anwar's breakthrough is temporary: that he can confront the Other only in moments of extreme, let us say *ecstatic*, experience. Indeed, he must defeat the defensive forces of the ego, find himself "possessed" by an unconscious drive to acknowledge the judgment rendered, however fleetingly, by what remains of his moral being. Indeed, one wonders how Anwar's wounded soul could ever confront that overwhelming Other: the reproachful eyes focused on his acts of killing by thousands of spectators across the world.

EPILOGUE

THERE IS an essential dimension to all the films in this study that I have not emphasized, perhaps because it is so obvious: each film stands as a piece of political discourse with quite specific political objectives. Andrzej Wajda is settling accounts with mendacious Russia, Poland's historic enemy, provoking it where it hurts the most: in its will to preserve the image of irreproachable heroism in the Great Patriotic War. Andrei Konchalovsky and Larisa Shepitko take aim at the crumbling myths of Stalinist positivism that persist like whited sepulchers in the Brezhnev era—attacks fueled by an archaic myth of origins or by an obsolete Christian iconography. Using techniques of textual deconstruction and living testimony, Yaël Hersonski touches the reality of the experience of the Warsaw Ghetto and exposes the lying images of a Nazi documentary that had been taken by many as transparent representation. Aware of the ultimate failure of his project to expose the crimes of the Pinochet dictatorship through his historical documentaries, Patricio Guzmán tries another tack: he undermines Chile's official history through a poetic meditation on the past in which subjective experience, including his own, emerges from memory and the mineral realities of the Atacama desert.

It is perhaps paradoxical to speak of these films as political discourse since they are not at all polemical, nor do they reduce historical realities to a closed narrative in which abstract social forces play out their destinies. They derive most of their power from atomized moments when historical experience speaks directly and fleetingly of itself and nothing else. Rithy Panh and Joshua Oppenheimer are both muckrakers in the sense that they aim to disturb the layers of sediment that time and political obfuscation have laid down to protect entrenched evil. Their projects are undeniably political, and the political repercussions of *S-21* and *The Act of Killing* were profound and continue to reverberate. Yet, as we have seen, Panh and Oppenheimer are particularly distinguished by the radical strategies they developed to recover the experience of the past. Is this perhaps the distinctive mark of innovative historical films in the twenty-first century, a paradoxical politics by other means? When the past and the present bring their heads together, does what we reexperience lead to a new kind of political discourse? Is this not the project of Susana de Sousa Diaz in her film *48* (2009), composed of the mug shots of political prisoners of Portugal's autocratic regime against which we hear the former prisoners' testimony recorded in the present?

These questions lead me to reflect again on the ideas of the philosophers and historians I have cited extensively throughout this book. First, I have been guided by Frank Ankersmit's fundamental insight that experience, in the historiographic tradition, has always been the acquiescent partner of interpretation, the process of producing meaning from the traces of human events. Experience is assumed to exist as a necessary substratum without which historic discourse would appear ungrounded in the material world of the past. Ankersmit's most important gesture is to "pull apart" *experience* from the *representation of meaning* and thereby give to experience "an autonomy it never had under the dispensation in which 'experience' and the 'representation of meaning' were always indiscriminately lumped together" as interpretation.[1] Historical representation always involves historicization and contextualization, that is, the logical reconstruction of what must have happened in the past and the circumstances that help explain why things happened as they did.

Experience of the past, on the other hand, appears in a flash of substantial reality, disconnected from the logical sequence of events and unconcerned about questions of motivation. To make this distinction clear, Ankersmit uses a simple metaphor. Imagine, he suggests, that you are in an airplane flying above a landscape whose topography you can reconstruct intellectually but which a dense cloud layer makes invisible. With the support of documents you are able to represent the landscape in your mind. Then, imagine a sudden break in the cloud cover that opens up a fragment of real space that you see in relief and in all its detail.[2] It is a *perception*, a fragment of space/time that strikes you the observer in its phenomenological richness. The constructed topography, by contrast, is a product of language. It is a product of *cognition*. Ankersmit is clear about language's failings—the obverse of its triumphs—and his words bring into focus what is at stake in the films in this study:

> Language presents us with an image of the world, but as such it can offer only the shadow of the terrors inhabiting the world itself and of the fears it may provoke. Language, the symbolic order, enables us to escape the perplexities of a direct confrontation with the world as it is given to us in experience.[3]

As I have attempted to show, what distinguishes *S-21* is that the film not only offers a reconstruction of the killing machine—its procedures and tactics, the testimony of its victims and perpetrators, its mission; it also gives us, at moments that Rithy Panh has carefully orchestrated, an immediate contact with events. We are confronted with "the terrors inhabiting the world itself" and the "fears it may provoke." We cannot occupy two positions at once: we cannot explain and experience at the same moment, although the best history concerns itself with both the outside and the inside of events. This double vision of history in which historical reconstruction alternates with immediate experience is equally characteristic of all the films in this study.

Paradoxically, the recovery of experience, which takes place momentarily and in the specific circumstances I have described, has a dramatic impact on our understanding of history and incites us to speak about the past in ways that scientific history closes off. The desire to avoid the pain of speaking publicly about brutal historical events, expressed in statements like "It happened so long ago," "It is time for reconciliation," "Why stir up the past?," loses its hold when it confronts historical experience. Because the past can be recovered in flashes of haunted memory or in the immutable figures of mythological thought, it is not entirely lost. Rather, it calls out to us to speak about what has been repressed from consciousness.

Therefore, experience instigates language, in particular a language of opposition or of revisionism, in which what has been suppressed or otherwise made invisible is brought to the surface of contemporary political discourse. It puts pressure on prohibitions, such as those fostered by the Khmer Rouge officials who continued (and still continue), with impunity, to occupy positions of power in the Cambodian government long after the fall of the regime. *The Act of Killing* is an even more striking example. Scandalous images of ruthless murderers indulging their murderous fantasies were profoundly shocking to international audiences. Particularly disturbing are the moments when real experience cracks the surface of the gangsters' contrived representations, and we feel the past take possession of the present, where it has resided all along. What *The Act of Killing* provoked after its first screening at the Telluride Film Festival was nothing short of a political explosion. The shock waves not only undermined the legitimacy of the Indonesian government and its then unquestioned methods of political repression; they set in motion renewed debates on American Cold War attitudes that could consider the deaths of hundreds of thousands of Indonesians as "good news."

These considerations bring me back to Timothy Snyder's *Bloodlands*, which is, to my mind, the best kind of history, for two reasons: because it is devoted to factual accuracy and to cleansing history of the ideologies of the twentieth century that have so long deformed it; and because it pays attention to the human experience of the catastrophic events it evokes. As Snyder observes, it is very important in analyzing Hitler's and Stalin's crimes against humanity to get the numbers right: How many victims did they murder, to what ethnicities or social classes did the victims belong, at whose hands did they perish, at which moments and in what contexts, what methods were used against them, and in the interest of what ends? It is equally important to represent the human costs of cataclysmic events. In the conclusion of *Bloodlands*, Snyder offers this reflection on what can be lost in the impersonal discourse of history:

Victims left behind mourners. Killers left behind numbers. To join in a large number after death is to be dissolved into a stream of anonymity. To be enlisted posthumously into competing national memories, bolstered by the numbers of which your life has become a part, is to sacrifice individuality. It is to be abandoned by history, which begins from the assumption that each person is irreducible. With all of its complexity, history is what we all have, and can all share. So even when we have the numbers right, we have to take care. The right number is not enough.[4]

That is one of the frustrations that Panh faces, for example, in wanting to bear witness to the immensity of human loss that the Khmer Rouge Killing Machine produced. So many dead, so few survivors, so little access to the individuals, such distortion of their histories. Under pressure, the perpetrators describe how they "helped" their victims construct their fictitious identities, creating portraits of saboteurs who fit the obsessions of the paranoid party apparatus that saw enemies everywhere. We learn the stories of the victimization of a few, and we see their faces—the mug shots that Panh's camera returns to repeatedly to reassert their humanity. But how are we to understand the scale of suffering? *S-21* asks this question cinematically through a single long take at the end of the film that takes place in the Tuong Sleng Museum of the Cambodian genocide. A tracking camera moves across the huge panels of photographic portraits representing thousands of the victims of the Khmer Rouge. Then, closing in, it isolates a single photo of a young woman. We have seen her before—in the repeated panning to her mug shot lying on the interrogation table.

Andrezj Wajda is similarly preoccupied by the scale of representation in *Katyn*. As we saw, he is careful to depict his focalized characters as representative of the much larger community of the Polish nation. To this end he employs rhetorical strategies in which the experience of the individual radiates out to lend subjectivity to the anonymous mass, as we saw in the way Wajda represents collective anxiety in a square in Krakow. Or he uses metaphor to enclose a group within a mythological space, like the monastery church where the Soviets hold the Polish officers prisoner. In the culminating moments of the film, however, Wajda's representation of the victims of Soviet murder runs counter to the direction of Panh's final sequence shot. Instead of moving toward

the recognizable face of a single victim, Wajda withdraws into an anonymity in which the Polish officers we have come to know lose their
identity in the brutality and despair of mass murder.

Joseph Mali tells us that the " 'crucial test' of mythistory, indeed of
any form of modern historiography, is whether it offers a new explanation of what is really 'modern' in contemporary history, to wit, the devastation of Western civilization in the totalitarian revolutions and wars
of the twentieth century."[5] Mali suggests that a "methodical 'recognition of myth' " is essential to an understanding of "that singular event
that so typifies this history and yet defies all the conventional categories of traditional historiography: the Holocaust."[6] Mythology reveals a
" 'poetic logic' by which men have made and written their own history."[7] Historians engage in a dialogue with myth in order to take account of "the mythical patterns of thought and action that reside in all
historical events and narratives (including their own)."[8] This does not
mean, especially in the context of the extreme events of the twentieth
century, that the historian remains uncritical about how myth as a political force is used. This is obviously essential, for example, in assess-
ing the impact of Swiss mythologist Johann Jakob Bachofen on Nazi
theorists like Alfred Baeumler. Indeed, Alon Confino argues convinc-
ingly that the valorization of Germanic mythology "liberated" the
Nazis from Judaism and made it possible "to open up new emotional,
historical, and moral horizons that enabled them to imagine and to
create their empire of death."[9]

Mali is obviously aware of the paradox of an exceptional event (the
Holocaust), which paradoxically "typifies" the extensive period of wars
and revolutions in the twentieth century. The Holocaust is certainly
exceptional—"an unassimilated and unassimilable and yet changing
reality," as Saul Friedländer puts it in *Reflections of Nazism: An Essay on
Kitsch and Death*.[10] It is an event beyond language. We could make the
argument, however, that the long history of Stalinist terror also typifies
twentieth-century history. It is also a reality that has not yet found its
language.

Stalinist crimes were not singular events in the same way as the Holocaust. They extended over decades of Soviet rule, and they were replicated in a host of regimes, whether under direct Soviet domination as
in Eastern Europe or in the Asian variants of Communism where, as

Martin Malia notes, they became increasingly violent. Communist terrorism cannot match the organized ferocity of the Final Solution and its genocidal ambition, but it has been in the long run more deadly: twenty million civilians died in the Soviet Union, sixty-five million in China, two million in North Korea, and approximately two million in Cambodia. Communism was dedicated, not to the destruction of a "racial" enemy, but to the destruction of a social class. The "Road to Socialism" is indeed littered with all the bodies sacrificed to the triumph of an ideology and a new world order. Successive Communist regimes sought to impose a collective phantasm in which class enemies—those constantly moving targets—could appear anywhere and at any time, particularly under the persuasive power of torture or the hysteria of denunciations.

As Rithy Panh makes clear, S-21 was dedicated to a perverse notion of political conversion. Reeducation of the masses consisted in coercing its "learners" into confessing their guilty roles in the paranoid drama of the party's struggle against internal enemies. Their "conversion" was, psychologically and culturally, extremely violent because it required those repenting to repudiate their experience, their own sense of themselves, and all the traditions and unspoken beliefs that sustained their membership in a community. In short they were compelled to renounce the mythological foundation that sustained their individual and communal life. Once "reeducated," the repentant were quickly murdered and their lives reduced to the avowals made under duress. Whereas the Moscow show trials made public display of the "crimes" of major party figures, the "traitors" who passed through S-21 were humble Cambodians who could not be distinguished, in terms of ethnicity or even of social class, from their guards, interrogators, and executioners. The victims of S-21, like all those Cambodians elsewhere who met their deaths through starvation, exhaustion, or murder, had nothing left to hold onto.

What motivates the filmmakers of all the films in this study is the desire to retrospectively defend the integrity of a tradition, to depict the heroes of resistance, and to revive the pathos of situations in which victims are threatened with annihilation. By "pathos" I do not mean the often denigrated appeal to the emotions in the rhetorical tradition but the effects produced when one reinvests human actions with the

sensations and feelings that originally adhered to them. Every attempt
to explain the extreme events of the twentieth century is bound to be
deficient if it is couched only in the discursive categories of the historical sciences. As Saul Friedländer contends, historical analysis that
is driven by economic and social categories alone proves inadequate to
describing Nazism after 1936, and the same can be said for the other
historical moments that have concerned us. Such events—excessive,
aberrant, monstrous—spill over and through whatever conceptual grid
is thrown up to contain them. The dispassionate historian observing
from the outside cannot take the full measure of such excess. Likewise,
sociology and psychology can only partially explain how an individual
can be caught up in the machinery of death. In analyzing the behavior
of perpetrators at S-21, it is certainly important to understand that Pol
Pot had a predilection, following Mao, for recruiting young uneducated
men, and that "the poor and the blank," responsive to indoctrination
and authority within what Erving Goffman describes as a total institution, showed little resistance to authorities when ordered to commit
atrocities and on many occasions went beyond all expectations. But the
young guard in S-21 is not just an example of the behavior of a given
social category in the specific conditions imposed by a ruthless Stalinist dictator. He is the instrument by means of which the agonizing experience of incarceration in S-21—lost to memory and to history—is
momentarily recovered. One senses the recovery in the texture of his
voice, in his manic gestures, and in the space he reinvests with the
presence he has long repressed.

In these intense moments of recovery, objects from the past—piles
of unexamined photographs of prisoners, voluminous archives of their
confessions and records of denunciations, the night landscape of the
execution ground echoing with the song of frogs, the coat button that
Vann Nath pulls from the debris on the floor of a cellblock, the imaginary can of water the young guard carries as he threatens to beat his
prisoners—are capable of returning the gaze, as Walter Benjamin so
insightfully put it. The gaze of the guard who reenters the space of his
own experience and our own as we accompany him.

This fusion of subject and object and of the past with the present is
what I have attempted to identify in the seven films under study. In
the final moments of *Katyn*, Andrzej Wajda, and we along with him,

confront the execution of the Polish officers in its unsparing brutality and reexperience the anguish of the death of the father as we are over-whelmed by the death of the nation. In *Siberiade* Andrei Konchalosky reinvests the Siberian landscape with its primal mythic power whose emotional, symbolic and aesthetic dimensions speak to us about hu-mankind's place in the cosmic order of things and thus constructs an elemental argument against the calculus of Stalinist history. In *The Ascent* Larisa Shepitko narrows the scale of representation. She shoots close to the human body creating an intimacy of contact: as Rybak pulls the wounded Sotnikov through the snow, he pulls us with him. So it is with her intimate depiction of the human physiognomy whose mobile features betray evolving emotions and transcendent states. In *A Film Unfinished*, Yaël Hersonski digs through the layers of the Nazi misrepresentation of the Warsaw Ghetto and exposes the nerve of ex-perience. We observe it in the involuntary gestures of survivors in a screening room who are caught by the indexical power of the image or, more directly, in the disturbing *frisson* we feel as the eyes of long-dead victims stare back at us from the darkness of history. In *Nostalgia for the Light* Patricio Guzmán searches for historical emotion through his disjointed reminiscence of personal experience, his rebellion against the irreversibility of time, his skepticism about the efficacy of narra-tive, his desire—and his protagonists' desire—to recover the materials of experience, to revisit a past long gone and perhaps (fleetingly) resur-rect it. In unguarded moments in *The Act of Killing*, Anwar Congo, the charismatic gangster and mass murderer, yields to his own pain. What strikes us is the incongruity of his gestures, how inadequate they are to express the enormity of his acts. We are justly scandalized by this failure of proportion. At the same time, it is through the shudder of experience—a trembling hand, sudden tears, dry retching—that we know the horror of a historical moment, in the etymological sense of the Latin *horrere*: the body's involuntary responses, like hair raising on our arms.

Timothy Snyder draws what I believe is the most important histori-cal lesson about extreme events of the twentieth century: what is cen-tral is life rather than death, "since life gives meaning to death, rather than the other way around." We should not be looking for closure, which is a "false harmony," Snyder tells us. "The important question is:

how could (and can) so many lives be brought to a violent end?"[11] Indeed, none of the seven films that have been the subject of this book seeks resolution. They expose us to uncomfortable realities but do not enclose them within a narrative frame. The mass execution of Poles at the end of *Katyn* shatters any hope of dénouement. The final close-ups of the suicidal traitor in *The Ascent* fade into snowy oblivion. The diminished figure of Anwar Congo slips into the dark streets of Medan bearing his unrelieved burden of guilt. As Ankersmit says, there are "wounds with which we should never cease to suffer."

In closing, I would like to turn to the work of the German poet and essayist W. G. Sebald, who has expressed, perhaps better than anyone, what is at stake in historical memory. In *The Rings of Saturn* the narrator, whom I will refer to simply as Sebald, recounts a walking tour that he made on the eastern coast of England. Essential to the successive visions his historical imagination evokes is the breaking loose not only from the routine of the academic job he holds in Britain but also from the constraints of historical distance: "At all events, in retrospect I became preoccupied not only with the unaccustomed sense of freedom but also with the paralysing horror that had come over me at various times when confronted with the traces of destruction, reaching far back into the past, that were evident even in that remote place."[12]

Sebald possesses an extraordinary sensitivity to historical landscapes, which he never objectifies but instead sees through the lens of his subjectivity. One of the grand metaphors of the text is the labyrinth: becoming lost on the featureless heath, he is forced "to retrace long stretches in that bewildering terrain." It is only in a dream that he discovers in Dunwich heath a point of view on a labyrinth, "a pattern simple in comparison with the tortuous trail I had behind me, but one which I knew in my dream, with absolute certainty, represented a cross-section of my brain."[13] "Confronted with the traces of destruction, reaching far back into the past,"[14] Sebald gives in to the emotional power of the historical traces he encounters, in a fusion of real perception and dream. He experiences panic on the heath, and indeed landscape often overwhelms him to the point of pathology. The same intense subjectivity characterizes his relationship to written texts and their power to awaken history. Sebald's searing evocation of European colonialism centers on his identification with Joseph Conrad—it is indeed difficult to separate Sebald the narrator from his character, Korzeniowski (Conrad's "real" Polish name), whose tortured life Sebald relates so personally. Identification with the words of figures such as Conrad or Chateaubriand are so close that Sebald does not shy away from reproducing them nearly verbatim without quotation marks.

Sebald's perceptions focus on details that are never described clinically but remain open to insights that can only be called poetic. Although he does not address the question in theoretical terms, the reader understands how skeptical he is of historical vision conceived as a retrospective account and of the dispassionate historian who, in the name of objectivity, stands his ground. Consider, for example, the memory that Sebald evokes of his visit to the memorial on the historical site of the Battle of Waterloo, "the very definition of ugliness, in my eyes." It is a bleak winter's day without visitors, the site deserted except for actors in Napoleonic costume who suddenly appear "tramping up and down the few streets, beating drums and blowing fifes."[15] Sebald buys a ticket for the Waterloo panorama, "housed in an immense domed rotunda, where from a raised platform in the middle one can view the battle. . . . It is like being at the centre of events." He describes the historical "landscape" with its "lifesize horses, and cutdown infantrymen, hussars and chevaux-légers, eyes rolling in pain or already extinguished,"[16] all molded out of wax. From the three-dimensional space of the horrific scene "on which the cold dust of time has settled," Sebald gazes toward the horizon where the immense diorama, painted by French marine artist Louis Dumontin in 1912, occupies a space a hundred yards by twelve. The panorama's two-dimensionality and the waxen figures it frames stand as a metaphor for the synoptic vision of history. It is worth quoting the passage at some length:

> This then, I thought, as I looked round about me, is the representation of history. It requires falsification of perspective. We, the survivors, see everything from above, see everything at once, and still we do not know how it was. The desolate field extends all around where once fifty thousand soldiers and ten thousand horses met their end within a few hours. The night after the battle, the air must have been filled with death rattles and groans. Now there is nothing but the silent brown soil. Whatever became of the corpses and mortal remains? Are they buried under the

memorial? Are we standing on a mountain of death? Is that our ultimate vantage point? Does one really have the much-vaunted historical overview from such a position?[17]

How can we know "how it was"? It is significant that Sebald is able to return to the reality of the scene only by obliterating the representation that stands before him: "Only when I had shut my eyes, I well recall, did I see a cannonball smash through a row of poplars at an angle, sending the green branches flying in tatters." This is the moment when history and fiction suddenly merge: "And then I saw Fabrizio, Stendhal's young hero, wandering about the battlefield, pale but with eyes aglow, and an unsaddled colonel getting to his feet and telling his sergeant: I can feel nothing but the old injury in my right hand."[18]

Metaphorically, Sebald loses himself in a historical landscape in order to find his way among the monuments he encounters. It is an adventure, reminiscent of Rimbaud's, in which the poet sets out to destabilize the mastery of the world held in place by language and the science of history. One must close one's eyes to historical representation as an organized discourse to reawaken the sensations that are the essential content of human experience. Sebald struggles, desperately, against loss and becomes the instrument through which the fugitive past can be experienced in the fullness of time. It is this rejection of loss and the desire for presence that animate all the films we have studied. History is alive only when a human subject, for a fleeting moment, makes contact with the past—a past that is capable of returning the subject's gaze.

NOTES

INTRODUCTION: MAKING EXPERIENCE SPEAK

1. Frank Ankersmit, *Meaning, Truth, and Reference in Historical Representation* (Ithaca: Cornell University Press, 2012), 175.
2. Henri-Irénée Marrou, *De la connaissance historique* (Paris: Seuil, 1954), 170–71. My translation.
3. Ankersmit, *Meaning, Truth, and Reference*, 176.
4. Frank Ankersmit, *Sublime Historical Experience* (Stanford: Stanford University Press, 2005), 101.
5. Ankersmit, *Meaning, Truth, and Reference*, 187.
6. Ibid., 203.
7. Jean-Marie Schaeffer, *Pourquoi la fiction?* (Paris: Seuil, 1999), 92.
8. Daniel Mendelsohn, *The Lost: A Search for Six of Six Million* (New York: Perennial, 2007), 501. Emphasis in original.
9. Richard Shusterman, *Pragmatist Aesthetics: Living Beauty, Rethinking Art* (Oxford: Blackwell, 1992), 124.
10. See Ankersmit's discussion of Wittgenstein's notion of the groan in *Sublime Historical Experience*, 193–97.
11. Ibid., 197. Emphasis in original.
12. Joseph Mali, *Mythistory: The Making of a Modern Historiography* (Chicago: University of Chicago Press, 2003), 11.
13. T. S. Eliot, quoted in ibid., 11–12.
14. Clifford Geertz, *The Interpretation of Cultures* (New York: Basic Books, 1973), 82.
15. Ankersmit, *Sublime Historical Experience*, 368.

16. Mali, *Mythistory*, 5.
17. Cited in ibid., 10.
18. Quoted in ibid., 22.
19. Cited in ibid., 12–13.
20. Ibid., 4.
21. Ibid., 232.
22. Tony Judt, *Postwar: A History of Europe Since 1945* (New York: Penguin, 2006), 425.
23. Ankersmit, *Sublime Historical Experience*, 321–24.
24. Paul Ricoeur, *Time and Narrative*, trans. Kathleen McLaughlin and David Pellauer (Chicago: University of Chicago Press, 1984) 1:200.
25. Ankersmit, *Sublime Historical Experience*, 323–24.
26. Ibid., 324.
27. Ibid., 343.
28. Shusterman, *Pragmatist Aesthetics*, 25.
29. John Dewey, *Art as Experience* (New York: Penguin, 2005), 2.
30. Shusterman, *Pragmatist Aesthetics*, 25.
31. Ibid., 28.
32. Dewey, *Art as Experience*, 103.
33. Ibid., 56.
34. Shusterman, *Pragmatist Aesthetics*, 90.
35. For a discussion of such strategies, see "Refiguring History" in my *Writing History in Film* (London: Routledge, 2006), 133–64.
36. Ankersmit, *Sublime Historical Experience*, 1.
37. Ibid., 2.
38. Ankersmit, *Meaning, Truth, and Reference*, 216.
39. Ibid., 217.
40. Ibid.
41. Marc Ferro, *Cinema and History*, trans. Naomi Greene (Detroit: Wayne State University Press, 1988), 23.
42. Ibid., 30–31.
43. Ibid., 23–46.
44. Ibid., 47.
45. Ibid., 159.
46. Robert Rosenstone, "The History Film as a Mode of Historical Thought," in *A Companion to the Historical Film*, ed. Robert Rosenstone and Constantin Parvulescu (Chichester, UK: Wiley-Blackwell, 2013), 71.
47. Natalie Zemon Davis, *Slaves on Screen: Film and Historical Vision* (Cambridge, Mass.: Harvard University Press, 2000), 6–7.
48. Robert Burgoyne, *The Hollywood Historical Film* (Malden, Mass.: Blackwell, 2008), 11.
49. Robert Burgoyne, "Generational Memory and Affect in *Letters from Iwo Jima*," in *A Companion to the Historical Film*, ed. Robert Rosenstone and Constantin Parvulescu (Chichester, UK: Wiley-Blackwell, 2013), 353.

50. Alison Landsberg, *Prosthetic Memory: The Transformation of American Remembrance in the Age of Mass Culture* (New York: Columbia University Press, 2004), 2.
51. Ibid., 113.
52. Ibid., 21.

1. YAËL HERSONSKI'S *A FILM UNFINISHED*

1. Laliv Melamed, "A Film Unraveled: An Interview with Yaël Hersonski," *International Journal of Politics, Culture and Society*, 26 (2013): 10.
2. Ibid.
3. Louis O. Mink, *Historical Understanding* (Ithaca: Cornell University Press, 1987), 56–57.
4. Michael Rothberg, *Traumatic Realism: The Demands of Holocaust Representation* (Minneapolis: University of Minnesota Press, 2000), 4.
5. Ibid.
6. Saul Friedländer, *Reflections of Nazism: An Essay on Kitsch and Death*, trans. Thomas Weyr (New York: Harper & Row, 1988), 106–7.
7. Ibid., 89.
8. Ibid., 125–26.
9. Frank Ankersmit, *Historical Representation* (Stanford: Stanford University Press, 2001), 161.
10. David Nirenberg, *Anti-Judaism: The Western Tradition* (New York: Norton, 2013), 404.
11. Ibid., 435.
12. Ibid., 437.
13. Alon Confino, *A World Without Jews: The Nazi Imagination from Persecution to Genocide* (New Haven: Yale University Press, 2014), 6.
14. Melamed, "A Film Unraveled," 15.
15. Ibid., 14.
16. Ibid., 12.
17. Statements quoted in voiceover.
18. Nirenberg, *Anti-Judaism*, 424.
19. Confino, *A World Without Jews*, 105.
20. Timothy Snyder, *Bloodlands: Europe Between Hitler and Stalin* (New York: Basic Books, 2010), 145.
21. Nirenberg, *Anti-Judaism*, 324.
22. William Guynn, *A Cinema of Nonfiction* (Cranbury, N.J.: Associated University Presses, 1990).
23. Shoshana Felman and Dori Laub, *Testimony: Crises of Witnessing in Literature, Psychoanalysis and History* (London: Routledge, Chapman and Hall, 1992), 205.

24. Ibid., 206.
25. Pierre Nora, introduction to *Realms of Memory: Conflict and Division*, trans. Arthur Goldhammer (New York: Columbia University Press, 1996), 1:3.
26. Melamed, "A Film Unraveled," 15.
27. Ibid., 19.
28. Frank Ankersmit, *Sublime Historical Experience* (Stanford: Stanford University Press, 2005), 186–87.
29. Ibid., 196–97. Emphasis in the original.
30. Melamed, "A Film Unraveled," 12.

2. ANDRZEJ WAJDA'S *KATYN*

1. Piotr Witek, "Andrzej Wajda as Historian," in *A Companion to the Historical Film*, ed. Robert Rosenstone and Constantin Parvulescu (Chichester, UK: Wiley-Blackstone, 2013), 154.
2. Available as a "bonus" on the DVD version of *Katyn*.
3. Timothy Snyder, *Bloodlands: Europe Between Hitler and Stalin* (New York: Basic Books, 2010), 124.
4. Ibid., 125.
5. Ibid., 126.
6. Ibid., 127–28.
7. Ibid., 386.
8. Ibid., 387.
9. Ibid., 287.
10. Robert Burgoyne, "Generational Memory and Affect in *Letters from Iwo Jima*," in *A Companion to the Historical Film*, ed. Robert Rosenstone and Constantin Parvulescu (Chichester, UK: Wiley-Blackwell, 2013), 353–59.
11. R. G. Collingwood, *The Idea of History* (Oxford: Clarendon Press, 1946), 213.
12. Ibid., 242.
13. Jean-Marie Schaeffer, *Pourquoi la fiction?* (Paris: Seuil, 1999), 81.
14. Collingwood, *The Idea of History*, 242.
15. Ibid., 217.
16. Arthur Danto, *Narration and Knowledge* (New York: Columbia University Press, 2007), 285.
17. Ibid., 296.
18. Ibid., 294.
19. Frank Ankersmit, *Sublime Historical Experience* (Stanford: Stanford University Press), 11.
20. Svetlana Boym, *The Future of Nostalgia* (New York: Basic Books, 2001), xvii.

21. Maurice Halbwachs, *The Collective Memory*, trans. Francis J. Ditter Jr. and Vida Yazdi Ditter (New York: Harper & Row, 1980), 56–57.

22. Boym, *The Future of Nostalgia*, xiii–xix.

23. Pierre Nora, *Realms of Memory: Conflict and Division*, trans. Arthur Goldhammer (New York: Columbia University Press, 1996), 1:3.

24. Interview with Jacques Le Goff, in Johan Huizinga, *L'Automne du Moyen Âge* (Paris: Payot & Rivages, 2015), 21.

25. Johan Huizinga, *The Autumn of the Middle Ages*, trans. Rodney J. Payton and Ulrich Mammitzsch (Chicago: University of Chicago Press, 1996), 1.

26. Ibid., 2.

27. Ibid., 312.

28. In Johan Huizinga, *L'Automne du Moyen Âge* (Paris: Payot & Rivages, 2015), 13.

29. Cited in Ankersmit, *Sublime Historical Experience*, 134.

30. Michael Taussig, *Mimesis and Alterity: A Particular History of the Senses* (London: Routledge, 1993), 20.

31. Ibid.

32. Walter Benjamin, *Illuminations*, trans. Harry Zohn (New York: Schocken Books, 1969), 336.

33. Cited in Taussig, *Mimesis and Alterity*, 2.

34. Robert Rosenstone, *Visions of the Past: The Challenge of Film to Our Idea of History* (Cambridge, Mass.: Harvard University Press, 1995), 70.

35. Natalie Zemon Davis, " 'Any Resemblance to Persons Living or Dead': Film and the Challenge of Authenticity," *Yale Review* 76, no. 4 (September 1987): 464.

36. William Guynn, *Writing History in Film* (Cranbury, N.J.: Associated University Presses, 1990), 133–63.

37. Cited in Taussig, *Mimesis and Alterity*, 1.

38. Cited in Antoine Prost, *Douze leçons sur l'histoire* (Paris: Seuil, 1996), 98.

39. Ankersmit, *Sublime Historical Experience*, 10.

40. Benjamin, *Illuminations*, 163.

41. Ibid., 158.

42. Ankersmit, *Sublime Historical Experience*, 109–40.

43. Ibid., 121.

44. Gérard Genette, *Fiction et diction* (Paris: Seuil, 1991), 19.

45. Robert Rosenstone and Constantin Parvulescu, introduction to *A Companion to the Historical Film* (Chichester, UK: Wiley-Blackwell, 2013), 7.

46. Paul Ricoeur, "Historical Intentionality," chap. 6 in *Time and Narrative*, trans. Kathleen McLaughlin and David Pellauer (Chicago: University of Chicago Press, 1984), 1:177 and passim.

47. Snyder, *Bloodlands*, 138.

48. Ankersmit, *Sublime Historical Experience*, 144–45. Emphasis in original.

49. Ibid., 146.

3. ANDREI KONCHALOVSKY'S *SIBERIADE*

1. Simon Schama, *Landscape and Memory* (New York: Knopf, 1995), 14.
2. Ibid., 18.
3. Tony Judt, *Postwar: A History of Europe Since 1945* (New York: Penguin, 2006), 425.
4. David Cook, *A History of Narrative Film* (New York: Norton, 2003), 699.
5. Katerina Clark, "Socialist Realism *with* Shores: The Conventions for the Positive Hero," in *Socialist Realism Without Shores*, ed. Thomas Lahusen and Evgeny Dobrenko (Durham: Duke University Press, 1997), 29.
6. Yuri Slezkine, "Primitive Communism and the Other Way Around," in *Socialist Realism Without Shores*, ed. Thomas Lahusen and Evgeny Dobrenko (Durham: Duke University Press, 1997), 310.
7. Ibid., 312.
8. Vasily Grossman, *Life and Fate*, trans. Robert Chandler (New York: New York Review Books, 2006), 55.
9. Svetlana Boym, "Paradoxes of Unified Culture: From Stalin's Fairy Tale to Molotov's Lacquer Box," in *Socialist Realism Without Shores*, ed. Thomas Lahusen and Evgeny Dobrenko (Durham: Duke University Press, 1997), 125.
10. Clark, "Socialist Realism *with* Shores," 30.
11. Leonid Heller, "A World of Prettiness: Socialist Realism and Its Aesthetic Categories," in *Socialist Realism Without Shores*, ed. Thomas Lahusen and Evgeny Dobrenko (Durham: Duke University Press, 1997), 51.
12. Ibid., 51–53.
13. Alexey Novikov-Priboi, quoted in ibid., 59.
14. Hans Günther, "Wise Father Stalin and His Family in Soviet Cinema," in *Socialist Realism Without Shores*, ed. Thomas Lahusen and Evgeny Dobrenko (Durham: Duke University Press, 1997), 179.
15. Joseph Mali, *Mythistory: The Making of a Modern Historiography* (Chicago: University of Chicago Press, 2003), 233.
16. Carlo Ginzberg, *Ecstasies: Deciphering the Witches' Sabbath* (New York: Pantheon Books, 1991), 24.
17. Cited by Mali, *Mythistory*, 12.
18. Ibid.
19. Walter Benjamin, "The Painter of Modern Life," cited in ibid., 251.
20. See in particular "On Some Motifs in Baudelaire" in Walter Benjamin, *Illuminations*, trans. Harry Zohn (New York: Schocken Books, 1969), 155–200.
21. Ibid., 186.
22. Ibid., 91.
23. Ibid., 96.
24. Mali, *Mythistory*, 276.
25. Benjamin, *Illuminations*, 188.

26. Ibid., 257–58.

27. Mali, *Mythistory*, 5.

4. LARISA SHEPITKO'S *THE ASCENT*

1. Vasily Grossman, *Everything Flows*, trans. Robert Chandler and Elizabeth Chandler (New York: New York Review Books, 2009), 193.

2. William Guynn, *Writing History in Film* (New York: Routledge, 2006), 80.

3. Robert Rosenstone, *Visions of the Past: The Challenge of Film to Our Idea of History* (Cambridge, Mass.: Harvard University Press, 1995), 61.

4. Paul Veyne, *Writing History* (Middletown, Conn.: Wesleyan University Press, 1984), 36.

5. Ann Rigney, *The Rhetoric of Historical Representation: Three Narrative Histories of the French Revolution* (Cambridge: Cambridge University Press, 1990), 77.

6. St. Augustine of Hippo, *The Homilies on John* (Altenmünster, Loschberg, Germany, 2012), Tractate XXV:16.

7. Hulliung, cited by Joseph Mali, *Mythistory: The Making of a Modern Historiography* (Chicago: University of Chicago Press, 2003), 55.

8. Benedict Anderson, *Imagined Communities: Reflections on the Origins and Spread of Nationalism* (London: Verso, 2006), 160.

9. Ibid., 2.

10. Eric Hobsbawn, *The Age of Extremes* (New York: Vintage Books, 1995), 477.

11. Vasily Grossman, *Life and Fate*, trans. Robert Chandler (New York: New York Review Books, 2006), 665.

12. Anderson, *Imagined Communities*, 7.

13. Grossman, *Life and Fate*, 665.

14. Andreas Huyssen, *Present Pasts: Urban Palimpsests and the Politics of Memory* (Stanford: Stanford University Press, 2003), 32.

15. Ibid., 38–39.

16. Ibid., 45.

17. See Pierre Nora, "The General Introduction," in *Realms of Memory*, trans. Arthur Goldhammer (New York: Columbia University Press, 1996), 1:1–20.

18. Hobsbawn, *The Age of Extremes*, 478.

19. Edmund Husserl, *The Cartesian Meditations* (The Hague: Martinus Nijhoff, 1960), 132.

20. Paul Ricoeur, *History, Memory, Forgetting*, trans. Kathleen Blamey and David Pellauer (Chicago: University of Chicago Press, 2004), 1:119.

21. Frank Ankersmit, *Historical Representation* (Stanford: Stanford University Press, 2001), 11.

22. Grossman, *Everything Flows*, 54.

23. Ibid., 55.

5. PATRICIO GUZMÁN'S *NOSTALGIA FOR THE LIGHT*

1. Rob White, "After-Effects: An Interview with Patricio Guzmán," *Film Quarterly*, July 2012, http://www.filmquarterly.com/2012/07/after-effects-interview-with-patricio-guzman/.
2. Ibid.
3. Frank Ankersmit, *Sublime Historical Experience* (Stanford: Stanford University Press, 2005), 307.
4. Svetlana Boym, *The Future of Nostalgia* (New York: Basic Books, 2001), xv.
5. Ibid., xviii.
6. Ankersmit, *Sublime Historical Experience*, 309.
7. William Guynn, *Writing History in Film* (New York: Routledge, 2006), 138–39.
8. T. V. F. Brogan, ed., *The Princeton Handbook of Poetic Terms* (Princeton: Princeton University Press, 1994), 233.
9. W. G. Sebald, *Austerlitz* (New York: Random House, 2011), 251.
10. Ibid., 257.
11. Ibid.
12. Ibid., 258.
13. Frank Ankersmit, *Historical Representation* (Stanford: Stanford University Press, 2001), 152.
14. Walter Benjamin, *Illuminations*, trans. Harry Zohn (New York: Schocken Books, 1969), 5.
15. Ibid., 6.

6. RITHY PANH'S *S-21:*
THE KHMER ROUGE KILLING MACHINE

1. Timothy Snyder, "Hitler vs. Stalin: Who Was Worse?" *New York Review of Books*, NYRblog, January 27, 2011, http://www.nybooks.com/daily/2011/01/27/hitler-vs-stalin-who-was-worse/.
2. Tony Judt, *Thinking the Twentieth Century*, with Timothy Snyder (New York: Penguin, 2012), 36.
3. Martin Malia, foreword to Stéphane Courtois et al., *The Black Book of Communism*, trans. Jonathan Murphy and Mark Kramer (Cambridge, Mass.: Harvard University Press, 1999).
4. Judt, 226.
5. Timothy Snyder, *Bloodlands: Europe Between Hitler and Stalin* (New York: Basic Books, 2010), 387.
6. Ibid., 388.
7. Rithy Panh, *The Elimination: A Survivor of the Khmer Rouge Confronts His Past and the Commandant of the Killing Fields*, with Christophe Bataille, trans. John Cullen (New York: Other Press, 2012), 33.

8. Erving Goffman, *Asylums: Essays on the Social Situation of Mental Patients and Other Inmates* (New York: Anchor Books, 1961), 4.

9. David Chandler, *Voices from S-21: Terror and History in Pol Pot's Secret Prison* (Berkeley: University of California Press, 1999), 126.

10. Ibid., 127.

11. Cited in ibid., 46.

12. Cited in Panh, *The Elimination*, 233–34.

13. Rithy Panh, "Je suis un arpenteur de mémoires," *Cahiers du Cinéma* 587 (February 2004): 14.

14. Ibid. 14.

15. Roger Chartier, foreword to Philippe Ariès, *Essais de mémoire: 1943–1983* (Paris: Seuil, 1993), 11.

16. Ibid.

17. Panh, *The Elimination*, 187.

18. Ibid., 164.

19. Chandler, *Voices from S-21*, 89.

20. Panh, *The Elimination*, 103. Emphasis in original.

21. Panh, "Je suis un arpenteur de mémoires," 16.

22. Ibid., 16.

23. Panh, *The Elimination*, 121.

24. Ibid., 255.

25. Joshua Oppenheimer, "Perpetrators' Testimony and the Restoration of Humanity: *S21*, Rithy Panh," in *Killer Images: Documentary Film, Memory, and the Performance of Violence*, ed. Joram Ten Brink and Joshua Oppenheimer (London: Wallflower Press, 2012), 244.

26. Panh, *The Elimination*, 73.

27. Ibid., 91.

28. Oppenheimer, "Perpetrators' Testimony and the Restoration of Humanity," 244.

29. Ibid., 254.

7. JOSHUA OPPENHEIMER'S *THE ACT OF KILLING*

1. Oppenheimer has since remedied this imbalance in his extraordinary *The Look of Silence* (2014), which he sees as the necessary complement to *The Act of Killing*. The film's courageous hero, Adi, confronts his brother's killers despite the threat such exposure entails for him and his family.

2. Octave Mannoni, *Clefs pour l'Imaginaire ou l'Autre Scène* (Paris: Seuil, 1969), 9–33.

3. For a key statement of his radical departure from classic ethnographic methodology, see Jean Rouch's "Mettre en circulation des objets inquiétants," *La Nouvelle Critique* 82 (March 1975): 74–78.

4. Arthur Danto, *The Transfiguration of the Commonplace* (Cambridge, Mass.: Harvard University Press, 1981), 14.
5. Octave Mannoni, *Clefs pour l'Imaginaire*, 181.
6. Danto, *The Transfiguration of the Commonplace*, 9.
7. Ibid., 9.
8. Ibid., 9.
9. Ibid., 11.
10. Ibid., 10.

EPILOGUE

1. Frank Ankersmit, *Sublime Historical Experience* (Stanford: Stanford University Press, 2005), 96.
2. Ibid., 256.
3. Ibid., 1.
4. Timothy Snyder, *Bloodlands: Europe Between Hitler and Stalin* (New York: Basic Books, 2010), 407.
5. Joseph Mali, *Mythistory: The Making of a Modern Historiography* (Chicago: University of Chicago Press, 2003), 29.
6. Ibid.
7. Ibid., 31.
8. Ibid., 18.
9. Alon Confino, *A World Without Jews* (New Haven: Yale University Press, 2014), 14.
10. Saul Friedländer, *Reflections of Nazism: An Essay on Kitsch and Death*, trans. Thomas Weyr (New York: Harper & Row, 1982), 11.
11. Snyder, *Bloodlands*, 387.
12. W. G. Sebald, *The Rings of Saturn*, trans. Michael Hulse (New York: New Directions Books, 1999), 3.
13. Ibid., 173.
14. Ibid., 1.
15. Ibid., 124.
16. Ibid.
17. Ibid., 125.
18. Ibid., 126.

BIBLIOGRAPHY

Anderson, Benedict. *Imagined Communities: Reflections on the Origins and Spread of Nationalism*. London: Verso, 2006.

Ankersmith, Frank R. *Historical Representation*. Stanford: Stanford University Press, 2001.

——. *Meaning, Truth, and Reference in Historical Representation*. Ithaca: Cornell University Press, 2012.

——. *Sublime Historical Experience*. Stanford: Stanford University Press, 2005.

Ariès, Philippe, *Essais de mémoire: 1943–1983*. Paris: Seuil, 1993.

Augustine of Hippo, St. *The Homilies on John*. Altenmünster, Loschberg, Germany: 2012.

Barthes, Roland. *Image-Music-Text*. New York: Hill & Wang, 1977.

Benjamin, Walter. *The Arcades Project*. Edited by Rolf Tiedemann. Cambridge, Mass.: Belknap Press of Harvard University Press.

——. *Illuminations*. Translated by Harry Zohn. New York: Schocken Books, 1969.

Boym, Svetlana. *The Future of Nostalgia*. New York: Basic Books, 2001.

——. "Paradoxes of Unified Culture: From Stalin's Fairy Tale to Molotov's Lacquer Box." In *Socialist Realism Without Shores*, edited by Thomas Lahusen and Evgeny Dobrenko, 120–34. Durham: Duke University Press, 1997.

Brink, Joram Ten, and Joshua Oppenheimer, eds. *Killer Images: Documentary Film, Memory and the Performance of Violence*. London: Wallflower Press, 2012.

Brogan, T. V. F., ed. *The New Princeton Handbook of Poetic Terms*. Princeton: Princeton University Press, 1994.

Burgoyne, Robert. "Generational Memory and Affect in *Letters from Iwo Jima*." In *A Companion to the Historical Film*, edited by Robert A. Rosenstone and Constantin Parvulescu, 349–64. Chichester, UK: Wiley-Blackwell, 2013.

——. *The Hollywood Historical Film*. Malden, Mass.: Blackwell, 2008.

Chandler, David. *Voices from S-21: Terror and History in Pol Pot's Secret Prison*. Berkeley: University of California Press, 1999.

Clark, Katerina. "Socialist Realism *with* Shores: The Conventions for the Positive Hero." In *Socialist Realism Without Shores*, edited by Thomas Lahusen and Evgeny Dobrenko, 27–50. Durham: Duke University Press, 1997.

Collingwood, R. G. *The Idea of History*. Oxford: Clarendon Press, 1946.

Confino, Alon. *A World Without Jews: The Nazi Imagination from Persecution to Genocide*. New Haven: Yale University Press, 2014.

Cook, David. *A History of Narrative Film*. New York: Norton, 2003.

Courtois, Stéphane, Nicolas Werth, Jean-Louis Panné, Andrzej Paczkowski, Karel Bertosek, and Jean-Louis Margolin. *The Black Book of Communism*. Translated by Jonathan Murphy and Mark Kramer. Foreword by Martin Malia. Cambridge, Mass.: Harvard University Press, 1999.

Danto, Arthur C. *Narration and Knowledge*. New York: Columbia University Press, 2007.

——. *The Transfiguration of the Commonplace*. Cambridge, Mass.: Harvard University Press, 1981.

Davis, Natalie Zemon. " 'Any Resemblance to Persons Living or Dead': Film and the Challenge of Authenticity." *Yale Review* 76, no. 4 (September 1987): 457–82.

——. *Slaves on Screen: Film and Historical Vision*. Cambridge, Mass.: Harvard University Press, 2000.

Deguy, Michel, ed. *Au sujet de Shoa: Le Film de Claude Lanzmann*. Paris: Belin, 1994.

Dewey, John. *Art as Experience*. New York: Penguin, 2005.

Felman, Shoshana. "A l'âge du témoignage: *Shoa*." In *Au sujet de Shoa: Le film de Claude Lanzmann*, edited by Michel Deguy, 74–194. Paris: Belin, 1990.

Felman, Shoshana, and Dori Laub. *Testimony: Crises of Witnessing in Literature, Psychoanalysis and History*. London: Routledge, Chapman and Hall, 1992.

Ferro, Marc. *Cinema and History*. Translated by Naomi Greene. Detroit, Mich.: Wayne State University Press, 1988.

Friedländer, Saul. *Reflections of Nazism: An Essay on Kitsch and Death*. Translated by Thomas Weyr. New York: Harper & Row, 1982.

Geertz, Clifford. *The Interpretation of Cultures*. New York: Basic Books, 1973.

Genette, Gérard. *Fiction et diction*. Paris: Seuil, 1991.

Ginzberg, Carlo. *Ecstasies: Deciphering the Witches' Sabbath*. New York: Pantheon Books, 1991.

Goffman, Erving. *Asylums: Essays on the Social Situation of Mental Patients and Other Inmates*. New York: Anchor Books, 1961.

Grossman, Vasily. *Everything Flows*. Translated by Robert Chandler and Elizabeth Chandler. New York: New York Review Books, 2009.

——. *Life and Fate*. Translated and with an introduction by Robert Chandler. New York: New York Review Books, 2006.

Gunther, Hans. "Wise Father Stalin and His Family in Soviet Cinema." In *Socialist Realism Without Shores*, edited by Thomas Lahusen and Evgeny Dobrenko, 178–90. Durham: Duke University Press, 1997.

Guynn, William. *A Cinema of Nonfiction*. Cranbury, N.J.: Associated University Presses, 1990.

——. *Writing History in Film*. London: Routledge, 2006.

Halbwachs, Maurice. *The Collective Memory*. Translated by Francis J. Ditter Jr. and Vida Yazdi Ditter. New York: Harper & Row, 1980.

Hamburger, Käte. *The Logic of Literature*. Translated by Marilynn J. Rose. Bloomington: Indiana University Press, 1993.

Heller, Leonid. "A World of Prettiness: Socialist Realism and Its Aesthetic Categories." In *Socialist Realism Without Shores*, edited by Thomas Lahusen and Evgeny Dobrenko, 51–75. Durham: Duke University Press, 1997.

Hobsbawn, Eric. *The Age of Extremes*. New York: Vintage Books, 1995.

Huizinga, Johan. *L'Automne du Moyen Age*. Preceded by a conversation with Jacques Le Goff. Paris: Payot & Rivages, 2015.

——. *The Autumn of the Middle Ages*. Translated by Rodney J. Payton and Ulrich Mammitzsch. Chicago: Chicago University Press, 1996.

Husserl, Edmund. *The Cartesian Meditations*. The Hague: Martinus Nijhoff, 1960.

Huyssen, Andreas. *Present Pasts: Urban Palimpsests and the Politics of Memory*. Stanford: Stanford University Press, 2003.

Judt, Tony. *Postwar: A History of Europe Since 1945*. New York: Penguin, 2006.

——. *Thinking the Twentieth Century*. With Timothy Snyder. New York: Penguin, 2012.

Koestler, Arthur. *Darkness at Noon*. 1941. Reprint, New York: Scribner, 2006.

Konchalovsky, Andrei, and Alexander Lipkov. *The Inner Circle: An Inside View of Soviet Life Under Stalin*. Translated by Jamey Gambrell. New York: Newmarket Press, 1991.

Lahusen, Thomas, and Evgeny Dobrenko, eds. *Socialist Realism Without Shores*. Durham: Duke University Press, 1997.

Landsberg, Alison. *Prosthetic Memory: The Transformation of American Remembrance in the Age of Mass Culture*. New York: Columbia University Press, 2004.

Le Goff, Jacques. *Histoire et mémoire*. Paris: Gallimard, 1977.

Mali, Joseph. *Mythistory: The Making of a Modern Historiography*. Chicago: University of Chicago Press, 2003.

Mannoni, Octave. *Clefs pour l'Imaginaire ou l'Autre Scène*. Paris: Seuil, 1969.

Marrou, Henri-Irénée. *De la connaissance historique*. Paris: Seuil, 1954.

Melamed, Laliv. "A Film Unraveled: An Interview with Yaël Hersonski." *International Journal of Politics, Culture, and Society* 23 (2013): 9–19.

Mendelsohn, Daniel. *The Lost: A Search for Six of Six Million*. New York: Perennial, 2007.

Mink, Louis O. *Historical Understanding*. Ithaca: Cornell University Press, 1987.

Nietzsche, Friedrich. *The Birth of Tragedy and Other Writings*. Edited by Raymond Geuss and Ronald Speirs. Cambridge: Cambridge University Press, 1999.

Nirenberg, David. *Anti-Judaism: The Western Tradition*. New York: Norton, 2013.

Nora, Pierre. *Realms of Memory: Conflict and Division*. Vol. 1. Translated by Arthur Goldhammer. New York: Columbia University Press, 1996.

Oppenheimer, Joshua. "Perpetrators' Testimony and the Restoration of Humanity: *S21*, Rithy Panh." In *Killer Images: Documentary Film, Memory, and the Performance of Violence,* edited by Joram Ten Brink and Joshua Oppenheimer, 243–55. London: Wallflower Press, 2012.

Panh, Rithy. *The Elimination: A Survivor of the Khmer Rouge Confronts His Past and the Commandant of the Killing Fields*. With Christophe Bataille. Translated by John Cullen. New York: Other Press, 2012.

——. "Je suis un arpenteur de mémoires." *Cahiers du Cinéma* 587 (February 2004): 14–17.

Platonov, Andrey. *The Foundation Pit*. Translated by Robert Chandler and Olga Meerson. New York: New York Review Books, 2009.

——. *Soul*. Translated by Robert and Elizabeth Chandler. New York: New York Review Books, 2008.

Prost, Antoine. *Douze leçons sur l'histoire*. Paris: Seuil, 1996.

Ricoeur, Paul. *History, Memory, Forgetting*. Translated by Kathleen Blamey and David Pellauer. Chicago: University of Chicago Press, 2004.

——. *Time and Narrative*. Translated by Kathleen McLaughlin and David Pellauer. Vol. 1. Chicago: University of Chicago Press, 1984.

Rigney, Ann. *The Rhetoric of Historical Representation: Three Narrative Histories of the French Revolution*. Cambridge: Cambridge University Press, 1990.

Rosenstone, Robert. *Visions of the Past: The Challenge of Film to Our Idea of History*. Cambridge, Mass.: Harvard University Press, 1995.

Rosenstone, Robert A., and Constantin Parvulescu, eds. *A Companion to the Historical Film*. Chichester, UK: Wiley-Blackwell, 2013.

Rothberg, Michael. *Traumatic Realism: The Demands of Holocaust Representation*. Minneapolis: University of Minnesota Press, 2000.

Rouch, Jean. "Mettre en circulation des objets inquiétants." *La Nouvelle Critique*, no. 82, nouvelle série (March 1973): 74–78.

Ruffinelli, Jorge. "Conversations with Patricio Guzmán: On Memories and Forgetfulness." http://www.patricioguzman.com/index.php?page=entrevista

Schaeffer, Jean-Marie. *Pourquoi la fiction?* Paris: Seuil, 1999.

Schama, Simon. *Landscape and Memory*. New York: Alfred A. Knopf, 1995.

Sebald, W. G. *Austerlitz*. Introduction by James Wood. New York: Random House, 2011.

——. *The Rings of Saturn*. Translated by Michael Hulse. New York: New Directions Books, 1999.

Shusterman, Richard. *Pragmatist Aesthetics: Living Beauty, Rethinking Art*. Oxford: Blackwell, 1992.

Slezkine, Yuri. "Primitive Communism and the Other Way Around." In *Socialist Realism Without Shores*, edited by Thomas Lahusen and Evgeny Dobrenko, Durham: Duke University Press, 1997.

Snyder, Timothy. *Bloodlands: Europe Between Hitler and Stalin*. New York: Basic Books, 2010.

——. "Hitler vs. Stalin: Who Was Worse?" *New York Review of Books*. NYRblog, January 27, 2011. http://www.nybooks.com/daily/2011/01/27/hitler-vs-stalin-who -was-worse/.

Taussig, Michael. *Mimesis and Alterity: A Particular History of the Senses*. New York: Routledge, 1993.

Veyne, Paul. *Writing History*. Middletown, Conn.: Wesleyan University Press, 1984.

White, Hayden. *Metahistory: The Historical Imagination in Nineteenth-Century Europe*. Baltimore: Johns Hopkins University Press, 1973.

——. *Tropics of Discourse*. Baltimore: Johns Hopkins University Press, 1978.

White, Rob. "After-Effects: An interview with Patricio Guzmán." *Film Quarterly*, July 2012. http://www.filmquarterly.com/2012/07/after-effects-interview-with -patricio-guzman/.

Witek, Piotr. "Andrzej Wajda as Historian." In *A Companion to the Historical Film*, edited by Robert Rosenstone and Constantin Parvulescu, 154–75. Chichester, UK: Wiley-Blackwell, 2013.

Wittgenstein, Ludwig. *Philosophical Investigations*. Translated by G. E. M. Anscombe. New York: Macmillan, 1953.

INDEX

FILM AND CULTURE

A series of Columbia University Press

EDITED BY JOHN BELTON

Orson Welles, Shakespeare, and Popular Culture
Michael Anderegg

Pre-Code Hollywood: Sex, Immorality, and Insurrection in American Cinema, 1930–1934
Thomas Doherty

Sound Technology and the American Cinema: Perception, Representation, Modernity
James Lastra

Melodrama and Modernity: Early Sensational Cinema and Its Contexts
Ben Singer

Wondrous Difference: Cinema, Anthropology, and Turn-of-the-Century Visual Culture
Alison Griffiths

Hearst Over Hollywood: Power, Passion, and Propaganda in the Movies
Louis Pizzitola

Masculine Interests: Homoerotics in Hollywood Film
Robert Lang

Special Effects: Still in Search of Wonder
Michele Pierson

Designing Women: Cinema, Art Deco, and the Female Form
Lucy Fischer

Cold War, Cool Medium: Television, McCarthyism, and American Culture
Thomas Doherty

Katharine Hepburn: Star as Feminist
Andrew Britton

Silent Film Sound
Rick Altman

Home in Hollywood: The Imaginary Geography of Hollywood
Elisabeth Bronfen

Hollywood and the Culture Elite: How the Movies Became American
Peter Decherney

Taiwan Film Directors: A Treasure Island
Emilie Yueh-yu Yeh and Darrell William Davis

Shocking Representation: Historical Trauma, National Cinema, and the Modern Horror Film
Adam Lowenstein